THE AYN RAND LIBRARY

Vol. I. PHILOSOPHY: WHO NEEDS IT
by Ayn Rand

Vol. II. THE EARLY AYN RAND:
A Selection from Her Unpublished Fiction
Edited by Leonard Peikoff

Vol. III. THE OMINOUS PARALLELS
by Leonard Peikoff, with an
Introduction by Ayn Rand

Vol. IV. THE AYN RAND LEXICON:
Objectivism from A to Z
by Harry Binswanger, with an
Introduction by Leonard Peikoff

Vol. V. THE VOICE OF REASON:
Essays in Objectivist Thought
by Ayn Rand
with additional essays by
Leonard Peikoff

Introduction to
Objectivist
Epistemology

by

Ayn Rand

With an Additional Essay
by Leonard Peikoff

Expanded Second Edition

Edited by
Harry Binswanger and
Leonard Peikoff

A MERIDIAN BOOK

MERIDIAN
Published by the Penguin Group
Penguin Books USA Inc., 375 Hudson Street, New York, New York 10014, U.S.A.
Penguin Books Ltd, 27 Wrights Lane, London W8 5TZ, England
Penguin Books Australia Ltd, Ringwood, Victoria, Australia
Penguin Books Canada Ltd, 10 Alcorn Avenue, Toronto, Ontario, Canada M4V 3B2
Penguin Books (N.Z.) Ltd, 182–190 Wairau Road, Auckland 10, New Zealand

Penguin Books Ltd, Registered Offices:
Harmondsworth, Middlesex, England

Published by Meridian, an imprint of Dutton Signet, a division of Penguin Books USA
Inc. Published simultaneously in Canada.

First Mentor Printing, April, 1979
First Meridian Printing (Expanded Second Edition), April, 1990
14 13 12 11 10 9 8 7 6 5

   REGISTERED TRADEMARK—MARCA REGISTRADA

Library of Congress Cataloging-in-Publication Data
Rand, Ayn.
    Introduction to objectivist epistemology / Ayn Rand : edited by
Harry Binswanger and Leonard Peikoff.—Expanded 2nd ed.
    p.   cm.
    ISBN 0-452-01030-6 (pbk.)
    0-452-01030-6 (pbk.)
    1. Philosophy.   I. Peikoff, Leonard.   II. Binswanger, Harry.   III.
Title.   IV. Title: Objectivist epistemology.
B945.R233167   1990
121—dc20   89-39565
                                                                      CIP

Printed in the United States of America
Set in Times Roman
Designed by Nissa Knuth

Contents

APPENDIX
Excerpts from the Epistemology Workshops

Foreword to the First Edition

(This work was first published in
The Objectivist July 1966–February 1967.)

This series of articles is presented "by popular demand."
We have had so many requests for information on Objectivist epistemology that I decided to put on record a summary
of one of its cardinal elements—the Objectivist theory of
concepts. These articles may be regarded as a preview of my
future book on Objectivism, and are offered here for the
guidance of philosophy students.

The issue of concepts (known as "the problem of universals") is philosophy's central issue. Since man's knowledge
is gained and held in conceptual form, the validity of man's
knowledge depends on the validity of concepts. But concepts are abstractions or universals, and everything that
man perceives is particular, concrete. What is the relationship between abstractions and concretes? To what precisely
do concepts refer in reality? Do they refer to something
real, something that exists—or are they merely inventions of
man's mind, arbitrary constructs or loose approximations
that cannot claim to represent knowledge?

"All knowledge is in terms of concepts. If these concepts
correspond to something that is to be found in reality they
are real and man's knowledge has a foundation in fact; if
they do not correspond to anything in reality they are not

1

real and man's knowledge is of mere figments of his own imagination." (Edward C. Moore, *American Pragmatism: Peirce, James, & Dewey,* New York: Columbia University Press, 1961, p. 27.)

To exemplify the issue as it is usually presented: When we refer to three persons as "men," what do we designate by that term? The three persons are three individuals who differ in every particular respect and may not possess a single *identical* characteristic (not even their fingerprints). If you list all their particular characteristics, you will not find one representing "manness." Where is the "manness" in men? What, in reality, corresponds to the concept "man" in our mind?

In the history of philosophy, there are, essentially, four schools of thought on this issue:

1. The "extreme realists" or Platonists, who hold that abstractions exist as real entities or archetypes in another dimension of reality and that the concretes we perceive are merely their imperfect reflections, but the concretes evoke the abstractions in our mind. (According to Plato, they do so by evoking the memory of the archetypes which we had known, before birth, in that other dimension.)

2. The "moderate realists," whose ancestor (unfortunately) is Aristotle, who hold that abstractions exist in reality, but they exist only *in* concretes, in the form of metaphysical *essences,* and that our concepts refer to these essences.

3. The "nominalists," who hold that all our ideas are only images of concretes, and that abstractions are merely "names" which we give to arbitrary groupings of concretes on the basis of vague resemblances.

4. The "conceptualists," who share the nominalists' view that abstractions have no actual basis in reality, but who hold that concepts exist in our minds as some sort of ideas, not as images.

(There is also the extreme nominalist position, the modern one, which consists of declaring that the problem is a meaningless issue, that "reality" is a meaningless term, that we can never know whether our concepts correspond to anything or not, that our knowledge consists of words—and that words are an arbitrary social convention.)

If, in the light of such "solutions," the problem might appear to be esoteric, let me remind you that the fate of human societies, of knowledge, of science, of progress and of every human life, depends on it. What is at stake here is the cognitive efficacy of man's mind.

As I wrote in *For the New Intellectual:* "To negate man's mind, it is the *conceptual* level of his consciousness that has to be invalidated. Under all the tortuous complexities, contradictions, equivocations, rationalizations of the post-Renaissance philosophy—the one consistent line, the fundamental that explains the rest, is: *a concerted attack on man's conceptual faculty.* Most philosophers did not intend to invalidate conceptual knowledge, but its defenders did more to destroy it than did its enemies. They were unable to offer a solution to the 'problem of universals,' that is: to define the nature and source of abstractions, to determine the relationship of concepts to perceptual data—and to prove the validity of scientific induction. . . . The philosophers were unable to refute the Witch Doctor's claim that their concepts were as arbitrary as his whims and that their scientific knowledge had no greater metaphysical validity than his revelations."

These are the reasons why I chose to introduce you to Objectivist epistemology by presenting my theory of concepts. I entitle this work an "Introduction," because the theory is presented outside of its full context. For instance, I do not include here a discussion of the validity of man's senses—since the arguments of those who attack the senses are merely variants of the fallacy of the "stolen concept."

For the purposes of this series, the validity of the senses must be taken for granted—and one must remember the axiom: *Existence exists.* (This, incidentally, is a way of translating into the form of a proposition, and thus into the form of an axiom, the primary fact which is existence.) Please bear in mind the full statement: "Existence exists—and the act of grasping that statement implies two corollary axioms:

that something exists which one perceives and that one
exists possessing consciousness, consciousness being the faculty of perceiving that which exists." *(Atlas Shrugged.)*

(For the reader's convenience, a summary of the text is
provided at the conclusion of this work.)

—Ayn Rand

New York, July 1966.

1. Cognition and Measurement

Consciousness, as a state of awareness, is not a passive state, but an active process that consists of two essentials: differentiation and integration.

Although, chronologically, man's consciousness develops in three stages: the stage of sensations, the perceptual, the conceptual—epistemologically, the base of all of man's knowledge is the *perceptual* stage.

Sensations, as such, are not retained in man's memory, nor is man able to experience a pure isolated sensation. As far as can be ascertained, an infant's sensory experience is an undifferentiated chaos. Discriminated awareness begins on the level of percepts.

A percept is a group of sensations automatically retained and integrated by the brain of a living organism. It is in the form of percepts that man grasps the evidence of his senses and apprehends reality. When we speak of "direct perception" or "direct awareness," we mean the perceptual level. Percepts, not sensations, are the given, the self-evident. The knowledge of sensations as components of percepts is not direct, it is acquired by man much later: it is a scientific, *conceptual* discovery.

The building-block of man's knowledge is the concept of an *"existent"*—of something that exists, be it a thing, an attribute or an action. Since it is a concept, man cannot grasp it *explicitly* until he has reached the conceptual stage. But it is implicit in every percept (to perceive a thing is to perceive

5

that it exists) and man grasps it *implicitly* on the perceptual level—i.e., he grasps the constituents of the concept "existent," the data which are later to be integrated by that concept. It is this implicit knowledge that permits his consciousness to develop further.

(It may be supposed that the concept "existent" is implicit even on the level of sensations—if and to the extent that a consciousness is able to discriminate on that level. A sensation is a sensation of *something,* as distinguished from the *nothing* of the preceding and succeeding moments. A sensation does not tell man *what* exists, but only *that* it exists.)

The (implicit) concept "existent" undergoes three stages of development in man's mind. The first stage is a child's awareness of objects, of things—which represents the (implicit) concept *"entity."* The second and closely allied stage is the awareness of specific, particular things which he can recognize and distinguish from the rest of his perceptual field—which represents the (implicit) concept *"identity."*

The third stage consists of grasping relationships among these entities by grasping the similarities and differences of their identities. This requires the transformation of the (implicit) concept "entity" into the (implicit) concept *"unit."*

When a child observes that two objects (which he will later learn to designate as "tables") resemble each other, but are different from four other objects ("chairs"), his mind is focusing on a particular attribute of the objects (their shape), then isolating them according to their differences, and integrating them as units into separate groups according to their similarities.

This is the key, the entrance to the conceptual level of man's consciousness. *The ability to regard entities as units is man's distinctive method of cognition,* which other living species are unable to follow.

A unit is an existent regarded as a separate member of a group of two or more similar members. (Two stones are two units; so are two square feet of ground, if regarded as distinct parts of a continuous stretch of ground.) Note that the concept "unit" involves an act of consciousness (a selective focus, a certain way of regarding things), but that it is *not* an arbitrary creation of consciousness: it is a method of identification or classification according to the attributes which a consciousness observes in reality. This method permits any number of classifications and cross-classifications: one may classify things according to their shape or color or weight or size or atomic structure; but the criterion of classification is not invented, it is perceived in reality. Thus the concept "unit" is a bridge between metaphysics and epistemology: units do not exist *qua* units, what exists are things, but *units are things viewed by a consciousness in certain existing relationships*.

With the grasp of the (implicit) concept "unit" man reaches the conceptual level of cognition, which consists of two interrelated fields: Conceptual and the Mathematical. The process of concept-formation is, in large part, a mathematical process.

Mathematics is the science of *measurement*. Before proceeding to the subject of concept-formation, let us first consider the subject of measurement.

Measurement is the identification of a relationship—a quantitative relationship establishd by means of a standard that serves as a unit. Entities (and their actions) are measured by their attributes (length, weight, velocity, etc.) and the standard of measurement is a concretely specified unit representing the appropriate attribute. Thus, one measures length in inches, feet and miles—weight in pounds—velocity by means of a given distance traversed in a given time, etc.

It is important to note that while the choice of a given standard is optional, the mathematical rules of using it are not. It makes no difference whether one measures length in terms of feet or meters; the standard provides only the form of notation, not the substance nor the result of the process of measuring. The facts established by measurement will be the same, regardless of the particular standard used; the standard can neither alter nor affect them. The requirements of a standard of measurement are: that it represent the appropriate attribute, that it be easily perceivable by man and that, once chosen, it remain immutable and absolute whenever used. (Please remember this; we will have reason to recall it.)

Now what is the purpose of measurement? Observe that measurement consists of relating an easily perceivable unit to larger or smaller quantities, then to infinitely larger or infinitely smaller quantities, which are not directly perceivable to man. (The word "infinitely" is used here as a mathematical, not a metaphysical, term.) The purpose of measurement is to expand the range of man's consciousness, of his knowledge, beyond the perceptual level: beyond the direct power of his senses and the immediate concretes of any given moment. Man can perceive the length of one foot directly; he cannot perceive ten miles. By establishing the relationship of feet to miles, he can grasp and know any distance on earth; by establishing the relationship of miles to light-years, he can know the distances of galaxies.

The process of measurement is a process of integrating an unlimited scale of knowledge to man's limited perceptual experience—a process of making the universe knowable by bringing it within the range of man's consciousness, by establishing its relationship to man. It is not an accident that man's earliest attempts at measurement (the evidence of which survives to this day) consisted of relating things to *himself*—as, for instance, taking the length of his foot as a standard of length, or adopting the decimal system, which is supposed to have its origin in man's ten fingers as units of counting.

It is here that Protagoras' old dictum may be given a new meaning, the opposite of the one he intended: "Man is the measure of all things." Man *is* the measure, epistemologically—*not* metaphysically. In regard to human knowledge, man has to be the measure, since he has to bring all things into the realm of the humanly knowable. But, far from leading to subjectivism, the methods which he has to employ require the most rigorous mathematical precision, the most rigorous compliance with objective rules and facts—if the end product is to be *knowledge*.

This is true of mathematical principles and of the principles by which man forms his concepts. Man's mathematical and conceptual abilities develop simultaneously. A child learns to count when he is learning his first words. And in order to proceed beyond the stage of counting his ten fingers, it is the *conceptual* level of his consciousness that man has to expand.

2. Concept-Formation

A *concept* is a mental integration of two or more units which are isolated according to a specific characteristic(s) and united by a specific definition.

The units involved may be any aspect of reality: entities, attributes, actions, qualities, relationships, etc.; they may be perceptual concretes or other, earlier-formed concepts. The act of isolation involved is a process of *abstraction:* i.e., a selective mental focus that *takes out* or separates a certain aspect of reality from all others (e.g., isolates a certain attibute from the entities possessing it, or a certain action from the entities performing it, etc.). The uniting involved is not a mere sum, but an *integration,* i.e., a blending of the units into a *single,* new *mental* entity which is used thereafter as a single unit of thought (but which can be broken into its component units whenever required).

In order to be used as a single unit, the enormous sum integrated by a concept has to be given the form of a single, specific, *perceptual* concrete, which will differentiate it from all other concretes and from all other concepts. This is the function performed by language. Language is a code of visual-auditory symbols that serves the psycho-epistemological function of converting concepts into the mental equivalent of concretes. Language is the exclusive domain and tool of concepts. Every word we use (with the exception of proper names) is a symbol that denotes a concept, i.e., that stands for an unlimited number of concretes of a certain kind.

(Proper names are used in order to identify and include particular entities in a conceptual method of cognition. Observe that even proper names, in advanced civilizations, follow the definitional principles of *genus* and *differentia:* e.g., John Smith, with "Smith" serving as *genus* and "John" as *differentia*—or New York, U.S.A.)

Words transform concepts into (mental) entities; *definitions* provide them with *identity*. (Words without definitions are not language but inarticulate sounds.) We shall discuss definitions later and at length.

The above is a general description of the nature of concepts as products of a certain mental process. But *the* question of epistemology is: what precisely is the nature of that process? To what precisely do concepts refer in reality?

Let us now examine the process of forming the simplest concept, the concept of a single attribute (chronologically, this is not the first concept that a child would grasp; but it is the simplest one epistemologically)—for instance, the concept *"length."* If a child considers a match, a pencil and a stick, he observes that length is the attribute they have in common, but their specific lengths differ. The *difference is one of measurement.* In order to form the concept "length," the child's mind retains the attribute and omits its particular measurements. Or, more precisely, if the process were identified in words, it would consist of the following: "Length must exist in *some* quantity, but may exist in *any* quantity. I shall identify as 'length' that attribute of any existent possessing it which can be quantitatively related to a unit of length, without specifying the quantity."

The child does not think in such words (he has, as yet, no knowledge of words), but *that* is the nature of the process which his mind performs wordlessly. And that is the principle which his mind follows, when, having grasped the concept "length" by observing the three objects, he uses it to identify the attribute of length in a piece of string, a ribbon, a belt, a corridor or a street.

The same principle directs the process of forming concepts of entities—for instance, the concept *"table."* The child's mind isolates two or more tables from other objects, by focusing on their distinctive characteristic: their shape. He observes that their shapes vary, but have one characteristic in common: a flat, level surface and support(s). He forms the concept "table" by retaining that characteristic and omitting *all* particular measurements, not only the measurements of the shape, but of all the other characteristics of tables (many of which he is not aware of at the time).

An adult definition of "table" would be: "A man-made object consisting of a flat, level surface and support(s), intended to support other, smaller objects." Observe what is specified and what is omitted in this definition: the distinctive characteristic of the shape is specified and retained; the particular geometrical measurements of the shape (whether the surface is square, round, oblong or triangular, etc., the number and shape of supports, etc.) are omitted; the measurements of size or weight are omitted; the fact that it is a material object is specified, but the material of which it is made is omitted, thus omitting the measurements that differentiate one material from another; etc. Observe, however, that the utilitarian requirements of the table set certain limits on the omitted measurements, in the form of "no larger than and no smaller than" required by its purpose. This rules out a ten-foot tall or a two-inch tall table (though the latter may be sub-classified as a toy or a miniature table) and it rules out unsuitable materials, such as non-solids.

Bear firmly in mind that the term "measurements omitted" does not mean, in this context, that measurements are regarded as non-existent; it means that *measurements exist, but are not specified.* That measurements *must* exist is an essential part of the process. The principle is: the relevant measurements must exist in *some* quantity, but may exist in *any* quantity.

A child is not and does not have to be aware of all these complexities when he forms the concept "table." He forms it by differentiating tables from all other objects *in the context of his knowledge.* As his knowledge grows, the definitions of his concepts grow in complexity. (We shall discuss this when we discuss definitions.) But the principle and pattern of concept-formation remain the same.

The first words a child learns are words denoting visual objects, and he retains his first concepts *visually*. Observe that the visual form he gives them is reduced to those *essentials* which distinguish the particular kind of entities from all others—for instance, the universal type of a child's drawing of man in the form of an oval for the torso, a circle for the head, four sticks for extremities, etc. Such drawings are a visual record of the process of abstraction and concept-formation in a mind's transition from the perceptual level to the full vocabulary of the conceptual level.

There is evidence to suppose that written language originated in the form of drawings—as the pictographic writing of the Oriental peoples seems to indicate. With the growth of man's knowledge and of his power of abstraction, a pictorial representation of concepts could no longer be adequate to his conceptual range, and was replaced by a fully symbolic code.

A concept is a mental integration of two or more units possessing the same distinguishing characteristic(s), with their particular measurements omitted.

The element of *similarity* is crucially involved in the formation of every concept; similarity, in this context, is the relationship between two or more existents which possess the same characteristic(s), but in different measure or degree.

Observe the multiple role of measurements in the process of concept-formation, in both of its two essential parts: differentiation and integration. Concepts cannot be formed at random. All concepts are formed by first differentiating two or more existents from other existents. All conceptual differentiations are made in terms of *commensurable characteristics* (i.e., characteristics possessing a common unit of measurement). No concept could be formed, for instance, by attempting to distinguish long objects from green objects. Incommensurable characteristics cannot be integrated into one unit.

Tables, for instance, are first differentiated from chairs,

beds and other objects by means of the characteristic of *shape,* which is an attribute possessed by all the objects involved. Then, their particular kind of shape is set as the distinguishing characteristic of tables—i.e., a certain category of geometrical measurements of shape is specified. Then, within that category, the particular measurements of individual table-shapes are omitted.

Please note the fact that a given shape represents a certain category or set of geometrical measurements. Shape is an attribute; differences of shape—whether cubes, spheres, cones or any complex combinations—are a matter of differing measurements; any shape can be reduced to or expressed by a set of figures in terms of *linear measurement.* When, in the process of concept-formation, man observes that shape is a commensurable characteristic of certain objects, he does not have to measure all the shapes involved *nor even to know how to measure them;* he merely has to observe the element of *similarity.*

Similarity is grasped *perceptually;* in observing it, man is not and does not have to be aware of the fact that it involves a matter of measurement. It is the task of philosophy and of science to identify that fact.

As to the actual process of measuring shapes, a vast part of higher mathematics, from geometry on up, is devoted to the task of discovering methods by which various shapes can be measured—complex methods which consist of reducing the problem to the terms of a simple, primitive method, the only one available to man in this field: linear measurement. (Integral calculus, used to measure the area of circles, is just one example.)

In this respect, concept-formation and applied mathematics have a similar task, just as philosophical epistemology and theoretical mathematics have a similar goal: the goal and task of bringing the universe within the range of man's knowledge—by identifying relationships to perceptual data.

Another example of implicit measurement can be seen in the process of forming concepts of colors. Man forms such concepts by observing that the various shades of blue are similar, as against the shades of red, and thus differentiating the range of blue from the range of red, of yellow, etc. Centuries passed before science discovered the unit by which colors could actually be measured: the wavelengths of light— a discovery that supported, in terms of mathematical proof, the differentiations that men were and are making in terms of visual similarities. (Any questions about "borderline cases" will be answered later.)

A commensurable characteristic (such as shape in the case of tables, or hue in the case of colors) is an essential element in the process of concept-formation. I shall designate it as the "Conceptual Common Denominator" and define it as "The characteristic(s) reducible to a unit of measurement, by means of which man differentiates two or more existents from other existents possessing it."

The distinguishing characteristic(s) of a concept represents a specified category of measurements within the "Conceptual Common Denominator" involved.

New concepts can be formed by integrating earlier-formed concepts into wider categories, or by subdividing them into narrower categories (a process which we shall discuss later). But all concepts are ultimately reducible to their base in perceptual entities, which are the base (the given) of man's cognitive development.

The first concepts man forms are concepts of entities— since entities are the only primary existents. (Attributes cannot exist by themselves, they are merely the characteristics of entities; motions are motions of entities; relationships are relationships among entities.)

In the process of forming concepts of entities, a child's mind has to focus on a distinguishing characteristic—i.e., on an attribute—in order to isolate one group of entities from all others. He is, therefore, aware of attributes while forming his first concepts, but he is aware of them *perceptually, not* conceptually. It is only after he has grasped a number of concepts of entities that he can advance to the stage of abstracting attributes from entities and forming separate concepts of attributes. The same is true of concepts of motion: a child is aware of motion *perceptually*, but cannot conceptualize "motion" until he has formed some concepts of that which moves, i.e., of entities.

(As far as can be ascertained, the perceptual level of a child's awareness is similar to the awareness of the higher animals: the higher animals are able to perceive entities, motions, attributes, and certain numbers of entities. But what an animal cannot perform is the process of abstraction—of mentally separating attributes, motions or numbers from entities. It has been said that an animal can perceive two oranges or two potatoes, but cannot grasp the concept "two.")

Concepts of *materials* are formed by observing the differences in the constituent materials of entities. (Materials exist only in the form of specific entities, such as a nugget of gold, a plank of wood, a drop or an ocean of water.) The concept of "gold," for instance, is formed by isolating gold objects from all others, then abstracting and retaining the material, the gold, and omitting the measurements of the objects (or of the alloys) in which gold may exist. Thus, the material is the same in all the concrete instances subsumed under the concept, and differs only in quantity.

Concepts of *motion* are formed by specifying the distinctive nature of the motion and of the entities performing it, and/or of the medium in which it is performed—and omitting the particular measurements of any given instance of such motion and of the entities involved. For instance, the concept "walking" denotes a certain kind of motion performed by living entities possessing legs, and does not apply to the motion of a snake or of an automobile. The concept "swimming" denotes the motion of any living entity propelling itself through water, and does not apply to the motion of a boat. The concept "flying" denotes the motion of any entity propelling itself through the air, whether a bird or an airplane.

Adverbs are concepts of the characteristics of motion (or action); they are formed by specifying a characteristic and omitting the measurements of the motion and of the entities involved—e.g., "rapidly," which may be applied to "walking" or "swimming" or "speaking," etc., with the measurement of what is "rapid" left open and depending, in any given case, on the type of motion involved.

Prepositions are concepts of relationships, predominantly of spatial or temporal relationships, among existents; they are formed by specifying the relationship and omitting the measurements of the existents and of the space or time involved—e.g., "on," "in," "above," "after," etc.

Adjectives are concepts of attributes or of characteristics. *Pronouns* belong to the category of concepts of entities. *Conjunctions* are concepts of relationships among thoughts, and belong to the category of concepts of consciousness.

As to concepts of consciousness, we shall discuss them later and at length. (To anticipate questions such as: "Can you measure love?"—I shall permit myself the very philosophical answer: "And how!")

Now we can answer the question: To what precisely do we refer when we designate three persons as "men"? We refer to the fact that they are living beings who possess the *same* characteristic distinguishing them from all other living species: a rational faculty—though the specific measurements of their distinguishing characteristic *qua* men, as well as of all their other characteristics *qua* living beings, are different. (As living beings of a certain kind, they possess innumerable characteristics in common: the same shape, the same range of size, the same facial features, the same vital organs, the same fingerprints, etc., and all these characteristics differ only in their measurements.)

Two links between the conceptual and the mathematical fields are worth noting at this point, apart from the obvious fact that the concept "unit" is the base and start of both.

1. A concept is not formed by observing every concrete subsumed under it, and does not specify the number of such concretes. A concept is like an arithmetical sequence of *specifically defined units,* going off in both directions, open at both ends and including *all* units of that particular kind. For instance, the concept "man" includes all men who live at

present, who have ever lived or will ever live. An arithmetical sequence extends into infinity, without implying that infinity actually exists; such extension means only that whatever number of units does exist, it is to be included in the same sequence. The same principle applies to concepts: the concept "man" does not (and need not) specify what number of men will ultimately have existed—it specifies only the characteristics of man, and means that any number of entities possessing these characteristics is to be identified as "men."

2. The basic principle of concept-formation (which states that the omitted measurements must exist in *some* quantity, but may exist in *any* quantity) is the equivalent of the basic principle of algebra, which states that algebraic symbols must be given *some* numerical value, but may be given *any* value. In this sense and respect, perceptual awareness is the arithmetic, but *conceptual awareness is the algebra of cognition.*

The relationship of concepts to their constituent particulars is the same as the relationship of algebraic symbols to numbers. In the equation $2a = a + a$, any number may be substituted for the symbol *"a"* without affecting the truth of the equation. For instance: $2 \times 5 = 5 + 5$, or: $2 \times 5,000,000 = 5,000,000 + 5,000,000$. In the same manner, by the same psycho-epistemological method, a concept is used as an algebraic symbol that stands for *any* of the arithmetical sequence of units it subsumes.

Let those who attempt to invalidate concepts by declaring that they cannot find "manness" in men, try to invalidate algebra by declaring that they cannot find *"a-ness"* in 5 or in 5,000,000.

3. Abstraction from Abstractions

Starting from the base of conceptual development—from the concepts that identify perceptual concretes—the process of cognition moves in two interacting directions: toward more extensive and more intensive knowledge, toward wider integrations and more precise differentiations. Following the process and *in accordance with cognitive evidence,* earlier-formed concepts are integrated into wider ones or subdivided into narrower ones.

The role of language (which we shall discuss at length when we discuss definitions) must be mentioned briefly at this point. The process of forming a concept is not complete until its constituent units have been integrated into a single mental unit by means of a specific word. The first concepts a child forms are concepts of perceptual entities; the first words he learns are words designating them. Even though a child does not have to perform the feat of genius performed by some mind or minds in the prehistorical infancy of the human race: the invention of language—every child has to perform independently the feat of grasping the nature of language, the process of symbolizing concepts by means of words.

Even though a child does not (and need not) originate and form every concept on his own, by observing every aspect of reality confronting him, he has to perform the process of differentiating and integrating perceptual concretes, in order to grasp the meaning of words. If a child's brain is physically damaged and unable to perform that process, he does not learn to speak.

Learning to speak does not consist of memorizing sounds—*that* is the process by which a parrot learns to "speak." Learning consists of grasping meanings, i.e., of grasping the *referents* of words, the kinds of existents that words denote in reality. In this respect, the learning of words is an invaluable accelerator of a child's cognitive development, but it is not a substitute for the process of concept-formation; nothing is.

After the first stage of learning certain fundamentals, there is no particular order in which a child learns new concepts; there is, for a while, a broad area of the optional, where he may learn simple, primary concepts and complex, derivative ones almost concurrently, depending on his own mental initiative and on the random influences of his environment. The particular order in which he learns new words is of no significance, at this stage, *provided he understands their meanings.* His full, independent conceptual development does not begin until he has acquired a sufficient vocabulary to be able to form sentences—i.e., *to be able to think* (at which time he can gradually bring order to his haphazard conceptual equipment). Up to that time, he is able to retain the referents of his concepts by perceptual, predominantly visual means; as his conceptual chain moves farther and farther away from perceptual concretes, the issue of verbal definitions becomes crucial. It is at this point that all hell breaks loose.

Apart from the fact that the educational methods of most of his elders are such that, instead of helping him, they tend to cripple his further development, a child's own choice and motivation are crucial at this point. There are many different ways in which children proceed to learn new words thereafter. Some (a very small minority) proceed straight on, by the same method as before, i.e., by treating words as concepts, by requiring a clear, first-hand understanding *(within the context of their knowledge)* of the exact meaning of every word they learn, never allowing a break in the chain linking their concepts to the facts of reality. Some proceed by the road of approximations, where the fog deepens with every step, where the use of words is guided by the feeling: "I kinda know what I mean." Some switch from cognition to imitation, substituting memorizing for understanding, and adopt something as close to a parrot's psycho-epistemology as a human brain can come—learning, not concepts nor words, but strings of sounds whose referents are not the facts of reality, but the facial expressions and emotional vibrations of their elders. And some (the overwhelming majority) adopt a precarious mixture of different degrees of all three methods.

But the question of how particular men happen to *learn* concepts and the question of what concepts *are,* are two different issues. In considering the nature of concepts and the process of abstracting from abstractions, we must assume a mind capable of performing (or of retracing and checking) that process. And we must remember that no matter how many men mouth a concept as a meaningless sound, *some* man had to originate it at some time.

The first stages of integrating concepts into wider concepts are fairly simple, because they still refer to perceptual concretes. For instance, man observes that the objects which he has identified by the concepts "table," "chair," "bed," "cabinet," etc. have certain similarities, but are different from the objects he has identified as "door," "window," "picture," "drapes"—and he integrates the former into the wider concept "furniture." In this process, concepts serve as units and are treated *epistemologically* as if each were a single (mental) concrete—always remembering that *metaphysically* (i.e., in reality) each unit stands for an unlimited number of actual concretes of a certain kind.

The distinguishing characteristics of these units are specified categories of measurements of shape, such as "a flat, level surface and support(s)" in the case of tables. In relation to the new concept, these distinguishing characteristics are now regarded in the same manner as the measurements of individual table-shapes were regarded in forming the concept "table": they are omitted, on the principle that a piece of furniture must have *some* shape, but may have *any* of the shapes characterizing the various units subsumed under the new concept.

The *distinguishing* characteristic of the new concept is determined by the nature of the objects from which its constituent units are being differentiated, i.e., by their "Conceptual Common Denominator," which, in this case, is: large objects inside a human habitation. The adult definition of "furniture" would be: "Movable man-made objects intended to be used in a human habitation, which can support the weight of the human body or support and/or store other, smaller objects." This differentiates "furniture" from architectural features, such as doors or windows, from ornamental objects, such as pictures or drapes, and from a variety of smaller objects that may be used inside a habitation, such as ashtrays, bric-a-brac, dishes, etc.

The distinguishing characteristics of "furniture" are a specified range of functions in a specified place (both are measurable characteristics): "furniture" must be no larger than can be placed inside a human habitation, no smaller than can perform the specified functions, etc.

Observe that the concept "furniture" is an abstraction one step further removed from perceptual reality than any of its constituent concepts. "Table" is an abstraction, since it designates *any* table, but its meaning can be conveyed simply by pointing to one or two perceptual objects. There is no such perceptual object as "furniture"; there are only tables, chairs, beds, etc. The meaning of "furniture" cannot be grasped unless one has first grasped the meaning of its constituent concepts; these are its link to reality. (On the lower levels of an unlimited conceptual chain, this is an illustration of the hierarchical structure of concepts.)

Observe also that the concept "furniture" involves a relationship to another concept which is not one of its constituent units, but which has to be grasped before one can grasp the meaning of "furniture": the concept "habitation." This kind of interrelationship among concepts grows progressively more complex as the level of concept-formation grows farther away from perceptual concretes.

Now let us examine the process of subdividing the concept "table." By observing the differences in the size and function of various tables, man subdivides the concept into: "dining table," "coffee table," "end table," "desk," etc. In the first three instances, the distinguishing characteristic of "table," its shape, is retained, and the differentiations are purely a matter of measurement: the range of the shape's measurements is reduced in accordance with the narrower utilitarian function. (Coffee tables are lower and smaller than dining tables; end tables are higher than coffee tables, but lower than dining tables, etc.) In the case of "desk," however, the distinguishing characteristic of "table" is retained, but combined with a new element: a "desk" is a table with drawers for storing stationery supplies. The first three instances are not actually new concepts, but qualified instances of the concept "table." "Desk," however, involves a significant difference in its distinguishing characteristic; it involves an additional category of measurements, and is given a new linguistic symbol. (As far as the process of concept-formation is concerned, it would make no difference if "desk" were designated as "office table," or if a new word were coined for each of the other sub-categories of "table." There is, however, an epistemological reason for the present designations, which we shall discuss when we discuss definitions.)

When concepts are integrated into a wider one, the new concept includes *all* the characteristics of its constituent units; but their distinguishing characteristics are regarded as omitted measurements, and one of their common characteristics determines the distinguishing characteristic of the new concept: the one representing their "Conceptual Common Denominator" with the existents from which they are being differentiated.

When a concept is subdivided into narrower ones, its distinguishing characteristic is taken as their "Conceptual Common Denominator"—and is given a narrower range of specified measurements or is combined with an additional characteristic(s), to form the individual distinguishing characteristics of the new concepts.

Let us observe these two principles on another example: the ramifications of the concept "man."

Man's particular type of consciousness is the distinguishing characteristic by which a child (at a certain level of development) differentiates him from all other entities. By observing the similarities among "cat," "dog," "horse," "bird," and by differentiating them from other entities, he integrates them into the wider concept "animal"—and, later, includes "man" in this wider concept. The definition of "animal" (in general terms) would be: "A living entity possessing the faculties of consciousness and locomotion."

Man's distinguishing characteristic, his rational faculty, is omitted from the definition of "animal"—on the principle that an animal must possess *some* type of consciousness, but may possess *any* of the types characterizing the various units subsumed under the new concept. (The standard of measurement that differentiates one type of consciousness from another is its *range.*)

The distinguishing characteristics of the new concept are characteristics possessed by all its constituent units: the attribute "living" and the faculties "consciousness and locomotion."

With further knowledge, by observing the similarities among animals, plants and certain sub-microscopic entities (and their differences from inanimate objects), man integrates them into the concept "organism." The definition of "organism" (in general terms) would be: "An entity possessing the capacities of internally generated action, of growth through metabolism, and of reproduction."

These distinguishing characteristics of the new concept are possessed by all its constituent units. The distinguishing characteristics of "animal" are omitted from the definition—on the principle that the "internally generated actions" must exist in *some* form (including "consciousness and locomotion"), but may exist in *any* of the forms characterizing the various units subsumed under the new concept.

With the growth of man's knowledge, a very broad concept, such as "animal," is subdivided into new concepts, such as: "mammal," "amphibian," "fish," "bird," etc. Each of these is then subdivided further and further into narrower sub-categories. The principle of concept-formation remains the same: the distinguishing characteristics of the concept "animal" (the faculties of "consciousness and locomotion") are the "Conceptual Common Denominator" of these subdivisions, and are retained but qualified by the addition of other (anatomical and physiological) characteristics to form the distinguishing characteristics of the new concepts.

(The chronological order in which man forms or learns these concepts is optional. A child, for instance, may first integrate the appropriate concretes into the concepts "animal," "bird," "fish," then later integrate them into a wider concept by expanding his concept of "animal." The principles involved and the ultimate choice of distinguishing characteristics will be the same, granting he reaches the same level of knowledge.)

Turning now to the process of conceptual subdivision, the concept "man" can be subdivided into innumerable subcategories, according to various aspects or attributes. For instance, such concepts as "child," "adolescent," "youth," "adult" are formed according to measurements of time, i.e., according to the number of years lived. These concepts retain the distinguishing characteristic of "rational animal" but narrowed by a specified range of years.

The concept "man" can be subdivided according to special characteristics, such as racial (anatomical) descent: "Caucasian," "Negro," "Mongolian," etc.—or national (politico-geographical) origin: "American," "Englishman," "Frenchman," etc.—or professional activity: "Engineer," "Doctor,"

"Artist," etc. (which involve concepts of consciousness)—or even according to such characteristics as the color of hair: "Blonde," "Brunette," "Redhead." In all such cases, the distinguishing characteristic of "rational animal" is retained but narrowed by specified characteristics which represent specified categories of measurements.

The concept "man" can be subdivided according to special relationships—for instance, according to a biological relationship ("Father," "Son," "Brother"), or a legal relationship ("Husband," "Wife"), or an economic relationship ("Employer," "Employee"), etc. In all such cases, the characteristic of "rational animal" is retained but combined with a specified relationship.

Some concepts of relationships (such as "legal" or "economic") involve concepts of consciousness. The most complex abstractions (both in regard to wider integrations and narrower subdivisions) are those which involve a combination of concepts of action with concepts of consciousness. (We shall discuss these in the next chapter.)

Two aspects of the cognitive content of abstractions are worth noting at this point.

1. The formation (or the learning) of wider concepts requires more knowledge (i.e., a wider range of conceptualized evidence) than was required by any one of the constituent concepts which they subsume. For instance, the concept "animal" requires more knowledge than the concept "man" —since it requires knowledge of man and of some of the other species. It requires a sufficient knowledge of man's characteristics and of the characteristics of other animals to differentiate man from other animals, and to differentiate animals from plants or from inanimate objects.

A widespread error, in this context, holds that the wider the concept, the less its cognitive content—on the ground that its distinguishing characteristic is more generalized than the distinguishing characteristics of its constituent concepts. The error lies in assuming that a concept consists of nothing but its distinguishing characteristic. But the fact is that in the process of abstracting from abstractions, one cannot know *what* is a distinguishing characteristic unless one has observed other characteristics of the units involved and of the existents from which they are differentiated.

Just as the concept "man" does not consist merely of "rational faculty" (if it did, the two would be equivalent and interchangeable, which they are not), but includes *all* the characteristics of "man," with "rational faculty" serving as the distinguishing characteristic—so, in the case of wider concepts, the concept "animal" does not consist merely of "consciousness and locomotion," but subsumes *all* the characteristics of all the animal species, with "consciousness and locomotion" serving as the distinguishing characteristic. (We shall discuss this further when we discuss definitions.)

An error of that kind is possible only on the basis of assuming that man learns concepts by memorizing their definitions, i.e., on the basis of studying the epistemology of a parrot. But that is not what we are here studying. To grasp a concept is to grasp and, in part, to retrace the process by which it was formed. To retrace that process is to grasp at least *some* of the units which it subsumes (and thus to link one's understanding of the concept to the facts of reality).

Just as wider integrations of concepts require a more *extensive* knowledge, so narrower subdivisions of concepts require a more *intensive* knowledge. For instance, the concept "father" requires more knowledge than the concept "man"—since it requires knowledge of man, of the act of reproduction, and of the consequent relationship.

2. The formation of a concept provides man with the means of identifying, not only the concretes he has observed, but all the concretes *of that kind* which he may encounter in the future. Thus, when he has formed or grasped the concept "man," he does not have to regard every man he meets thereafter as a new phenomenon to be studied from scratch: he identifies him as "man" and applies to him the knowledge he has acquired about man (which

leaves him free to study the particular, individual character-istics of the newcomer, i.e., the individual measurements within the categories established by the concept "man").

This process of conceptual identification (of subsuming a new concrete under an appropriate concept) is learned as one learns to speak, and it becomes automatic in the case of existents given in perceptual awareness, such as "man," "table," "blue," "length," etc. But it grows progressively more difficult as man's concepts move farther away from direct perceptual evidence, and involve complex combina-tions and cross-classifications of many earlier concepts. (Ob-serve the difficulties of identifying a given political system, or of diagnosing a rare disease.) In such cases, the knowl-edge of whether a concrete is or is not to be subsumed under a certain concept does not come automatically, but requires a new cognitive effort.

Thus the process of forming and applying concepts con-tains the essential pattern of two fundamental methods of cognition: *induction* and *deduction*.

The process of observing the facts of reality and of inte-grating them into concepts is, in essence, a process of induc-tion. The process of subsuming new instances under a known concept is, in essence, a process of deduction.

4. Concepts of Consciousness

Consciousness is the faculty of awareness—the faculty of perceiving that which exists.

Awareness is not a passive state, but an active process. On the lower levels of awareness, a complex neurological process is required to enable man to experience a sensation and to integrate sensations into percepts; that process is automatic and non-volitional: man is aware of its results, but not of the process itself. On the higher, conceptual level, the process is psychological, conscious and volitional. In either case, awareness is achieved and maintained by continuous *action*.

Directly or indirectly, every phenomenon of consciousness is derived from one's awareness of the external world. Some object, i.e., some *content,* is involved in every state of awareness. Extrospection is a process of cognition directed outward—a process of apprehending some existent(s) of the external world. Introspection is a process of cognition directed inward—a process of apprehending one's own psychological actions in regard to some existent(s) of the external world, such actions as thinking, feeling, reminiscing, etc. It is only in relation to the external world that the various actions of a consciousness can be experienced, grasped, defined or communicated. Awareness is awareness of something. A content-less state of consciousness is a contradiction in terms.

Two fundamental attributes are involved in every state,

aspect or function of man's consciousness: content and action—the content of awareness, and the action of consciousness in regard to that content.

These two attributes are the fundamental Conceptual Common Denominator of all concepts pertaining to consciousness.

On the perceptual level of awareness, a child merely experiences and performs various psychological processes; his full conceptual development requires that he learn to conceptualize them (after he has reached a certain stage in his extrospective conceptual development).

To form concepts of consciousness, one must isolate the action from the content of a given state of consciousness, by a process of abstraction. Just as, extrospectively, man can abstract attributes from entities—so, introspectively, he can abstract the actions of his consciousness from its contents, and observe the *differences* among these various actions.

For instance (on the adult level), when a man sees a woman walking down the street, the action of his consciousness is *perception;* when he notes that she is beautiful, the action of his consciousness is *evaluation;* when he experiences an inner state of pleasure and approval, of admiration, the action of his consciousness is *emotion;* when he stops to watch her and draws conclusions, from the evidence, about her character, age, social position, etc., the action of his consciousness is *thought;* when, later, he recalls the incident, the action of his consciousness is *reminiscence;* when he projects that her appearance would be improved if her hair were blond rather than brown, and her dress were blue rather than red, the action of his consciousness is *imagination.*

He can also observe the *similarities* among the actions of his consciousness on various occasions, by observing the fact that these same actions—in different sequences, combinations and degrees—are, have been or can be applicable to other objects: to a man, a dog, an automobile, or the entire street; to the reading of a book, the learning of a new skill, the choice of a job, or to any object within the scope of his awareness.

Such is the pattern of the process by which (in slower, gradual steps) man learns to form concepts of consciousness.

In the realm of introspection, the concretes, the *units* which are integrated into a single concept, are the specific instances of a given psychological process. The measurable attributes of a psychological process are its object or *content* and its *intensity*.

The content is some aspect of the external world (or is derived from some aspect of the external world) and is measurable by the various methods of measurement applicable to the external world. The intensity of a psychological process is the automatically summed up result of many factors: of its scope, its clarity, its cognitive and motivational context, the degree of mental energy or effort required, etc.

There is no exact method of measuring the intensity of all psychological processes, but—as in the case of forming concepts of colors—conceptualization does not require the knowledge of exact measurements. Degrees of intensity can be and are measured approximately, on a comparative scale. For instance, the intensity of the emotion of joy in response to certain facts varies according to the importance of these facts in one's *hierarchy* of values; it varies in such cases as buying a new suit, or getting a raise in pay, or marrying the person one loves. The intensity of a process of thought and of the intellectual effort required varies according to the *scope* of its content; it varies when one grasps the concept "table" or the concept "justice," when one grasps that $2 + 2 = 4$ or that $e = mc^2$.

The formation of introspective concepts follows the same principles as the formation of extrospective concepts. A concept pertaining to consciousness is a mental integration of two or more instances of a psychological process possessing the same distinguishing characteristics, with the particular contents and the measurements of the action's intensity omitted—on the principle that these omitted measurements must exist in *some* quantity, but may exist in *any* quantity (i.e., a given psychological process must possess *some* con-

tent and *some* degree of intensity, but may possess *any*
content or degree of the appropriate category).

For instance, the concept "thought" is formed by retaining the distinguishing characteristics of the psychological
action (a purposefully directed process of cognition) and by
omitting the particular contents as well as the degree of the
intellectual effort's intensity. The concept "emotion" is formed
by retaining the distinguishing characteristics of the psychological action (an automatic response proceeding from an
evaluation of an existent) and by omitting the particular
contents (the existents) as well as the degree of emotional
intensity.

Now observe that I have mentioned the terms *scope* and
hierarchy in connection with the intensity of psychological
processes. These are terms that belong to the category of
measurements—and they indicate more precise methods of
measuring some psychological phenomena.

In regard to the concepts pertaining to cognition ("thought,"
"observation," "reasoning," "learning," etc.), the scope of
the content provides a method of measurement. The scope is
gauged by two interrelated aspects: by the scope of the
factual material involved in a given cognitive process, and
by *the length of the conceptual chain* required to deal with
that material. Since concepts have a hierarchical structure,
i.e., since the higher, more complex abstractions are derived
from the simpler, basic ones (starting with the concepts of
perceptually given concretes), the distance from the perceptual level of the concepts used in a given cognitive process
indicates the scope of that process. (The level of abstraction
with which a man is able to deal indicates how much he had
to know in order to reach that level. I am not speaking here
of men who mouth memorized floating abstractions, but
only of those who actually grasp all the steps involved.)

In regard to the concepts pertaining to evaluation ("value,"
"emotion," "feeling," "desire," etc.), the hierarchy involved
is of a different kind and requires an entirely different type
of measurement. It is a type applicable only to the psychological process of evaluation, and may be designated as *"teleological measurement."*

Measurement is the identification of a relationship—a quantitative relationship established by means of a standard that serves as a unit. Teleological measurement deals, not with cardinal, but with *ordinal* numbers—and the standard serves to establish a graded relationship of means to end.

For instance, a moral code is a system of teleological measurement which grades the choices and actions open to man, according to the degree to which they achieve or frustrate the code's standard of value. The standard is the end, to which man's actions are the means.

A moral code is a set of abstract principles; to practice it, an individual must translate it into the appropriate concretes —he must choose the particular goals and values which he is to pursue. This requires that he define his particular hierarchy of values, in the order of their importance, and that he act accordingly. Thus all his actions have to be guided by a process of teleological measurement. (The degree of uncertainty and contradictions in a man's hierarchy of values is the degree to which he will be unable to perform such measurements and will fail in his attempts at value calculations or at purposeful action.)

Teleological measurement has to be performed in and against an enormous context: it consists of establishing the relationship of a given choice to all the other possible choices and to one's hierarchy of values.

The simplest example of this process, which all men practice (with various degrees of precision and success), may be seen in the realm of material values—in the (implicit) principles that guide a man's spending of money. On any level of income, a man's money is a limited quantity; in spending it, he weighs the value of his purchase against the value of every other purchase open to him for the same amount of money, he weighs it against the hierarchy of all his other goals, desires and needs, then makes the purchase or not accordingly.

The same kind of measurement guides man's actions in the wider realm of moral or spiritual values. (By "spiritual" I mean "pertaining to consciousness." I say "wider" because it is man's hierarchy of values in this realm that determines his hierarchy of values in the material or economic realm.) But the currency or medium of exchange is different. In the spiritual realm, the currency—which exists in limited quantity and must be teleologically measured in the pursuit of any value—is *time*, i.e., *one's life.*

Since a value is that which one acts to gain and/or keep, and the amount of possible action is limited by the duration of one's lifespan, it is a part of one's life that one invests in everything one values. The years, months, days or hours of thought, of interest, of action devoted to a value are the currency with which one pays for the enjoyment one receives from it.

Now let us answer the question: "Can you measure love?"

The concept "love" is formed by isolating two or more instances of the appropriate psychological process, then retaining its distinguishing characteristics (an emotion proceeding from the evaluation of an existent as a positive value and as a source of pleasure) and omitting the object and the measurements of the process's intensity.

The object may be a thing, an event, an activity, a condition or a person. The intensity varies according to one's evaluation of the object, as, for instance, in such cases as one's love for ice cream, or for parties, or for reading, or for freedom, or for the person one marries. The concept "love" subsumes a vast range of values and, consequently, of intensity: it extends from the lower levels (designated by the sub-category "liking") to the higher level (designated by the sub-category "affection," which is applicable only in regard to persons) to the highest level, which includes romantic love.

If one wants to measure the intensity of a particular instance of love, one does so by reference to the hierarchy of values of the person experiencing it. A man may love a woman, yet may rate the neurotic satisfactions of sexual promiscuity higher than her value to him. Another man may love a woman, but may give her up, rating his fear of the disapproval of others (of his family, his friends or any random strangers) higher than her value. Still another man may risk his life to save the woman he loves, because all his other values would lose meaning without her. The emotions in these examples are not emotions of the same intensity or dimension. Do not let a James Taggart type of mystic tell you that love is immeasurable.

Certain categories of concepts of consciousness require special consideration. These are concepts pertaining to the *products* of psychological processes, such as "knowledge," "science," "idea," etc.

These concepts are formed by retaining their distinguishing characteristics and omitting their content. For instance, the concept "knowledge" is formed by retaining its distinguishing characteristics (a mental grasp of a fact(s) of reality, reached either by perceptual observation or by a process of reason based on perceptual observation) and omitting the particular fact(s) involved.

The intensity of the psychological processes which led to the products is irrelevant here, but the *nature* of these processes is included in the distinguishing characteristics of the concepts, and serves to differentiate the various concepts of this kind.

It is important to note that these concepts are not the equivalent of their existential content—and that they belong to the category of epistemological concepts, with their metaphysical component regarded as their content. For instance, the concept "the science of physics" is not the same thing as the physical phenomena which are the content of the science. The phenomena exist independent of man's knowledge; the science is an organized body of knowledge about these phenomena, acquired by and communicable to a human consciousness. The phenomena would continue to exist, even if no human consciousness remained in existence; the science would not.

A special sub-category of concepts pertaining to the products of consciousness, is reserved for concepts of *method*. Concepts of method designate systematic courses of action devised by men for the purpose of achieving certain goals. The course of action may be purely psychological (such as a method of using one's consciousness) or it may involve a combination of psychological and physical actions (such as a method of drilling for oil), according to the goal to be achieved.

Concepts of method are formed by retaining the distinguishing characteristics of the purposive course of action and of its goal, while omitting the particular measurements of both.

For instance, *the* fundamental concept of method, the one on which all the others depend, is *logic*. The distinguishing characteristic of logic (the art of non-contradictory identification) indicates the nature of the actions (actions of consciousness required to achieve a correct identification) and their goal (knowledge)—while omitting the length, complexity or specific steps of the process of logical inference, as well as the nature of the particular cognitive problem involved in any given instance of using logic.

Concepts of method represent a large part of man's conceptual equipment. Epistemology is a science devoted to the discovery of the proper methods of acquiring and validating knowledge. Ethics is a science devoted to the discovery of the proper methods of living one's life. Medicine is a science devoted to the discovery of the proper methods of curing disease. All the applied sciences (i.e., technology) are sciences devoted to the discovery of methods.

The concepts of method are the link to the vast and complex category of concepts that represent integrations of existential concepts with concepts of consciousness, a category that includes most of the concepts pertaining to man's actions. Concepts of this category have no direct referents on the perceptual level of awareness (though they include perceptual components) and can neither be formed nor grasped without a long antecedent chain of concepts.

For instance, the concept "marriage" denotes a certain moral-legal relationship between a man and a woman, which entails a certain pattern of behavior, based on a mutual agreement and sanctioned by law. The concept "marriage" cannot be formed or grasped merely by observing the behavior of a couple: it requires the integration of their actions with a number of concepts of consciousness, such as "contractual agreement," "morality" and "law."

The concept "property" denotes the relationship of a man to an object (or an idea): his right to use it and to dispose of it—and involves a long chain of moral-legal concepts, including the procedure by which the object was acquired. The mere observation of a man in the act of using an object will not convey the concept "property."

Composite concepts of this kind are formed by isolating the appropriate existents, relationships and actions, then retaining their distinguishing characteristics and omitting the type of measurements appropriate to the various categories of concepts involved.

Now a word about grammar. Grammar is a science dealing with the formulation of the proper methods of verbal expression and communication, i.e., the methods of organizing words (concepts) into sentences. Grammar pertains to the actions of consciousness, and involves a number of special concepts—such as conjunctions, which are concepts denoting relationships among thoughts ("and," "but," "or," etc.). These concepts are formed by retaining the distinguishing characteristics of the relationship and omitting the particular thoughts involved. The purpose of conjunctions is verbal economy: they serve to integrate and/or condense the content of certain thoughts.

For instance, the word "and" serves to integrate a number of facts into one thought. If one says: "Smith, Jones and Brown are walking," the "and" indicates that the observation "are walking" applies to the three individuals named. Is there an object in reality corresponding to the word "and"? No. Is there a fact in reality corresponding to the word "and"? Yes. The fact is that three men are walking—and that the word "and" integrates into one thought a fact which otherwise would have to be expressed by: "Smith is walking. Jones is walking. Brown is walking."

The word "but" serves to indicate an exception to or a contradiction of the possible implications of a given thought.

If one says: "She is beautiful, but dumb," the "but" serves to condense the following thoughts: "This girl is beautiful. Beauty is a positive attribute, a value. Before you conclude that this girl is valuable, you must consider also her negative attribute: she is dumb." If one says: "I work every day, but not on Sunday," the "but" indicates an exception and condenses the following: "I work on Monday. I work on Tuesday. (And so on, four more times.) My activity on Sunday is different: I do not work on Sunday."

(These examples are for the benefit of those victims of modern philosophy who are taught by Linguistic Analysis that there is no way to derive conjunctions from experience, i.e., from the facts of reality.)

A certain aspect of the epistemological state of today's culture is worth noting at this point.

Observe that the attacks on the conceptual level of man's consciousness, i.e., on reason, come from the same ideological quarters as the attacks on *measurement*. When discussing man's consciousness, particularly his emotions, some persons use the word "measurement" as a pejorative term—as if an attempt to apply it to the phenomena of consciousness were a gross, insulting, "materialistic" impropriety. The question "Can you measure love?" is an example and a symptom of that attitude.

As in many other issues, the two allegedly opposite camps are merely two variants growing out of the same basic premises. The old-fashioned mystics proclaim that you cannot measure love in pounds, inches or dollars. They are aided and abetted by the neo-mystics who—punch-drunk with undigested concepts of measurement, proclaiming measurement to be the sole tool of science—proceed to measure knee-jerks, statistical questionnaires, and the learning time of rats, as indices to the human psyche.

Both camps fail to observe that *measurement requires an appropriate standard,* and that in the physical sciences—which one camp passionately hates, and the other passionately envies—one does not measure length in pounds, or weight in inches.

Measurement is the identification of a relationship in numerical terms—and the complexity of the science of measurement indicates the complexity of the relationships which exist in the universe and which man has barely begun to investigate. They exist, even if the appropriate standards and methods of measurement are not always as easily apparent nor the degree of achievable precision as great as in the case of measuring the basic, perceptually given attributes of matter. If anything were actually "immeasurable," it would bear no relationship of any kind to the rest of the universe, it would not affect nor be affected by anything else in any manner whatever, it would enact no causes and bear no consequences—in short, it would not exist.

The motive of the anti-measurement attitude is obvious: it is the desire to preserve a sanctuary of the indeterminate for the benefit of the irrational—the desire, epistemologically, to escape from the responsibility of cognitive precision and wide-scale integration; and, metaphysically, the desire to escape from the absolutism of existence, of facts, of reality and, above all, of *identity*.

5. Definitions

A definition is a statement that identifies the nature of the units subsumed under a concept.

It is often said that definitions state the meaning of words. This is true, but it is not exact. A word is merely a visual-auditory symbol used to represent a concept; a word has no meaning other than that of the concept it symbolizes, and the meaning of a concept consists of its units. It is not words, but concepts that man defines—by specifying their referents.

The purpose of a definition is to distinguish a concept from all other concepts and thus to keep its units differentiated from all other existents.

Since the definition of a concept is formulated in terms of other concepts, it enables man, not only to identify and *retain* a concept, but also to establish the relationships, the hierarchy, the *integration* of all his concepts and thus the integration of his knowledge. Definitions preserve, not the chronological order in which a given man may have learned concepts, but the *logical* order of their hierarchical interdependence.

With certain significant exceptions, every concept can be defined and communicated in terms of other concepts. The exceptions are concepts referring to sensations, and metaphysical axioms.

Sensations are the primary material of consciousness and, therefore, cannot be communicated by means of the material which is derived from them. The existential causes of sensations can be described and defined in conceptual terms (e.g., the wavelengths of light and the structure of the human eye, which produce the sensations of color), but one cannot communicate what color is like, to a person who is born blind. To define the meaning of the concept "blue," for instance, one must point to some blue objects to signify, in effect: "I mean *this*." Such an identification of a concept is known as an "ostensive definition."

Ostensive definitions are usually regarded as applicable only to conceptualized sensations. But they are applicable to axioms as well. Since axiomatic concepts are identifications of irreducible primaries, the only way to define one is by means of an ostensive definition—e.g., to define "existence," one would have to sweep one's arm around and say: "I mean *this*." (We shall discuss axioms later.)

The rules of correct definition are derived from the process of concept-formation. The units of a concept were differentiated—by means of a distinguishing characteristic(s)—from other existents possessing a commensurable characteristic, a "Conceptual Common Denominator." A definition follows the same principle: it specifies the distinguishing characteristic(s) of the units, and indicates the category of existents from which they were differentiated.

The distinguishing characteristic(s) of the units becomes the *differentia* of the concept's definition; the existents possessing a "Conceptual Common Denominator" become the *genus*.

Thus a definition complies with the two essential functions of consciousness: differentiation and integration. The differentia isolates the units of a concept from all other existents; the genus indicates their connection to a wider group of existents.

For instance, in the definition of table ("An item of furniture, consisting of a flat, level surface and supports, intended to support other, smaller objects"), the specified shape is the differentia, which distinguishes tables from the other entities belonging to the same genus: furniture. In the definition of man ("A rational animal"), "rational" is the differentia, "animal" is the genus.

Just as a concept becomes a unit when integrated with others into a wider concept, so a genus becomes a single unit, a *species*, when integrated with others into a wider genus. For instance, "table" is a species of the genus "furniture," which is a species of the genus "household goods," which is a species of the genus "man-made objects." "Man" is a species of the genus "animal," which is a species of the genus "organism," which is a species of the genus "entity."

A definition is not a description; it *implies*, but does not mention all the characteristics of a concept's units. If a definition were to list all the characteristics, it would defeat its own purpose: it would provide an indiscriminate, undifferentiated and, in effect, pre-conceptual conglomeration of characteristics which would not serve to distinguish the units from all other existents, nor the concept from all other concepts. A definition must identify the *nature* of the units, i.e., the *essential* characteristics without which the units would not be the kind of existents they are. But it is important to remember that a definition implies *all* the characteristics of the units, since it identifies their *essential*, not their *exhaustive*, characteristics; since it designates *existents*, not their isolated aspects; and since it is a condensation of, not a substitute for, a wider knowledge of the existents involved.

This leads to a crucial question: since a group of existents may possess more than one characteristic distinguishing them from other existents, how does one determine the essential characteristic of an existent and, therefore, the proper defining characteristic of a concept?

The answer is provided by the process of concept-formation.

Concepts are not and cannot be formed in a vacuum; they are formed in a context; the process of conceptualization consists of observing the differences and similarities of the existents *within the field of one's awareness* (and organizing them into concepts accordingly). From a child's grasp of the simplest concept integrating a group of perceptually given concretes, to a scientist's grasp of the most complex abstractions integrating long conceptual chains—all conceptualization is a contextual process; the context is the entire field of a mind's awareness or knowledge at any level of its cognitive development.

This does not mean that conceptualization is a subjective process or that the content of concepts depends on an individual's subjective (i.e., arbitrary) choice. The only issue open to an individual's choice in this matter is how much knowledge he will seek to acquire and, consequently, what conceptual complexity he will be able to reach. But so long as and to the extent that his mind deals with concepts (as distinguished from memorized sounds and floating abstractions), the content of his concepts is determined and dictated by the cognitive content of his mind, i.e., by his grasp of the facts of reality. If his grasp is non-contradictory, then even if the scope of his knowledge is modest and the content of his concepts is primitive, *it will not contradict the content of the same concepts in the mind of the most advanced scientists.*

The same is true of definitions. *All definitions are contextual,* and a primitive definition *does not contradict* a more advanced one: the latter merely expands the former.

As an example, let us trace the development of the concept "man."

On the pre-verbal level of awareness, when a child first learns to differentiate men from the rest of his perceptual field, he observes distinguishing characteristics which, if translated into words, would amount to a definition such as: "A thing that moves and makes sounds." Within the context of his awareness, this is a valid definition: man, in fact, does move and make sounds, and this distinguishes him from the inanimate objects around him.

When the child observes the existence of cats, dogs and automobiles, his definition ceases to be valid: it is still true that man moves and makes sounds, but these characteristics do not distinguish him from other entities in the field of the child's awareness. The child's (wordless) definition then changes to some equivalent of: "A living thing that walks on two legs and has no fur," with the characteristics of "moving and making sounds" remaining implicit, but no longer defining. Again, this definition is valid—within the context of the child's awareness.

When the child learns to speak and the field of his awareness expands still further, his definition of man expands accordingly. It becomes something like: "A living being that speaks and does things no other living beings can do."

This type of definition will suffice for a long time (a great many men, some modern scientists among them, never progress beyond some variant of this definition). But this ceases to be valid at about the time of the child's adolescence, when he observes (if his conceptual development continues) that his knowledge of the "things no other living beings can do" has grown to an enormous, incoherent, unexplained collection of activities, some of which are performed by all men, but some are not, some of which are even performed by animals (such as building shelters), but in some significantly different manner, etc. He realizes that his definition is neither applicable equally to all men, nor does it serve to distinguish men from all other living beings.

It is at this stage that he asks himself: What is the common characteristic of all of man's varied activities? What is their root? What capacity enables man to perform them and thus distinguishes him from all other animals? When he grasps that man's distinctive characteristic is his type of consciousness—a consciousness able to abstract, to form concepts, to apprehend reality by a process of reason—he reaches the one and only valid definition of man, within the context of his knowledge and of all of mankind's knowledge to date: "*A rational animal.*"

("Rational," in this context, does not mean "acting invariably in accordance with reason"; it means "possessing the faculty of reason." A full biological definition of man would include many sub-categories of "animal," but the general category and the ultimate definition remain the same.)

Observe that all of the above versions of a definition of man were *true*, i.e., were correct identifications of the facts of reality—and that they were valid *qua* definitions, i.e., were correct selections of distinguishing characteristics in a given context of knowledge. None of them was contradicted by subsequent knowledge: they were included implicitly, as non-defining characteristics, in a more precise definition of man. It is still true that man is a rational animal who speaks, does things no other living beings can do, walks on two legs, has no fur, moves and makes sounds.

The specific steps given in this example are not necessarily the literal steps of the conceptual development of every man, there may be many more steps (or fewer), they may not be as clearly and consciously delimited—but this is the *pattern* of development which most concepts and definitions undergo in a man's mind with the growth of his knowledge. It is the pattern which makes intensive study and, therefore, the growth of knowledge—*and of science*—possible.

Now observe, on the above example, the process of determining an essential characteristic: the rule of *fundamentality*. When a given group of existents has more than one characteristic distinguishing it from other existents, man must observe the relationships among these various characteristics and discover the one on which all the others (or the greatest number of others) depend, i.e., the fundamental characteristic without which the others would not be possible. This fundamental characteristic is the *essential* distinguishing characteristic of the existents involved, and the proper *defining* characteristic of the concept.

Metaphysically, a fundamental characteristic is that distinctive characteristic which makes the greatest number of others possible; epistemologically, it is the one that explains the greatest number of others.

For instance, one could observe that man is the only animal who speaks English, wears wristwatches, flies airplanes, manufactures lipstick, studies geometry, reads newspapers, writes poems, darns socks, etc. None of these is an essential characteristic: none of them explains the others; none of them applies to all men; omit any or all of them, assume a man who has never done any of these things, and he will still be a *man*. But observe that all these activities (and innumerable others) require a *conceptual grasp* of reality, that an animal would not be able to understand them, that they are the expressions and consequences of man's rational faculty, that an organism without that faculty would *not* be a man—and you will know why man's rational faculty is his *essential* distinguishing and defining characteristic.

If definitions are contextual, how does one determine an objective definition valid for all men? It is determined according to the widest context of knowledge available to man on the subjects relevant to the units of a given concept.

Objective validity is determined by reference to the facts of reality. But it is man who has to identify the facts; objectivity requires discovery by man—and cannot precede man's knowledge, i.e., cannot require omniscience. Man *cannot* know more than he has discovered—and he *may not* know less than the evidence indicates, if his concepts and definitions are to be objectively valid.

In this issue, an ignorant adult is in the same position as a child or adolescent. He has to act within the scope of such knowledge as he possesses and of his correspondingly primitive conceptual definitions. When he moves into a wider field of action and thought, when new evidence confronts him, he has to expand his definitions according to the evidence, if they are to be objectively valid.

An objective definition, valid for all men, is one that designates the *essential* distinguishing characteristic(s) and genus of the existents subsumed under a given concept—according to all the relevant knowledge available at that stage of mankind's development.

(Who decides, in case of disagreements? As in all issues pertaining to objectivity, there is no ultimate authority, except reality and the mind of every individual who judges the evidence by the *objective* method of judgment: logic.)

This does not mean that every man has to be a universal scholar and that every discovery of science affects the definitions of concepts: when science discovers some previously unknown aspects of reality, it forms *new* concepts to identify them (e.g., "electron"); but insofar as science is concerned with the intensive study of previously known and conceptualized existents, its discoveries are identified by means of conceptual sub-categories. For instance, man is classified biologically in several sub-categories of "animal," such as "mammal," etc. But this does not alter the fact that rationality is his essential distinguishing and defining characteristic, and that "animal" is the wider genus to which he belongs. (And it does not alter the fact that when a scientist and an illiterate use the concept "man," they are referring to the same kind of entities.)

Only when and if some discovery were to make the definition "rational animal" inaccurate (i.e., no longer serving to distinguish man from all other existents) would the question of expanding the definition arise. "Expanding" does not mean negating, abrogating or contradicting; it means demonstrating that some other characteristics are more distinctive of man than rationality and animality—in which unlikely case these two would be regarded as non-defining characteristics, but would still remain true.

Remember that concept-formation is a method of cognition, man's method, and that concepts represent classifications of observed existents according to their relationships to other observed existents. Since man is not omniscient, a definition cannot be changelessly absolute, because it cannot establish the relationship of a given group of existents to everything else in the universe, including the undiscovered and unknown. And for the very same reasons, a definition is false and worthless if it is not *contextually* absolute—if it does not specify the known relationships among existents (in terms of the known *essential* characteristics) or if it contradicts the known (by omission or evasion).

The nominalists of modern philosophy, particularly the logical positivists and linguistic analysts, claim that the alternative of true or false is not applicable to definitions, only to "factual" propositions. Since words, they claim, represent arbitrary human (social) conventions, and concepts have no objective referents in reality, a definition can be neither true nor false. The assault on reason has never reached a deeper level or a lower depth than this.

Propositions consist of words—and the question of how a series of sounds unrelated to the facts of reality can produce a "factual" proposition or establish a criterion of discrimination between truth and falsehood, is a question not worth debating. Nor can it be debated by means of inarticulate sounds that switch meanings at the whim of any speaker's mood, stupor or expediency of any given moment. (But the results of that notion can be observed in university classrooms, in the offices of psychiatrists, or on the front pages of today's newspapers.)

Truth is the product of the recognition (i.e., identification) of the facts of reality. Man identifies and integrates the facts of reality by means of concepts. He retains concepts in his mind by means of definitions. He organizes concepts into propositions—and the truth or falsehood of his propositions rests, not only on their relation to the facts he asserts, but also on the truth or falsehood of the definitions of the concepts he uses to assert them, which rests on the truth or falsehood of his designations of *essential* characteristics.

Every concept stands for a number of propositions. A concept identifying perceptual concretes stands for some implicit propositions; but on the higher levels of abstraction, a concept stands for chains and paragraphs and pages of *explicit* propositions referring to complex factual data. *A definition is the condensation of a vast body of observations— and stands or falls with the truth or falsehood of these observations.* Let me repeat: *a definition is a condensation.* As a legal preamble (referring here to *epistemological* law), every definition begins with the implicit proposition: "After full consideration of all the known facts pertaining to this group of existents, the following has been demonstrated to be their essential, therefore defining, characteristic . . ."

In the light of this fact, consider some modern examples of proposed definitions. A noted anthropologist, writing in a national magazine, suggests that man's essential distinction from all other animals, the essential characteristic responsible for his unique development and achievements, is the possession of a thumb. (The same article asserts that the dinosaur also possessed a thumb, but "somehow failed to develop.") What about man's type of consciousness? Blank out.

An article in a reputable encyclopedia suggests that man might be defined as "a language-having animal." Is "language-having" a primary characteristic, independent of any other characteristic or faculty? Does language consist of the ability to articulate sounds? If so, then parrots and myna-birds should be classified as men. If they should not, then what human faculty do they lack? Blank out.

There is no difference between such definitions and those chosen by individuals who define man as "a Christian (or Jewish or Mohammedan) animal" or "a white-skinned animal" or "an animal of exclusively Aryan descent," etc.—no difference in epistemological principle or in practical consequences (or in psychological motive).

The truth or falsehood of all of man's conclusions, inferences, thought and knowledge rests on the truth or falsehood of his definitions.

(The above applies only to valid concepts. There are such things as invalid concepts, i.e., words that represent attempts to integrate errors, contradictions or false propositions, such as concepts originating in mysticism—or words without specific definitions, without referents, which can mean anything to anyone, such as modern "anti-concepts." Invalid concepts appear occasionally in men's languages, but are usually—though not necessarily—short-lived, since they lead to cognitive dead-ends. An invalid concept invalidates every proposition or process of thought in which it is used as a cognitive assertion.)

Above the level of conceptualized sensations and metaphysical axioms, every concept requires a verbal definition. Paradoxically enough, it is the simplest concepts that most people find it hardest to define—the concepts of the perceptual concretes with which they deal daily, such as "table," "house," "man," "walking," "tall," "number," etc. There is a good reason for it: such concepts are, chronologically, the first concepts man forms or grasps, and can be defined verbally only by means of later concepts—as, for instance, one grasps the concept "table" long before one can grasp such concepts as "flat," "level," "surface," "supports." Most people, therefore, regard formal definitions as unnecessary and treat simple concepts as if they were pure sense data, to be identified by means of ostensive definitions, i.e., simply by pointing.

There is a certain psychological justification for this policy. Man's discriminated awareness begins with *percepts;* the conceptual identifications of daily-observed percepts have become so thoroughly automatized in men's minds that they seem to require no definitions—and men have no difficulty in identifying the referents of such concepts ostensively.

(This, incidentally, is one instance demonstrating the grotesque inversions of Linguistic Analysis: the stock-in-trade of linguistic analysts consists of reducing people to stammering helplessness by demanding that they define "house" or "which" or "but," then proclaiming that since people cannot define *even* such simple words, they cannot be expected to define more complex ones, and, therefore, there can be no such things as definitions—or concepts.)

In fact and in practice, so long as men *are* able to identify with full certainty the perceptual referents of simple concepts, it is not necessary for them to devise or memorize the verbal definitions of such concepts. What *is* necessary is a knowledge of the rules by which the definitions can be formulated; and what is *urgently* necessary is a clear grasp of that dividing line beyond which ostensive definitions are no longer sufficient. (That dividing line begins at the point where a man uses words with the feeling "I kinda know what I mean.") Most people have no grasp of that line and no inkling of the necessity to grasp it—and the disastrous, paralyzing, stultifying consequences are the greatest single cause of mankind's intellectual erosion.

(As an illustration, observe what Bertrand Russell was able to perpetrate because people thought they "kinda knew" the meaning of the concept "number"—and what the collectivists were able to perpetrate because people did not even pretend to know the meaning of the concept "man.")

To know the exact meaning of the concepts one is using, one must know their correct definitions, one must be able to retrace the specific (logical, not chronological) steps by which they were formed, and one must be able to demonstrate their connection to their base in perceptual reality.

When in doubt about the meaning or the definition of a concept, the best method of clarification is to look for its referents—i.e., to ask oneself: What fact or facts of reality gave rise to this concept? What distinguishes it from all other concepts?

For instance: what fact of reality gave rise to the concept "justice"? The fact that man must draw conclusions about the things, people and events around him, i.e., must judge and evaluate them. Is his judgment automatically right? No. What causes his judgment to be wrong? The lack of sufficient evidence, or his evasion of the evidence, or his inclusion of considerations other than the facts of the case. How, then, is he to arrive at the right judgment? By basing it exclusively on the factual evidence and by considering all the relevant evidence available. But isn't this a description of "objectivity"? Yes, "objective judgment" is one of the wider categories to which the concept "justice" belongs. What distinguishes "justice" from other instances of objective judgment? When one evaluates the nature or actions of inanimate objects, the criterion of judgment is determined by the particular purpose for which one evaluates them. But how does one determine a criterion for evaluating the character and actions of men, in view of the fact that men possess the faculty of volition? What science can provide an objective criterion of evaluation in regard to volitional matters? Ethics. Now, do I need a concept to designate the act of judging a man's character and/or actions exclusively on the basis of all the factual evidence available, and of evaluating it by means of an objective moral criterion? Yes. That concept is "justice."

Note what a long chain of considerations and observations is condensed into a single concept. And the chain is much longer than the abbreviated pattern presented here—because every concept used in this example stands for similar chains.

Please bear this example in mind. We shall discuss this issue further when we discuss the cognitive role of concepts.

Let us note, at this point, the radical difference between Aristotle's view of concepts and the Objectivist view, particularly in regard to the issue of essential characteristics.

It is Aristotle who first formulated the principles of correct definition. It is Aristotle who identified the fact that only concretes exist. But Aristotle held that definitions refer to metaphysical *essences,* which exist *in* concretes as a special element or formative power, and he held that the process of concept-formation depends on a kind of direct intuition by which man's mind grasps these essences and forms concepts accordingly.

Aristotle regarded "essence" as metaphysical; Objectivism regards it as *epistemological.*

Objectivism holds that the essence of a concept is that fundamental characteristic(s) of its units on which the greatest number of other characteristics depend, and which distinguishes these units from all other existents within the field of man's knowledge. Thus the essence of a concept is determined *contextually* and may be altered with the growth of man's knowledge. The metaphysical referent of man's concepts is not a special, separate metaphysical essence, but the *total* of the facts of reality he has observed, and this total determines which characteristics of a given group of existents he designates as *essential.* An essential characteristic is factual, in the sense that it does exist, does determine other characteristics and does distinguish a group of existents from all others; it is *epistemological* in the sense that the classification of "essential characteristic" is a device of man's method of cognition—a means of classifying, condensing and integrating an ever-growing body of knowledge.

Now refer to the four historical schools of thought on the issue of concepts, which I listed in the foreword to this work—and observe that the dichotomy of "intrinsic or subjective" has played havoc with this issue, as it has with every issue involving the relationship of consciousness to existence.

The extreme realist (Platonist) and the moderate realist (Aristotelian) schools of thought regard the referents of concepts as *intrinsic,* i.e., as "universals" inherent in things (either as archetypes or as metaphysical essences), as special existents unrelated to man's consciousness—to be perceived by man directly, like any other kind of concrete existents, but perceived by some non-sensory or extra-sensory means.

The nominalist and the conceptualist schools regard concepts as *subjective,* i.e., as products of man's consciousness, unrelated to the facts of reality, as mere "names" or notions arbitrarily assigned to arbitrary groupings of concretes on the ground of vague, inexplicable resemblances.

The extreme realist school attempts, in effect, to preserve the primacy of existence (of reality) by dispensing with consciousness—i.e., by converting concepts into concrete existents and reducing consciousness to the perceptual level, i.e., to the automatic function of grasping percepts (by supernatural means, since no such percepts exist).

The extreme nominalist (contemporary) school attempts to establish the primacy of consciousness by dispensing with existence (with reality)—i.e., by denying the status of existents even to concretes and converting concepts into conglomerates of fantasy, constructed out of the debris of other, lesser fantasies, such as words without referents or incantations of sounds corresponding to nothing in an unknowable reality.

To compound the chaos: it must be noted that the Platonist school begins by accepting the primacy of consciousness, by reversing the relationship of consciousness to existence, by assuming that reality must conform to the content of consciousness, not the other way around—on the premise that the presence of any notion in man's mind proves the existence of a corresponding referent in reality. But the Platonist school still retains some vestige of respect for reality, if only in unstated motivation: it distorts reality into a mystical construct in order to extort its sanction and validate subjectivism. The nominalist school begins, with empiricist humility, by negating the power of consciousness to form any valid generalizations about existence—and ends up with a subjectivism that requires no sanction, a consciousness freed from the "tyranny" of reality.

None of these schools regards concepts as *objective,* i.e., as neither revealed nor invented, but as produced by man's consciousuess in accordance with the facts of reality, as mental integrations of factual data computed by man—as the products of a cognitive method of classification whose processes must be performed by man, but whose content is dictated by reality.

It is as if, philosophically, mankind is still in the stage of transition which characterizes a child in the process of learning to speak—a child who is using his conceptual faculty, but has not developed it sufficiently to be able to examine it self-consciously and discover that what he is using is *reason.*

6. Axiomatic Concepts

Axioms are usually considered to be propositions identifying a fundamental, self-evident truth. But explicit propositions as such are not primaries: they are made of concepts. The base of man's knowledge—of all other concepts, all axioms, propositions and thought—consists of axiomatic concepts.

An axiomatic concept is the identification of a primary fact of reality, which cannot be analyzed, i.e., reduced to other facts or broken into component parts. It is implicit in all facts and in all knowledge. It is the fundamentally given and directly perceived or experienced, which requires no proof or explanation, but on which all proofs and explanations rest.

The first and primary axiomatic concepts are "existence," "identity" (which is a corollary of "existence") and "consciousness." One can study what exists and how consciousness functions; but one cannot analyze (or "prove") existence as such, or consciousness as such. These are irreducible primaries. (An attempt to "prove" them is self-contradictory: it is an attempt to "prove" existence by means of non-existence, and consciousness by means of unconsciousness.)

Existence, identity and consciousness are concepts in that they require identification in conceptual form. Their peculiarity lies in the fact that *they are perceived or experienced directly, but grasped conceptually.* They are implicit in every state of awareness, from the first sensation to the first percept to the sum of all concepts. After the first discriminated sensation (or percept), man's subsequent knowledge adds nothing to the basic facts designated by the terms "existence," "identity," "consciousness"—these facts are contained in any single state of awareness; but what *is* added by subsequent knowledge is *the epistemological need to identify them consciously and self-consciously.* The awareness of this need can be reached only at an advanced stage of conceptual development, when one has acquired a sufficient volume of knowledge—and the identification, the fully conscious grasp, can be achieved only by a process of abstraction.

It is not the abstraction of an attribute from a group of existents, but of a basic fact from all facts. Existence and identity are *not attributes* of existents, they *are* the existents. Consciousness is an attribute of certain living entities, but it is not an attribute of a given state of awareness, it *is* that state. Epistemologically, the formation of axiomatic concepts is an act of abstraction, a selective focusing on and mental isolation of metaphysical fundamentals; but metaphysically, it is an act of integration—*the widest integration possible to man:* it unites and embraces the total of his experience.

The units of the concepts "existence" and "identity" are every entity, attribute, action, event or phenomenon (including consciousness) that exists, has ever existed or will ever exist. The units of the concept "consciousness" are every state or process of awareness that one experiences, has ever experienced or will ever experience (as well as similar units, a similar faculty, which one infers in other living entities). The measurements omitted from axiomatic concepts are all the measurements of all the existents they subsume; what is retained, metaphysically, is only a fundamental fact; what is retained, epistemologically, is only one category of measurement, omitting its particulars: *time*—i.e., the fundamental fact is retained independent of any particular moment of awareness.

Axiomatic concepts are the *constants* of man's consciousness, the *cognitive integrators* that identify and thus protect its continuity. They identify explicitly the omission of psychological time measurements, which is implicit in all other concepts.

It must be remembered that conceptual awareness is the only type of awareness capable of integrating past, present and future. Sensations are merely an awareness of the present and cannot be retained beyond the immediate moment; percepts are retained and, through automatic memory, provide a certain rudimentary link to the past, but cannot project the future. It is only conceptual awareness that can grasp and hold the total of its experience—extrospectively, the continuity of existence; introspectively, the continuity of consciousness—and thus enable its possessor to project his course long-range. It is by means of axiomatic concepts that man grasps and holds this continuity, bringing it into his conscious awareness and *knowledge*. It is axiomatic concepts that identify the precondition of knowledge: the distinction between existence and consciousness, between reality and the awareness of reality, between the object and the subject of cognition. Axiomatic concepts are the foundation of *objectivity*.

Axiomatic concepts identify explicitly what is merely implicit in the consciousness of an infant or of an animal. (Implicit knowledge is passively held material which, to be grasped, requires a special focus and process of consciousness—a process which an infant learns to perform eventually, but which an animal's consciousness is unable to perform.)

If the state of an animal's perceptual awareness could be translated into words, it would amount to a disconnected succession of random moments such as "Here now table— here now tree—here now man—I now see—I now feel," etc.—with the next day or hour starting the succession all over again, with only a few strands of memory in the form of "This now food" or "This now master." What a man's consciousness does with the same material, by means of axiomatic concepts, is: "The table exists—the tree exists— man exists—I am conscious."

(The above projection of an animal's awareness is what

certain modern philosophers, such as logical positivists and logical atomists, ascribe to man, as his start and his only contact with reality—except that they reject the concept "reality," substitute sensations for percepts, and regard everything above this sub-animal level as an arbitrary human "construct.")

Since axiomatic concepts are not formed by differentiating one group of existents from others, but represent an integration of all existents, they have no Conceptual Common Denominator with anything else. They have no contraries, no alternatives. The contrary of the concept "table"—a non-table—is every other kind of existent. The contrary of the concept "man"—a non-man—is every other kind of existent. "Existence," "identity" and "consciousness" have no contraries—only a void.

It may be said that existence can be differentiated from non-existence; but non-existence is not a fact, it is the *absence* of a fact, it is a derivative concept pertaining to a relationship, i.e., a concept which can be formed or grasped only in relation to some existent that has ceased to exist. (One can arrive at the concept "absence" starting from the concept "presence," in regard to some particular existent(s); one cannot arrive at the concept "presence" starting from the concept "absence," with the absence including everything.) Non-existence as such is a zero with no sequence of numbers to follow it, it is the nothing, the total blank.

This gives us a lead to another special aspect of axiomatic concepts: although they designate a fundamental *metaphysical* fact, axiomatic concepts are the products of an *epistemological* need—the need of a volitional, conceptual consciousness which is capable of error and doubt. An animal's perceptual awareness does not need and could not grasp an equivalent of the concepts "existence," "identity" and "consciousness": it deals with them constantly, it is aware of existents, it recognizes various identities, but it takes them (and itself) as the given and can conceive of no alternative. It is only man's consciousness, a consciousness capable of conceptual errors, that needs a special identification of the directly given, to embrace and delimit the entire field of its awareness—to delimit it from the void of unreality to which conceptual errors can lead. Axiomatic concepts are epistemological guidelines. They sum up the essence of all human cognition: something *exists* of which I am *conscious;* I must discover its *identity.*

The concept "existence" does not indicate what existents it subsumes: it merely underscores the primary fact that they *exist.* The concept "identity" does not indicate the particular natures of the existents it subsumes: it merely underscores the primary fact that *they are what they are.* The concept "consciousness" does not indicate what existents one is conscious of: it merely underscores the primary fact that one is *conscious.*

This underscoring of primary facts is one of the crucial epistemological functions of axiomatic concepts. It is also the reason why they can be translated into a statement only in the form of a repetition (as a base and a reminder): Existence exists—Consciousness is conscious—A is A. (This converts axiomatic concepts into formal axioms.)

That special underscoring, which is of no concern to animals, is a matter of life or death for man—as witness, modern philosophy, which is a monument to the results of the attempt to evade or bypass such reminders.

Since axiomatic concepts refer to facts of reality and are not a matter of "faith" or of man's arbitrary choice, there is a way to ascertain whether a given concept is axiomatic or not: one ascertains it by observing the fact that an axiomatic concept cannot be escaped, that it is implicit in all knowledge, that it has to be accepted and used even in the process of any attempt to deny it.

For instance, when modern philosophers declare that axioms are a matter of arbitrary choice, and proceed to choose complex, derivative concepts as the alleged axioms of their alleged reasoning, one can observe that their statements imply and depend on "existence," "consciousness," "identity," which they profess to negate, but which are smuggled into their arguments in the form of unacknowledged, "stolen" concepts.

It is worth noting, at this point, that what the enemies of reason seem to know, but its alleged defenders have not discovered, is the fact that *axiomatic concepts are the guardians of man's mind and the foundation of reason*—the keystone, touchstone and hallmark of reason—and if reason is to be destroyed, it is axiomatic concepts that have to be destroyed.

Observe the fact that in the writings of every school of mysticism and irrationalism, amidst all the ponderously unintelligible verbiage of obfuscations, rationalizations and equivocations (which include protestations of fidelity to reason, and claims to some "higher" form of rationality), one finds, sooner or later, a clear, simple, explicit denial of the validity (of the metaphysical or ontological status) of axiomatic concepts, most frequently of "identity." (For example, see the works of Kant and Hegel.) You do not have to guess, infer or interpret: they tell you. But what you do have to know is the full meaning, implications and consequences of such denials—which, in the history of philosophy, seem to be better understood by the enemies of reason than by its defenders.

One of the consequences (a vulgar variant of concept stealing, prevalent among avowed mystics and irrationalists) is a fallacy I call the *Reification of the Zero*. It consists of regarding "nothing" as a *thing*, as a special, different kind of *existent*. (For example, see Existentialism.) This fallacy breeds such symptoms as the notion that presence and absence, or being and non-being, are metaphysical forces of equal power, and that being is the absence of non-being. E.g., "Nothingness is prior to being." (Sartre)—"Human finitude is the presence of the *not* in the being of man." (William Barrett)—"Nothing is more real than nothing." (Samuel Beckett)—*"Das Nichts nichtet"* or "Nothing noughts." (Heidegger). "Consciousness, then, is not a stuff, but a *negation*. The subject is not a thing, but a *non*-thing. The subject carves its own world out of Being by means of negative determinations. Sartre describes consciousness as a 'noughting nought' *(néant néantisant)*. It is a form of being other than its own: a mode 'which has yet to be what it is, that is to say, which is what it is, that is to say, which is what it is not and which is not what it is.' " (Hector Hawton, *The Feast of Unreason,* London: Watts & Co., 1952, p. 162.)

(The motive? "Genuine utterances about the nothing must always remain unusual. It cannot be made common. It dissolves when it is placed in the cheap acid of mere logical acumen." Heidegger.)

A man's protestations of loyalty to reason are meaningless as such: "reason" is not an axiomatic, but a complex, derivative concept—and, particularly since Kant, the philosophical technique of concept stealing, of attempting to negate reason by means of reason, has become a general bromide, a gimmick worn transparently thin. Do you want to assess the rationality of a person, a theory or a philosophical system? Do not inquire about his or its stand on the validity of reason. Look for the stand on axiomatic concepts. It will tell the whole story.

7. The Cognitive Role of Concepts

The story of the following experiment was told in a university classroom by a professor of psychology. I cannot vouch for the validity of the specific numerical conclusions drawn from it, since I could not check it first-hand. But I shall cite it here, because it is the most illuminating way to illustrate a certain fundamental aspect of consciousness—of any consciousness, animal or human.

The experiment was conducted to ascertain the extent of the ability of birds to deal with numbers. A hidden observer watched the behavior of a flock of crows gathered in a clearing of the woods. When a man came into the clearing and went on into the woods, the crows hid in the tree tops and would not come out until he returned and left the way he had come. When three men went into the woods and only two returned, the crows would not come out: they waited until the third one had left. But when five men went into the woods and only four returned, the crows came out of hiding. Apparently, their power of discrimination did not extend beyond three units—and their perceptual-mathematical ability consisted of a sequence such as: one-two-three-many.

Whether this particular experiment is accurate or not, the truth of the principle it illustrates can be ascertained *introspectively:* if we omit all conceptual knowledge, including the ability to count in terms of numbers, and attempt to see how many units (or existents of a given kind) we can discriminate, remember and deal with by purely perceptual means (e.g., visually or auditorially, but *without counting)*, we will discover that the range of man's *perceptual* ability may be greater, but not much greater, than that of the crow: we may grasp and hold five or six units at most.

This fact is the best demonstration of the cognitive role of concepts.

Since consciousness is a specific faculty, it has a specific nature or identity and, therefore, its range is limited: it cannot perceive everything at once; since awareness, on all its levels, requires an active process, it cannot do everything at once. Whether the units with which one deals are percepts or concepts, the range of what man can hold in the focus of his conscious awareness at any given moment, is limited. The essence, therefore, of man's incomparable cognitive power is the ability to reduce a vast amount of information to a minimal number of units—which is the task performed by his conceptual faculty. And the principle of *unit-economy* is one of that faculty's essential guiding principles.

Observe the operation of that principle in the field of mathematics. If the above described experiment were performed on a man, instead of on crows, he would be able to *count* and thus to remember a large number of men crossing the clearing (how large a number, would depend on the time available to perceive them all and to count).

A "number" is a mental symbol that integrates units into a single larger unit (or subdivides a unit into fractions) with reference to the basic number of "one," which is the basic mental symbol of "unit." Thus "5" stands for $\| \| \| \| \|$. (Metaphysically, the referents of "5" are any five existents of a specified kind; epistemologically, they are represented by a single symbol.)

Counting is an automatized, lightning-like process of reducing the number of mental units one has to hold. In the process of counting—"one, two, three, four, etc."—a man's consciousness holds only one mental unit at any one moment, the particular mental unit that represents the sum he has identified in reality (without having to retain the perceptual image of the existents composing that sum). If he reaches, say, the sum of 25 (or 250), it is still a single unit, easy to remember and to deal with. But project the state of your own consciousness, if I now proceeded to give you that sum by means of perceptual units, thus: ||||||||||| . . . etc.

Observe the principle of unit-economy in the structure of the decimal system, which demands of man's mind that it hold only ten symbols (including the zero) and one simple rule of notation for larger numbers or fractions. Observe the algebraic methods by which pages of complex calculations are reduced to a simple, single equation. Mathematics is a science of *method* (the science of measurement i.e., of establishing quantitative relationships), a cognitive method that enables man to perform an unlimited series of integrations. Mathematics indicates the pattern of the cognitive role of concepts and the *psycho-epistemological* need they fulfill. Conceptualization is a *method* of expanding man's consciousness by reducing the number of its content's units—a systematic means to an unlimited integration of cognitive data.

A concept substitutes one symbol (one word) for the enormity of the perceptual aggregate of the concretes it subsumes. In order to perform its unit-reducing function, the symbol has to become automatized in a man's consciousness, i.e., the enormous sum of its referents must be instantly (implicitly) available to his conscious mind whenever he uses that concept, without the need of perceptual visualization or mental summarizing—in the same manner as the concept "5" does not require that he visualize five sticks every time he uses it.

For example, if a man has fully grasped the concept "justice," he does not need to recite to himself a long treatise on its meaning, while he listens to the evidence in a court case. The mere sentence "I must be just" holds that meaning in his mind automatically, and leaves his conscious attention free to grasp the evidence and to evaluate it according to a complex set of principles. (And, in case of doubt, the conscious recall of the precise meaning of "justice" provides him with the guidelines he needs.)

It is the principle of unit-economy that necessitates the definition of concepts in terms of *essential* characteristics. If, when in doubt, a man recalls a concept's definition, the essential characterstic(s) will give him an instantaneous grasp of the concept's meaning, i.e., of the nature of its referents. For example, if he is considering some social theory and recalls that "man is a rational animal," he will evaluate the validity of the theory accordingly; but if, instead, he recalls that "man is an animal possessing a thumb," his evaluation and conclusion will be quite different.

Learning to speak is a process of automatizing the use (i.e., the meaning and the application) of concepts. And more: all learning involves a process of automatizing, i.e., of first acquiring knowledge by fully conscious, focused attention and observation, then of establishing mental connections which make that knowledge automatic (instantly available as a context), thus freeing man's mind to pursue further, more complex knowledge.

The status of automatized knowledge in his mind is experienced by man as if it had the direct, effortless, self-evident quality (and certainty) of perceptual awareness. But it is *conceptual* knowledge—and its validity depends on the precision of his concepts, which require as strict a precision of meaning (i.e., as strict a knowledge of what specific referents they subsume) as the definitions of mathematical terms. (It is obvious what disasters will follow if one automatizes errors, contradictions and undefined approximations.)

This leads us to a crucial aspect of the cognitive role of concepts: *concepts represent condensations of knowledge, which make further study and the division of cognitive labor possible.*

Remember that the perceptual level of awareness is the base of man's conceptual development. Man forms concepts, as a system of classification, whenever the scope of perceptual data becomes too great for his mind to handle. Concepts stand for specific kinds of existents, including *all* the characteristics of these existents, observed and not-yet-observed, known and unknown.

It is crucially important to grasp the fact that a concept is an "open-end" classification which includes the yet-to-be-discovered characteristics of a given group of existents. All of man's knowledge rests on that fact.

The pattern is as follows: when a child grasps the concept "man," the knowledge represented by that concept in his mind consists of perceptual data, such as man's visual appearance, the sound of his voice, etc. When the child learns to differentiate between living entities and inanimate matter, he ascribes a new characteristic, "living," to the entity he designates as "man." When the child learns to differentiate among various types of consciousness, he includes a new characteristic in his concept of man, "rational"—and so on. The implicit principle guiding this process, is: "I know that there exists such an entity as man; I know many of his characteristics, but he has many others which I do not know and must discover." The same principle directs the study of every other kind of perceptually isolated and conceptualized existents.

The same principle directs the accumulation and transmission of mankind's knowledge. From a savage's knowledge of man, which was not much greater than a child's, to the present level, when roughly half the sciences (the humanities) are devoted to the study of man, the *concept* "man" has not changed: it refers to the same kind of entities. What has changed and grown is the knowledge of these entities. The definitions of concepts may change with the changes in the designation of essential characteristics, and conceptual reclassifications may occur with the growth of knowledge, but these changes are made possible by and do not alter the fact that a concept subsumes *all* the characteristics of its referents, including the yet-to-be-discovered.

Since concepts represent a system of cognitive classification, a given concept serves (speaking metaphorically) as a file folder in which man's mind files his knowledge of the existents it subsumes. The content of such folders varies from individual to individual, according to the degree of his knowledge—it ranges from the primitive, generalized infor-

mation in the mind of a child or an illiterate to the enormously detailed sum in the mind of a scientist—but it pertains
to the same referents, to the same kind of existents, and is
subsumed under the same concept. This filing system makes
possible such activities as learning, education, research—the
accumulation, transmission and expansion of knowledge. (It
is the epistemological obligation of every individual to know
what his mental file contains in regard to any concept he
uses, to keep it integrated with his other mental files, and to
seek further information when he needs to check, correct or
expand his knowledge.)

The extent of today's confusion about the nature of man's
conceptual faculty, is eloquently demonstrated by the following: it is precisely the "open-end" character of concepts,
the essence of their cognitive function, that modern philosophers cite in their attempts to demonstrate that concepts
have no cognitive validity. "*When* can we claim that we
know what a concept stands for?" they clamor—and offer,
as an example of man's predicament, the fact that one may
believe all swans to be white, then discover the existence of
a black swan and thus find one's concept invalidated.

This view implies the unadmitted presupposition that concepts are not a cognitive device of man's type of consciousness, but a repository of closed, out-of-context omniscience
—and that concepts refer, not to the existents of the external world, but to the frozen, arrested state of knowledge
inside any given consciousness at any given moment. On
such a premise, every advance of knowledge is a setback, a
demonstration of man's ignorance. For example, the savages knew that man possesses a head, a torso, two legs and
two arms; when the scientists of the Renaissance began to
dissect corpses and discovered the nature of man's internal
organs, they invalidated the savages' concept "man"; when
modern scientists discovered that man possesses internal
glands, they invalidated the Renaissance concept "man,"
etc.

Like a spoiled, disillusioned child, who had expected
predigested capsules of automatic knowledge, a logical posi-

tivist stamps his foot at reality and cries that context, integration, mental effort and first-hand inquiry are too much to
expect of him, that he rejects so demanding a method of
cognition, and that he will manufacture his own "constructs"
from now on. (This amounts, in effect, to the declaration:
"Since the intrinsic has failed us, the subjective is our only
alternative.") The joke is on his listeners: it is this exponent
of a primordial mystic's craving for an effortless, rigid, automatic omniscience that modern men take for an advocate of
a free-flowing, dynamic, *progressive* science.

It is the "open-end" character of concepts that permits
the division of cognitive labor among men. A scientist could
not specialize in a particular branch of study without a wider
context, without the correlation and integration of his work
to the other aspects of the same subject. Consider, for
example, the science of medicine. If the concept "man" did
not stand as the unifying concept of that science (if some
scientists studied only man's lungs; others, only the stomach; still others, only the blood circulation; and still others,
only the retina of the eye), if all new discoveries were not to
be ascribed to the same entity and, therefore, were not to
be integrated in strict compliance with the law of non-
contradiction, the collapse of medical science would not
take long to follow.

No single mind can hold all the knowledge available to
mankind today, let alone hold it in minute detail. Yet that
knowledge has to be integrated and has to be kept open to
individual understanding and verification, if science is not to
collapse under the weight of uncorrelated, unproved, contradictory minutiae. Only the most rigorous epistemological
precision can implement and protect the advance of science.
Only the strictest, contextually absolute definitions of concepts, can enable men to integrate their knowledge, to keep
expanding their conceptual structure in severely hierarchical
order by forming new concepts, when and as needed—and
thus to condense information and to reduce the number of
mental units with which they have to deal.

Instead, men are taught by the guardians of scientific

epistemology, the philosophers, that conceptual precision is impossible, that integration is undesirable, that concepts have no factual referents, that a concept denotes nothing but its defining characteristic, which represents nothing but an arbitrary social convention—and that a scientist should take public polls to discover the meaning of the concepts he uses. ("Don't look for the meaning, look for the use.") The consequences of such doctrines are becoming apparent in every branch of science today, most obviously in the humanities.

Concepts represent a system of mental filing and cross-filing, so complex that the largest electronic computer is a child's toy by comparison. This system serves as the context, the frame-of-reference, by means of which man grasps and classifies (and studies further) every existent he encounters and every aspect of reality. Language is the physical (visual-auditory) implementation of this system.

Concepts and, therefore, language are *primarily* a tool of cognition—*not* of communication, as is usually assumed. Communication is merely the consequence, not the cause nor the primary purpose of concept-formation—a crucial consequence, of invaluable importance to men, but still only a consequence. *Cognition precedes communication;* the necessary precondition of communication is that one have something to communicate. (This is true even of communication among animals, or of communication by grunts and growls among inarticulate men, let alone of communication by means of so complex and exacting a tool as language.) The primary purpose of concepts and of language is to provide man with a system of cognitive classification and organization, which enables him to acquire knowledge on an unlimited scale; this means: to keep order in man's mind and enable him to think.

Many kinds of existents are integrated into concepts and represented by special words, but many others are not and are identified only by means of verbal descriptions. What determines man's decision to integrate a given group of existents into a concept? The requirements of cognition (and the principle of unit-economy).

There is a great deal of latitude, on the periphery of man's conceptual vocabulary, a broad area where the choice is optional, but in regard to certain central categories of existents the formation of concepts is mandatory. This includes such categories as: (a) the perceptual concretes with which men deal daily, represented by the first level of abstractions; (b) new discoveries of science; (c) new manmade objects which differ in their essential characteristics from the previously known objects (e.g., "television"); (d) complex human relationships involving combinations of physical and psychological behavior (e.g., "marriage," "law," "justice").

These four categories represent existents with which men have to deal constantly, in many different contexts, from many different aspects, either in daily physical action or, more crucially, in mental action and further study. The mental weight of carrying these existents in one's head by means of perceptual images or lengthy verbal descriptions is such that no human mind could handle it. The need of condensation, of unit-reduction, is obvious in such cases.

For an example, I refer you to my brief analysis of the need to form the concept "justice" (in the chapter on "Definitions"). If that concept did not exist, *what number* of considerations would a man have to bear in mind simultaneously, at every step of the process of judging another man? Or if the concept "marriage" did not exist, what number of considerations would a man have to bear in mind and express, when proposing to a woman? (Ask yourself what that concept subsumes and condenses in your own mind.)

The descriptive complexity of a given group of existents, the frequency of their use, and the requirements of cognition (of further study) are the main reasons for the formation of new concepts. Of these reasons, the requirements of cognition are the paramount one.

The requirements of cognition forbid the arbitrary grouping of existents, both in regard to isolation and to integration. They forbid the random coining of special concepts to designate any and every group of existents with any possible combination of characteristics. For example, there is no concept to designate "Beautiful blondes with blue eyes, 5'5" tall and 24 years old." Such entities or groupings are identified *descriptively*. If such a special concept existed, it would lead to senseless duplication of cognitive effort (and to conceptual chaos): everything of significance discovered about that group would apply to all other young women as well. There would be no cognitive justification for such a concept— unless some *essential* characteristic were discovered, distinguishing such blondes from all other women and requiring special study, in which case a special concept would become necessary.

(This is the reason why such conceptual subdivisions as "dining table," "coffee table," etc. are not designated by special concepts, but are treated as qualified instances of the concept "table"—as mentioned in the chapter on "Abstraction from Abstractions.")

In the process of determining conceptual classification, neither the essential similarities nor the essential differences among existents may be ignored, evaded or omitted once they have been observed. Just as the requirements of cognition forbid the arbitrary subdivision of concepts, so they forbid the arbitrary integration of concepts into a wider concept by means of obliterating their *essential* differences— which is an error (or falsification) proceeding from definitions by non-essentials. (This is the method involved in the obliteration of valid concepts by means of "anti-concepts.")

For example, if one took the capacity to run as man's essential characteristic and defined him as "a running animal," the next step would be the attempt to eliminate "non-essential" distinctions and to form a single, higher-level concept out of "running entities," such as a running man, a running river, a running stocking, a running movie, a running commentary, etc. (on some such grounds as the notion that entities have no epistemological priority over actions). The result would be cognitive stultification and epistemological disintegration.

Cognitively, such an attempt would produce nothing but a

bad hash of equivocations, shoddy metaphors and unacknowledged "stolen" concepts. Epistemologically, it would produce the atrophy of the capacity to discriminate, and the
panic of facing an immense, undifferentiated chaos of unintelligible data—which means: the retrogression of an adult
mind to the *perceptual* level of awareness, to the helpless
terror of primitive man. (This is happening today in certain
schools of biology and psychology, whose false definition of
the concept "learning" has led to attempts to equate the
"behavior" of a piece of magnetized iron with the "behavior" of man.)

The requirements of cognition determine the *objective*
criteria of conceptualization. They can be summed up best
in the form of an epistemological "razor": *concepts are not
to be multiplied beyond necessity*—the corollary of which is:
nor are they to be integrated in disregard of necessity.

As to the optional area of concept-formation, it consists
predominantly of subdivisions that denote subtle shades of
meaning, such as adjectives which are almost, but not fully,
synonymous. This area is the special province of literary
artists: it represents a form of unit-economy that permits an
enormous eloquence of expression (including emotional evo-
cation). Most languages have words that have no single-
word equivalent in other languages. But since words do
have objective referents, such "optional" concepts of one
language can be and are translated into another by means of
descriptive phrases.

The optional area includes also the favorite category (and
straw man) of modern philosophers: the "Borderline Case."

By "Borderline Case," they mean existents which share
some characteristics with the referents of a given concept,
but lack others; or which share some characteristics with the
referents of two different concepts and are, in effect, epistemological middle-of-the-road'ers—e.g., certain primitive organisms that biologists are unable to classify fully as either
animals or plants.

The modern philosophers' favorite examples of this "problem" are expressed by such questions as: "What precise

shade of color represents the conceptual borderline between 'red' and 'orange'?" Or: "If you had never seen any swans but white ones, and then discovered a black one, by what criteria would you decide whether to classify it as a 'swan' or to give it a different name and coin a new concept?" Or: "If you discovered the existence of a Martian who had a rational mind, but a spider's body, would you classify him as a rational animal, i.e., as 'man'?"

All this is accompanied by the complaint that "Nature doesn't tell us which choice to make," and purports to demonstrate that concepts represent arbitrary groupings formed by human (social) whim, that they are not determined by objective criteria and have no cognitive validity.

What these doctrines do demonstrate is the failure to grasp the cognitive role of concepts—i.e., the fact that the requirements of cognition determine the objective criteria of concept-formation. The conceptual classification of newly discovered existents depends on the nature and extent of their differences from and similarities to the previously known existents.

In the case of black swans, it is objectively mandatory to classify them as "swans," because virtually all their characteristics are similar to the characteristics of the white swans, and the difference in color is of no cognitive significance. (Concepts are not to be multiplied beyond necessity.) In the case of the rational spider from Mars (if such a creature were possible), the differences between him and man would be so great that the study of one would scarcely apply to the other and, therefore, the formation of a new concept to designate the Martians would be objectively mandatory. (Concepts are not to be integrated in disregard of necessity.)

In the case of existents whose characteristics are equally balanced between the referents of two different concepts— such as primitive organisms, or the transitional shades of a color continuum—there is no cognitive necessity to classify them under either (or any) concept. The choice is optional: one may designate them as a sub-category of either concept, or (in the case of a continuum) one may draw approximate dividing lines (on the principle of "no more than x and no less than y"), or one may identify them *descriptively*—as the nominalists are doing when they present the "problem."

(This "problem" is a straw man, in the sense that it is a problem only to the traditional-realist theories of universals, which claim that concepts are determined by and refer to archetypes or metaphysical "essences.")

If it should be asked, at this point: Who, then, is to keep order in the organization of man's conceptual vocabulary, suggest the changes or expansions of definitions, formulate the principles of cognition and the criteria of science, protect the objectivity of methods and of communications within and among the special sciences, and provide the guidelines for the integration of mankind's knowledge?—the answer is: *philosophy*. These, precisely, are the tasks of epistemology. The highest responsibility of philosophers is to serve as the guardians and integrators of human knowledge.

This is the responsibility on which modern philosophy has not merely defaulted, but worse: which it has reversed. It has taken the lead in the disintegration and destruction of knowledge—and has all but committed suicide in the process.

Philosophy is the foundation of science; epistemology is the foundation of philosophy. It is with a new approach to epistemology that the rebirth of philosophy has to begin.

8. Consciousness and Identity

The organization of concepts into propositions, and the wider principles of language—as well as the further problems of epistemology—are outside the scope of this work, which is concerned only with the nature of concepts. But a few aspects of these issues must be indicated.

Since concepts, in the field of cognition, perform a function similar to that of numbers in the field of mathematics, the function of a proposition is similar to that of an equation: it applies conceptual abstractions to a specific problem.

A proposition, however, can perform this function only if the concepts of which it is composed have precisely defined meanings. If, in the field of mathematics, numbers had no fixed, firm values, if they were mere approximations determined by the mood of their users—so that "5," for instance, could mean five in some calculations, but six-and-a-half or four-and-three-quarters in others, according to the users' "convenience"—there would be no such thing as the science of mathematics.

Yet *this* is the manner in which most people use concepts, and are taught to do so.

Above the first-level abstractions of perceptual concretes, most people hold concepts as loose approximations, without firm definitions, clear meanings or specific referents; and the greater a concept's distance from the perceptual level, the vaguer its content. Starting from the mental habit of learning words without grasping their meanings, people find

it impossible to grasp higher abstractions, and their conceptual development consists of condensing fog into fog into
thicker fog—until the hierarchical structure of concepts breaks
down in their minds, losing all ties to reality; and, as they
lose the capacity to understand, their education becomes a
process of memorizing and imitating. This process is encour-
aged and, at times, demanded by many modern teachers
who purvey snatches of random, out-of-context information
in undefined, unintelligible, contradictory terms.

The result is a mentality that treats the first-level abstractions, the concepts of physical existents, as if they were
percepts, and is unable to rise much further, unable to
integrate new knowledge or to identify its own experience—a
mentality that has not discovered the process of conceptualization in conscious terms, has not learned to adopt it as an
active, continuous, self-initiated policy, and is left arrested
on a concrete-bound level, dealing only with the given, with
the concerns of the immediate moment, day or year, anx-
iously sensing an abyss of the unknowable on all sides.

To such mentalities, higher concepts are indeterminate
splinters flickering in the abyss, which they seize and use at
random, with a nameless sense of guilt, with the chronic
terror of a dreadful avenger that appears in the form of the
question: "What do you mean?"

Words, as such people use them, denote unidentified feelings, unadmitted motives, subconscious urges, chance asso-
ciations, memorized sounds, ritualistic formulas, second-hand
cues—all of it hung, like barnacles, on some swimming
suggestion of some existential referent. Consequently (since
one cannot form concepts of consciousness without reference
to their existential content), the field of introspection, to
such people, is an untouched jungle in which no conceptual
paths have yet been cut. They are unable to distinguish
thought from emotion, cognition from evaluation, observation from imagination, unable to discriminate between
existence and consciousness, between object and subject,
unable to identify the meaning of any inner state—and they
spend their lives as cowed prisoners inside their own skulls,

afraid to look out at reality, paralyzed by the mystery of their own consciousness.

These are the mentalities that modern philosophy now asks us to accept as the criterion of the meaning of concepts.

There is an element of grim irony in the emergence of Linguistic Analysis on the philosophical scene. The assault on man's conceptual faculty has been accelerating since Kant, widening the breach between man's mind and reality. The cognitive function of concepts was undercut by a series of grotesque devices—such, for instance, as the "analytic-synthetic" dichotomy which, by a route of tortuous circumlocutions and equivocations, leads to the dogma that a "necessarily" true proposition cannot be factual, and a factual proposition cannot be "necessarily" true. The crass skepticism and epistemological cynicism of Kant's influence have been seeping from the universities to the arts, the sciences, the industries, the legislatures, saturating our culture, decomposing language and thought. If ever there was a need for a Herculean philosophical effort to clean up the Kantian stables—particularly, to redeem language by establishing objective criteria of meaning and definition, which average men could not attempt—the time was *now*. As if sensing that need, Linguistic Analysis came on the scene for the avowed purpose of "clarifying" language—and proceeded to declare that the meaning of concepts is determined in the minds of average men, and that the job of philosophers consists of observing and reporting on how people use words.

The *reductio ad absurdum* of a long line of mini-Kantians, such as pragmatists and positivists, Linguistic Analysis holds that words are an arbitrary social product immune from any principles or standards, an irreducible primary not subject to inquiry about its origin or purpose—and that we can "dissolve" all philosophical problems by "clarifying" the use of these arbitrary, causeless, meaningless sounds which hold ultimate power over reality. (The implicit psychological confession is obvious: it is an attempt to formalize and elevate second-handedness into a philosophical vocation.)

Proceeding from the premise that words (concepts) are

created by whim, Linguistic Analysis offers us a choice of whims: individual or collective. It declares that there are two kinds of definitions: "stipulative," which may be anything anyone chooses, and "reportive," which are ascertained by polls of popular use.

As reporters, linguistic analysts were accurate: Wittgenstein's theory that a concept refers to a conglomeration of things vaguely tied together by a "family resemblance" is a perfect description of the state of a mind out of focus.

Such is the current condition of philosophy. If, in recent decades, there has been an enormous "brain-drain" from the humanities, with the best minds seeking escape and *objective* knowledge in the physical sciences (as demonstrated by the dearth of great names or achievements in the humanities), one need look no further for its causes. The escape, however, is illusory. It is not the special sciences that teach man to think; it is philosophy that lays down the epistemological criteria of all special sciences.

To grasp and reclaim the power of philosophy, one must begin by grasping why concepts and definitions cannot and may not be arbitrary. To grasp that fully, one must begin by grasping the reason why man needs such a science as epistemology.

Man is neither infallible nor omniscient; if he were, a discipline such as epistemology—the theory of knowledge—would not be necessary nor possible: his knowledge would be automatic, unquestionable and total. But such is not man's nature. Man is a being of volitional consciousness: beyond the level of percepts—a level inadequate to the cognitive requirements of his survival—man has to acquire knowledge by his own effort, which he may exercise or not, and by a process of reason, which he may apply correctly or not. Nature gives him no automatic guarantee of his mental efficacy; he is capable of error, of evasion, of psychological distortion. He needs a *method* of cognition, which he himself has to discover: he must discover how to use his rational faculty, how to validate his conclusions, how to distinguish truth from falsehood, how to set the criteria of *what* he may accept as knowledge. Two questions are involved in his every conclusion, conviction, decision, choice or claim: *What do I know?*—and: *How do I know it?*

It is the task of epistemology to provide the answer to the "How?"—which then enables the special sciences to provide the answers to the "What?"

In the history of philosophy—with some very rare exceptions—epistemological theories have consisted of attempts to escape one or the other of the two fundamental questions which cannot be escaped. Men have been taught either that knowledge is impossible (skepticism) or that it is available without effort (mysticism). These two positions appear to be antagonists, but are, in fact, two variants on the same theme, two sides of the same fraudulent coin: the attempt to escape the responsibility of rational cognition and the absolutism of reality—the attempt to assert the primacy of consciousness over existence.

Although skepticism and mysticism are ultimately interchangeable, and the dominance of one always leads to the resurgence of the other, they differ in the form of their inner contradiction—the contradiction, in both cases, between their philosophical doctrine and their psychological motivation. Philosophically, the mystic is usually an exponent of the *intrinsic* (revealed) school of epistemology; the skeptic is usually an advocate of epistemological *subjectivism*. But, psychologically, the mystic is a subjectivist who uses intrinsicism as a means to claim the primacy of *his* consciousness over that of others. The skeptic is a disillusioned intrinsicist who, having failed to find automatic supernatural guidance, seeks a substitute in the collective subjectivism of others.

The motive of all the attacks on man's rational faculty—from any quarter, in any of the endless variations, under the verbal dust of all the murky volumes—is a single, hidden premise: the desire to exempt consciousness from the law of identity. The hallmark of a mystic is the savagely stubborn refusal to accept the fact that consciousness, like any other existent, possesses identity, that it is a faculty of a specific nature, functioning through specific means. While the advance of civilization has been eliminating one area of magic after another, the last stand of the believers in the miraculous consists of their frantic attempts to regard *identity* as the *disqualifying* element of consciousness.

The implicit, but unadmitted premise of the neo-mystics of modern philosophy, is the notion that only an ineffable consciousness can acquire a valid knowledge of reality, that "true" knowledge has to be causeless, i.e., acquired without any means of cognition.

The entire apparatus of Kant's system, like a hippopotamus engaged in belly-dancing, goes through its gyrations while resting on a single point: that man's knowledge is not valid because his consciousness possesses identity. "His argument, in essence, ran as follows: man is *limited* to a consciousness of a specific nature, which perceives by specific means and no others, therefore, his consciousness is not valid; man is blind, because he has eyes—deaf, because he has ears—deluded, because he has a mind—and the things he perceives do not exist, *because* he perceives them." *(For the New Intellectual.)*

This is a negation, not only of man's consciousness, but of *any* consciousness, of consciousness as such, whether man's, insect's or God's. (If one supposed the existence of God, the negation would still apply: either God perceives through no means whatever, in which case he possesses no identity—or he perceives by some divine means and no others, in which case his perception is not valid.) As Berkeley negated existence by claiming that "to be, is to be perceived," so Kant negates consciousness by implying that to be perceived, is not to be.

What Kant implied through coils of obfuscating verbiage, his more consistent followers declared explicitly. The following was written by a Kantian: "With him [Kant] all is phenomenal [mere appearance] which is relative, and all is relative which is an object to a conscious subject. The conceptions of the understanding as much depend on the constitution of our thinking faculties, as the perceptions of the senses do on the constitution of our intuitive faculties. Both *might* be different, were our mental constitution changed; both probably *are* different to beings differently constituted. The *real* thus becomes identical with the *absolute,* with the object as it is in itself, out of all relation to a subject; and, as all consciousness is a relation between subject and object, it follows that to attain a knowledge of the real we must go out of consciousness." (Henry Mansel, "On the Philosophy of Kant," reprinted in Henry Mansel, *Letters, Lectures and Reviews,* ed. H. W. Chandler, London: John Murray, 1873, p. 171.)

From primordial mysticism to this, its climax, the attack on man's consciousness and particularly on his conceptual faculty has rested on the unchallenged premise that any knowledge acquired by a *process* of consciousness is necessarily subjective and cannot correspond to the facts of reality, since it is *"processed* knowledge."

Make no mistake about the actual meaning of that premise: it is a revolt, not only against being conscious, but against being alive—since in fact, in reality, on earth, every aspect of being alive involves a process of self-sustaining and self-generated action. (This is an example of the fact that the revolt against identity is a revolt against existence. "The desire not to be anything, is the desire not to be." *Atlas Shrugged.*)

All knowledge *is* processed knowledge—whether on the sensory, perceptual or conceptual level. An "unprocessed" knowledge would be a knowledge acquired without means of cognition. Consciousness (as I said in the first sentence of this work) is not a passive state, but an active process. And more: the satisfaction of every need of a living organism requires an act of *processing* by that organism, be it the need of air, of food or of knowledge.

No one would argue (at least, not yet) that since man's body has to *process* the food he eats, no objective rules of proper nutrition can ever be discovered—that "true nutrition" has to consist of absorbing some ineffable substance without the participation of a digestive system, but since man is incapable of "true feeding," nutrition is a subjective matter open to his whim, and it is merely a social convention that forbids him to eat poisonous mushrooms.

No one would argue that since nature does not tell man automatically what to eat—as it does not tell him automatically how to form concepts—he should abandon the illusion that there is a right or wrong way of eating (or he should revert to the safety of the time when he did not have to "trust" objective evidence, but could rely on dietary laws prescribed by a supernatural power).

No one would argue that man eats bread rather than stones purely as a matter of "convenience."

It is time to grant to man's consciousness the same cognitive respect one grants to his body—i.e., the same *objectivity*.

Objectivity begins with the realization that man (including his every attribute and faculty, including his consciousness) is an entity of a specific nature who must act accordingly; that there is no escape from the law of identity, neither in the universe with which he deals nor in the working of his own consciousness, and if he is to acquire knowledge of the first, he must discover the proper method of using the second; that there is no room for the *arbitrary* in any activity of man, least of all in his method of cognition—and just as he has learned to be guided by objective criteria in making his physical tools, so he must be guided by objective criteria in forming his tools of cognition: his concepts.

Just as man's physical existence was liberated when he grasped the principle that "nature, to be commanded, must be obeyed," so his consciousness will be liberated when he grasps that *nature, to be apprehended, must be obeyed*—that the rules of cognition must be derived from the nature of existence and the nature, the *identity*, of his cognitive faculty.

Summary

1. Cognition and Measurement. The base of all of man's knowledge is the perceptual level of awareness. It is in the form of percepts that man grasps the evidence of his senses and apprehends reality. The building-block of man's knowledge is the concept of "existent" which is implicit in every percept. The (implicit) concept "existent" undergoes three stages of development in man's mind: *entity-identity-unit.* The ability to regard entities as units is man's distinctive method of cognition. A unit is an existent regarded as a separate member of a group of two or more similar members. Measurement is the identification of a quantitative relationship, by means of a standard that serves as a unit. The purpose of measurement is to expand the range of man's knowledge beyond the directly perceivable concretes.

2. Concept-Formation. Similarity is the relationship between two or more existents which possess the same characteristic(s), but in different measure or degree. The process of concept-formation consists of mentally isolating two or more existents by means of their distinguishing characteristic, and retaining this characteristic while omitting their particular measurements—on the principle that these measurements must exist in *some* quantity, but may exist in *any* quantity. A concept is a mental integration of two or more units possessing the same distinguishing characteristic(s), with their particular measurements omitted.

3. Abstraction from Abstractions. When concepts are integrated into a wider concept, they serve as units and are treated *epistemologically* as if each were a single (mental) concrete—always remembering that *metaphysically* (i.e., in reality) each unit stands for an unlimited number of concretes of a certain kind. When concepts are integrated into a wider one, the new concept includes *all* the characteristics of its constituent units; but their distinguishing characteristics are regarded as omitted measurements, and one of their common characteristics becomes the distinguishing characteristic of the new concept. When a concept is subdivided into narrower ones, its distinguishing characteristic is retained and is given a narrower range of specified measurements or is combined with an additional characteristic(s) to form the individual distinguishing characteristics of the new concepts.

4. *Concepts of Consciousness.* Every state of consciousness involves two fundamental attributes: the *content* (or object) of awareness, and the *action* (or process) of consciousness in regard to that content. A concept pertaining to consciousness is a mental integration of two or more instances of a psychological process possessing the same distinguishing characteristic(s), with the particular contents and the measurements of the action's intensity omitted. The intensity of a psychological process is measured on a comparative scale. Concepts pertaining to cognition are measured by the scope of their factual content and by the length of the conceptual chain required to grasp it. Concepts pertaining to evaluation are measured by reference to a person's hierarchy of values; this involves a process of "teleological measurement" which deals, not with cardinal, but with *ordinal* numbers, establishing a graded relationship of means to ends, i.e., of actions to a standard of value. A special category of concepts of consciousness consists of concepts pertaining to the *products* of consciousness (e.g., "knowledge"), and concepts of *method* (e.g., "logic").

5. *Definitions.* A definition is a statement that identifies the nature of a concept's units. A correct definition must specify the distinguishing characteristic(s) of the units (the

differentia), and indicate the category of existents from which they were differentiated (the genus). The *essential* distinguishing characteristic(s) of the units and the proper defining characteristic(s) of the concept must be a *fundamental* characteristic(s)—i.e., that distinctive characteristic(s) which, metaphysically, makes the greatest number of other distinctive characteristics possible and which, epistemologically, explains the greatest number of others. Just as the process of concept-formation is contextual, so *all definitions are contextual.* The designation of an essential characteristic depends on the context of man's knowledge; a primitive definition, if correct, does not contradict a more advanced one: the latter merely expands the former. An objective definition, valid for all men, is determined according to all the relevant knowledge available at that stage of mankind's development. Definitions are not changelessly absolute, but they are *contextually absolute.* A definition is false if it does not specify the known relationships among existents (in terms of the known *essential* characteristics) or if it contradicts the known.

Every concept stands for a number of implicit propositions. A definition is the *condensation* of a vast body of observations—and its validity depends on the truth or falsehood of these observations, as represented and summed up by the designation of a concept's essential, defining characteristic(s). The truth or falsehood of all of man's conclusions, inferences and knowledge rests on the truth or falsehood of his definitions. The radical difference between the Aristotelian view of concepts and the Objectivist view lies in the fact that Aristotle regarded "essence" as metaphysical; Objectivism regards it as epistemological.

6. *Axiomatic Concepts.* An axiomatic concept is the identification of a primary fact of reality, which is implicit in all facts and in all knowledge. It is perceived or experienced directly, but grasped conceptually. The first and primary axiomatic concepts are "existence," "identity" and "consciousness." They identify explicitly the omission of psychological time measurements, which is implicit in all concepts—and

serve as constants, as cognitive integrators and epistemological guidelines. They embrace the entire field of man's awareness, delimiting it from the void of unreality to which
conceptual errors can lead. Axiomatic concepts are not a
matter of arbitrary choice; one ascertains whether a given
concept is axiomatic or not by observing the fact that an
axiomatic concept has to be accepted and used even in the
process of any attempt to deny it. Axiomatic concepts are
the foundation of objectivity.

7. *The Cognitive Role of Concepts.* The range of what man
can hold in the focus of his conscious awareness at any given
moment is limited. The essence of his cognitive power is the
ability to reduce a vast amount of information to a minimal
number of units; this is the task performed by his conceptual
faculty. Concepts represent condensations of knowledge,
"open-end" classifications that subsume *all* the characteristics of their referents, the known and the yet-to-be-
discovered; this permits further study and the division of
cognitive labor. The requirements of cognition control the
formation of new concepts, and forbid arbitrary conceptual
groupings. In the process of determining conceptual classifications, neither the essential differences nor the essential
similarities among existents may be ignored once they have
been observed. To sum up in the form of an epistemological
"razor": *concepts are not to be multiplied beyond necessity,
nor are they to be integrated in disregard of necessity.*

8. *Consciousness and Identity.* The assault on man's conceptual faculty has been accelerating since Kant, widening
the breach between man's mind and reality. To reclaim the
power of philosophy, one must grasp the reason why man
needs epistemology. Since man is neither infallible nor omniscient, he has to *discover* a valid method of cognition.
Two questions are involved in his every conclusion or decision: *What* do I know?—and: *How* do I know it? It is the
task of epistemology to provide the answer to the "How?"
—which then enables the special sciences to provide the
answer to the "What?" In the history of philosophy, epistemological theories have consisted predominantly of attempts

to escape one or the other of these two questions—by means of skepticism or mysticism. The motive of all the attacks on man's rational faculty, is a single basic premise: the desire to exempt consciousness from the law of identity. The implicit, but unadmitted premise of modern philosophy is the notion that "true" knowledge must be acquired without any means of cognition, and that identity is the *disqualifying* element of consciousness. This is the essence of Kant's doctrine, which represents the negation of *any* consciousness, of consciousness as such. Objectivity begins with the realization that man (including his consciousness) is an entity of a specific nature who must act accordingly; that there is no escape from the law of identity; that there is no room for the arbitrary in any activity of man, least of all in his method of cognition—and that he must be guided by objective criteria in forming his tools of cognition: his concepts. Just as man's physical existence was liberated when he grasped that "nature, to be commanded, must be obeyed," so his consciousness will be liberated when he grasps that *nature, to be apprehended, must be obeyed*—that the rules of cognition must be derived from the nature of existence and the nature, the *identity*, of his cognitive faculty.

The Analytic-Synthetic Dichotomy
by Leonard Peikoff

(This work was first published in
The Objectivist May–September 1967.)

Introduction

Some years ago, I was defending capitalism in a discussion with a prominent professor of philosophy. In answer to his charge that capitalism leads to coercive monopolies, I explained that such monopolies are caused by government intervention in the economy and are logically impossible under capitalism. (For a discussion of this issue, see *Capitalism: The Unknown Ideal.*) The professor was singularly unmoved by my argument, replying, with a show of surprise and disdain:

"*Logically* impossible? Of course—granted your definitions. You're merely saying that, no matter what proportion of the market it controls, you won't call a business a 'coercive monopoly' if it occurs in a system you call 'capitalism.' Your view is true by arbitrary fiat, it's a matter of semantics, it's *logically* true but not *factually* true. Leave logic aside now; be serious and consider the actual empirical facts on this matter."

To the philosophically uninitiated, this response will be baffling. Yet they meet its equivalents everywhere today. The tenets underlying it permeate our intellectual atmosphere like the germs of an epistemological black plague waiting to infect and cut down any idea that claims the support of conclusive logical argumentation, a plague that spreads subjectivism and conceptual devastation in its wake.

This plague is a formal theory in technical philosophy; it is called: *the analytic-synthetic dichotomy.* It is accepted, in some form, by virtually every influential contemporary philosopher—pragmatist, logical positivist, analyst and existentialist alike.

The theory of the analytic-synthetic dichotomy penetrates every corner of our culture, reaching, directly or indirectly, into every human life, issue and concern. Its carriers are many, its forms subtly diverse, its basic causes complex and hidden—and its early symptoms prosaic and seemingly benign. But it is deadly.

The comparison to a plague is not, however, fully exact. A plague attacks man's body, not his conceptual faculty. And it is not launched by the profession paid to protect men from it.

Today, each man must be his own intellectual protector. In whatever guise the theory of the analytic-synthetic dichotomy confronts him, he must be able to detect it, to understand it, and to answer it. Only thus can he withstand the onslaught and remain epistemologically untouched.

The theory in question is not a philosophical primary; one's position on it, whether it be agreement or opposition, derives, in substantial part, from one's view of the nature of concepts. The Objectivist theory of concepts is presented above, in Ayn Rand's *Introduction to Objectivist Epistemology*. In the present discussion, I shall build on this foundation. I shall summarize the theory of the analytic-synthetic dichotomy as it would be expounded by its contemporary advocates, and then answer it point by point.

The theory was originated, by implication, in the ancient world, with the views of Pythagoras and Plato, but it achieved real prominence and enduring influence only after its advocacy by such modern philosophers as Hobbes, Leibniz, Hume and Kant. (The theory was given its present name by Kant.) In its dominant contemporary form, the theory states that there is a fundamental cleavage in human knowledge, which divides propositions or truths into two mutually exclusive (and jointly exhaustive) types. These types differ, it is claimed, in their origins, their referents, their cognitive status, and the means by which they are validated. In particular, four central points of difference are alleged to distinguish the two types.

(a) Consider the following pairs of true propositions:

   i) A man is a rational animal.
  ii) A man has only two eyes.

   i) Ice is a solid.
  ii) Ice floats on water.

   i) 2 plus 2 equals 4.
  ii) 2 qts. of water mixed with 2 qts. of ethyl alcohol yield 3.86 qts. of liquid, at 15.56°C.

The *first* proposition in each of these pairs, it is said, can be validated *merely by an analysis of the meaning of its constituent concepts* (thus, these are called *"analytic"* truths). If one merely specifies the definitions of the relevant concepts in any of these propositions, and then applies the laws of logic, one can see that the truth of the proposition follows directly, and that to deny it would be to endorse a logical contradiction. Hence, these are also called "logical truths," meaning that they can be validated merely by correctly applying the laws of logic.

Thus, if one were to declare that "A man is *not* a rational animal," or that "2 plus 2 does *not* equal 4," one would be maintaining by implication that "A rational animal is *not* a rational animal," or that "1 plus 1 plus 1 plus 1, does *not* equal 1 plus 1 plus 1 plus 1"—both of which are self-contradictory. (The illustration presupposes that "rational animal" is the definition of "man.") A similar type of self-contradiction would occur if one denied that "Ice is a solid."

Analytic truths represent concrete instances of the Law of Identity; as such, they are also frequently called "tautologies" (which, etymologically, means that the proposition repeats "the same thing"; e.g., "A rational animal is a rational animal," "The solid form of water is a solid"). Since all of the propositions of logic and mathematics can ultimately be analyzed and validated in this fashion, these two subjects, it is claimed, fall entirely within the "analytic" or "tautological" half of human knowledge.

Synthetic propositions, on the other hand—illustrated by the *second* proposition in each of the above pairs, and by most of the statements of daily life and of the sciences—are said to be entirely different on all these counts. A "synthetic" proposition is defined as one which *cannot* be validated merely by an analysis of the meanings or definitions of its constituent concepts. For instance, conceptual or definitional analysis alone, it is claimed, could not tell one whether ice floats on water, or what volume of liquid results when various quantities of water and ethyl alcohol are mixed.

In this type of case, said Kant, the predicate of the proposition (e.g., "floats on water") states something about the subject ("ice") which is not already contained in the meaning of the subject-concept. (The proposition represents a *synthesis* of the subject with a new predicate, hence the name.) Such truths cannot be validated merely by correctly applying the laws of logic; they do not represent concrete instances of the Law of Identity. To deny such truths is to maintain *a falsehood,* but *not a self-contradiction.* Thus, it is false to assert that "A man has three eyes," or that "Ice sinks in water"—but, it is said, these assertions are not self-contradictory. It is the *facts* of the case, not the laws of logic, which condemn such statements. Accordingly, synthetic truths are held to be "factual," as opposed to "logical" or "tautological" in character.

(b) Analytic truths are *necessary;* no matter what region of space or what period of time one considers, such propositions *must* hold true. Indeed, they are said to be true not only throughout the universe which actually exists, but in "all possible worlds"—to use Leibniz's famous phrase. Since its denial is self-contradictory, the opposite of any analytic truth is unimaginable and inconceivable. A visitor from an alien planet might relate many unexpected marvels, but his claims would be rejected out-of-hand if he announced that, in his world, ice was a gas, man was a postage stamp, and 2 plus 2 equaled 7.3.

Synthetic truths, however, are declared *not* to be necessary; they are called *"contingent."* This means: As a matter of fact, in the actual world that men now observe, such propositions *happen to be* true—but they do not *have to be* true. They are not true in "all possible worlds." Since its denial is not self-contradictory, the opposite of any synthetic truth is at least imaginable or conceivable. It is imaginable or conceivable that men should have an extra eye (or a baker's dozen of such eyes) in the back of their heads, or that ice should sink in water like a stone, etc. These things do not occur in our experience but, it is claimed, there is no logical necessity about this. The facts stated by synthetic truths are "brute" facts, which no amount of logic can make fully intelligible.

Can one conclusively *prove* a synthetic proposition? Can one ever be logically *certain* of its truth? The answer given is: "No. As a matter of logic, no synthetic proposition 'has to be' true; the opposite of any is conceivable." (The most uncompromising advocates of the analytic-synthetic dichotomy continue: "You cannot even be certain of the direct evidence of your senses—for instance, that you now see a patch of red before you. In classifying what you see as 'red,' you are implicitly declaring that it is similar in color to certain of your past experiences—and how do you know that you have remembered these latter correctly? That man's memory is reliable, is not a tautology; the opposite is conceivable.") Thus, the most one can ever claim for synthetic, contingent truths is some measure of probability; they are more-or-less-likely hypotheses.

(c) Since analytic propositions are "logically" true, they can, it is claimed, be validated *independently of experience;* they are "non-empirical" or "a priori" (today, these terms mean: "independent of experience"). Modern philosophers grant that some experience is required to enable a man to form concepts; their point is that, once the appropriate concepts have been formed (e.g., "ice," "solid," "water," etc.), no *further* experience is required to validate their combination into an analytically true proposition (e.g., "Ice is solid water"). The proposition follows simply from an analysis of definitions.

Synthetic truths, on the other hand, are said to be *dependent upon experience* for their validation; they are "empirical" or "a posteriori." Since they are "factual," one can discover their truth initially only by observing the appropriate facts directly or indirectly; and since they are "contingent," one can find out whether yesterday's synthetic truths are still holding today, only by scrutinizing the latest empirical data.

(d) Now we reach the climax: the characteristically twentieth-century *explanation* of the foregoing differences. It is: *Analytic propositions provide no information about reality, they do not describe facts, they are "non-ontological"* (i.e., do not pertain to reality). Analytic truths, it is held, are created and sustained by men's arbitrary decision to use words (or concepts) in a certain fashion, they merely record the implications of linguistic (or conceptual) *conventions.* This, it is claimed, is what accounts for the characteristics of analytic truths. They are non-empirical—because they say nothing about the world of experience. No fact can ever cast doubt upon them, they are immune from future correction—because they are immune from reality. They are necessary—because men make them so.

"The propositions of logic," said Wittgenstein in the *Tractatus*, "all say the same thing: that is, nothing." "The principles of logic and mathematics," said A. J. Ayer in *Language, Truth and Logic*, "are true universally simply because we never allow them to be anything else."

Synthetic propositions, on the other hand, *are* factual— and for this, man pays a price. The price is that they are contingent, uncertain and unprovable.

The theory of the analytic-synthetic dichotomy presents men with the following choice: If your statement is proved, it says nothing about that which exists; if it is about existents, it cannot be proved. If it is demonstrated by logical argument, it represents a subjective convention; if it asserts a fact, logic cannot establish it. If you validate it by an appeal to the meanings of your *concepts,* then it is cut off from reality; if you validate it by an appeal to your *percepts,* then you cannot be certain of it.

Objectivism rejects the theory of the analytic-synthetic dichotomy as false—in principle, at root, and in every one of its variants.

Now, let us analyze and answer this theory point by point.

"Analytic" and "Synthetic" Truths

An analytic proposition is defined as one which can be validated merely by an analysis of the meaning of its constituent concepts. The critical question is: *What is included in "the meaning of a concept"?* Does a concept mean the *existents* which it subsumes, including *all* their characteristics? Or does it mean only certain aspects of these existents, designating some of their characteristics but excluding others?

The latter viewpoint is fundamental to every version of the analytic-synthetic dichotomy. The advocates of this dichotomy divide the characteristics of the existents subsumed under a concept into two groups: those which are *included* in the meaning of the concept, and those—the great majority—which, they claim, are *excluded* from its meaning. The dichotomy among propositions follows directly. If a proposition links the "included" characteristics with the concept, it can be validated merely by an "analysis" of the concept; if it links the "excluded" characteristics with the concept, it represents an act of "synthesis."

For example: it is commonly held that, out of the vast number of man's characteristics (anatomical, physiological, psychological, etc.), *two*—"rationality" and "animality"—constitute the entire meaning of the *concept* "man." All the rest, it is held, are outside the concept's meaning. On this view, it is "analytic" to state that "A man is a rational animal" (the predicate is "included" in the subject-concept), but "synthetic" to state that "A man has only two eyes" (the predicate is "excluded").

The primary historical source of the theory that a concept includes some of an entity's characteristics but excludes others, is the Platonic realist theory of universals. Platonism holds that concepts designate non-material essences (universals) subsisting in a supernatural dimension. Our world, Plato claimed, is only the reflection of these essences, in a material form. On this view, a physical entity possesses two very different types of characteristics: those which reflect its supernatural essence, and those which arise from the fact that, in this world, the essence is manifest in material form. The first are "essential" to the entity, and constitute its real nature; the second are matter-generated "accidents." Since concepts are said to designate essences, the concept of an entity includes its "essential" characteristics, but excludes its "accidents."

How does one differentiate "accidents" from "essential" characteristics in a particular case? The Platonists' ultimate answer is: By an act of "intuition."

(A more plausible and naturalistic variant of the essence-accident dichotomy is endorsed by Aristotelians; on this point, their theory of concepts reflects a strong Platonic influence.)

In the modern era, Platonic realism lost favor among philosophers; nominalism progressively became the dominant theory of concepts. The nominalists reject supernaturalism as unscientific, and the appeal to "intuition" as a thinly veiled subjectivism. They do not, however, reject the crucial consequence of Plato's theory: *the division of an entity's characteristics into two groups,* one of which is excluded from the concept designating the entity.

Denying that concepts have an objective basis in the facts of reality, nominalists declare that the source of concepts is a subjective human decision: men *arbitrarily* select certain characteristics to serve as the basis (the "essentials") for a classification; thereafter, they agree to apply the same term to any concretes that happen to exhibit these "essentials," no matter how diverse these concretes are in other respects. On this view, the concept (the term) means only those characteristics initially decreed to be "essential." The other characteristics of the subsumed concretes bear no necessary connection to the "essential" characteristics, and are excluded from the concept's meaning.

Observe that, while condemning Plato's *mystic* view of a concept's meaning, the nominalists embrace the same view in a *skeptic* version. Condemning the essence-accident dichotomy as implicitly arbitrary, they institute an *explicitly* arbitrary equivalent. Condemning Plato's "intuitive" selection of essences as a disguised subjectivism, they spurn the disguise and adopt subjectivism as their official theory—as though a concealed vice were heinous, but a brazenly flaunted one, rational. Condemning Plato's supernaturally determined essences, they declare that essences are *socially* determined, thus transferring to the province of *human whim* what had once been the prerogative of Plato's divine realm. The nominalists' "advance" over Plato consisted of *secularizing* his theory. To secularize an error is still to commit it.

Its form, however, changes. Nominalists do not say that a concept designates only an entity's "essence," excluding its "accidents." Their secularized version is: A concept is only a shorthand tag for the characteristics stated in its definition; a concept and its definition are interchangeable; *a concept means only its definition.*

It is the Platonic-nominalist approach to concept-formation, expressed in such views as these, that gives rise to the theory of the analytic-synthetic dichotomy. Yet its advocates commonly advance the dichotomy as a self-contained primary, independent of any particular theory of concepts. Indeed, they usually insist that the issue of concept-formation—since it is "empirical," not "logical"—is outside the province of philosophy. (!) (Thus, they use the dichotomy to discredit in advance any inquiry into the issues on which the dichotomy itself depends.)

In spite of this, however, they continue to advocate "conceptual analysis," and to distinguish which truths can—or cannot—be validated by its practice. One is expected to analyze concepts, without a knowledge of their source and nature—to determine their meaning, while ignorant of their relationship to concretes. How? The answer implicit in contemporary philosophical practice is: "Since people have already given concepts their meanings, we need only study common usage." In other words, paraphrasing Galt: "The concepts are here. How did they get here? Somehow." *(Atlas Shrugged)*

Since concepts are complex products of man's consciousness, any theory or approach which implies that they are irreducible primaries is invalidated by that fact alone. Without a theory of concepts as a foundation, one cannot, in reason, adopt *any* theory about the nature or kinds of propositions; propositions are only combinations of concepts.

The Objectivist theory of concepts undercuts the theory of the analytic-synthetic dichotomy at its root.

According to Objectivism, concepts "represent classifications of observed existents according to their relationships to other observed existents." (Ayn Rand, *Introduction to Objectivist Epistemology;* all further quotations in this section, unless otherwise identified, are from this work.) To form a concept, one mentally *isolates* a group of concretes (of distinct perceptual units), on the basis of observed similarities which distinguish them from all other known concretes (similarity is "the relationship between two or more existents which possess the same characteristic(s), but in different measure or degree"); then, by a process of omitting the particular measurements of these concretes, one *integrates* them into a single new mental unit: the concept, which subsumes all concretes of this kind (a potentially unlimited number). The integration is completed and retained by the selection of a perceptual symbol (a word) to designate it. "A concept is a mental integration of two or more units possessing the same distinguishing characteristic(s), with their particular measurements omitted."

By isolating and integrating perceived concretes, by reducing the number of mental units with which he has to deal, man is able to break up and organize his perceptual field, to engage in specialized study, and to retain an unlimited amount of information pertaining to an unlimited number of concretes. Conceptualization is a method of acquiring and retaining knowledge of that which exists, on a scale inaccessible to the perceptual level of consciousness.

Since a word is a symbol for a concept, it has no meaning apart from the content of the concept it symbolizes. And since a concept is an integration of units, *it* has no content or meaning apart from its units. *The meaning of a concept consists of the units—the existents—which it integrates, including all the characteristics of these units.*

Observe that concepts mean *existents,* not arbitrarily selected portions of existents. There is no basis whatever— neither metaphysical nor epistemological, neither in the nature of reality nor of a conceptual consciouness—for a division of the characteristics of a concept's units into two groups, one of which is excluded from the concept's meaning.

Metaphysically, an entity is: all of the things which it is. Each of its characteristics has the same metaphysical status: each constitutes a part of the entity's identity.

Epistemologically, all the characteristics of the entities subsumed under a concept are discovered by the same basic method: by observation of these entities. The initial similarities, on the basis of which certain concretes were isolated and conceptually integrated, were grasped by a process of observation; all subsequently discovered characteristics of these concretes are discovered by the same method (no matter how complex the inductive procedures involved may become).

The fact that certain characteristics are, at a given time, *unknown* to man, does not indicate that these characteristics are excluded from the entity—*or from the concept*. A is A; existents are what they are, independent of the state of human knowledge; and a concept means the existents which it integrates. Thus, a concept subsumes and includes *all* the characteristics of its referents, known and not-yet-known.

(This does not mean that man is omniscient, or that he can capriciously ascribe any characteristics he chooses to the referents of his concepts. In order to discover that an entity possesses a certain characteristic, one must engage in a process of scientific study, observation and validation. Only then does one know that that characteristic is true of the entity and, therefore, is subsumed under the concept.)

"It is crucially important to grasp the fact that a concept is an 'open-end' classification which includes the yet-to-be-discovered characteristics of a given group of existents. All of man's knowledge rests on that fact.

"The pattern is as follows: When a child grasps the concept 'man,' the knowledge represented by that concept in his mind consists of perceptual data, such as man's visual appearance, the sound of his voice, etc. When the child learns to differentiate between living entities and inanimate matter, he ascribes a new characteristic, 'living,' to the entity he designates as 'man.' When the child learns to differentiate among various types of consciousness, he includes a new characteristic in his concept of man, 'rational' —and so on. The implicit principle guiding this process, is: 'I know that there exists such an entity as man; I know many of his characteristics, but he has many others which I do not know and must discover.' The same principle directs the study of every other kind of perceptually isolated and conceptualized existents.

"The same principle directs the accumulation and transmission of mankind's knowledge. From a savage's knowledge of man . . . [to the present level], the *concept* 'man' has not changed: it refers to the same kind of entities. What has changed and grown is the knowledge of these entities."

What, then, is the meaning of the concept "man"? "Man" means a certain type of entity, a rational animal, including *all* the characteristics of this entity (anatomical, physiological, psychological, etc., as well as the relations of these characteristics to those of other entities)—all the characteristics already known, and all those ever to be discovered. Whatever is true of the entity, is meant by the concept.

It follows that there are no grounds on which to distinguish "analytic" from "synthetic" propositions. Whether one states that "A man is a rational animal," or that "A man has only two eyes"—in both cases, the predicated characteristics are true of man and are, therefore, included in the concept "man." The meaning of the first statement is: "A certain type of entity, including all its characteristics (among which are rationality and animality) is: a rational animal." The meaning of the second is: "A certain type of entity, including all its characteristics (among which is the possession of only two eyes) has: only two eyes." Each of these statements is an instance of the Law of Identity; each is a "tautology"; to deny either is to contradict the meaning of the concept "man," and thus to endorse a self-contradiction.

A similar type of analysis is applicable to *every* true statement. Every truth about a given existent(s) reduces, in basic pattern, to: "X is: one or more of the things which it is." The predicate in such a case states some characteristic(s) of the subject; but since it *is* a characteristic of the subject, the *concept(s)* designating the subject in fact includes the predicate from the outset. If one wishes to use the term "tautology" in this context, then *all* truths are "tautological." (And, by the same reasoning, all falsehoods are self-contradictions.)

When making a statement about an existent, one has, ultimately, only two alternatives: "X (which means X, the existent, including all its characteristics) *is* what it is"—or:

"X *is not* what it is." The choice between truth and falsehood is the choice between "tautology" (in the sense explained) and self-contradiction.

In the realm of propositions, there is only one basic epistemological distinction: *truth vs. falsehood,* and only one fundamental issue: By what method is truth discovered and validated? To plant a dichotomy at the base of human knowledge—to claim that there are opposite *methods* of validation and opposite *types* of truth—is a procedure without grounds or justification.

In one sense, *no* truths are "analytic." No proposition can be validated merely by "conceptual analysis"; the content of the concept—i.e., the characteristics of the existents it integrates—must be discovered and validated by observation, before any "analysis" is possible. In another sense, *all* truths are "analytic." When some characteristic of an entity *has* been discovered, the proposition ascribing it to the entity will be seen to be "logically true" (its opposite would contradict the meaning of the concept designating the entity). In either case, the analytic-logical-tautological vs. synthetic-factual dichotomy collapses.

To justify their view that some of an entity's characteristics are excluded from the concept designating it, both Platonists and nominalists appeal to the distinction between the "essential" and the "non-essential" characteristics of an entity. For the Platonists, this distinction represents a *metaphysical* division, *intrinsic* to the entity, independent of man and of man's knowledge. For the nominalists, it represents a *subjective* human decree, independent of the facts of reality. For both schools, whatever their terminological or other differences, a concept means only the essential (or defining) characteristics of its units.

Neither school provides an *objective* basis for the distinction between an entity's "essential" and "non-essential" characteristics. (Supernaturalism—in its avowed or secularized form—is not an objective basis for anything.) Neither school explains why such a distinction is objectively required in the process of conceptualization.

This explanation is provided by Objectivism, and exposes the basic error in the Platonic-nominalist position.

When a man reaches a certain level of conceptual complexity, he needs to discover a method of organizing and interrelating his concepts; he needs a method that will enable him to keep each of his concepts clearly distinguished from all the others, each connected to a specific group of existents clearly distinguished from the other existents he knows. (In the early stages of conceptual development, when a child's concepts are comparatively few in number and designate directly perceivable concretes, "ostensive definitions" are sufficient for this purpose.) The method consists of *defining* each concept, by specifying the characteristic(s) of its units upon which the greatest number of their other known characteristics depends, and which distinguishes the units from all other known existents. The characteristic(s) which fulfills this requirement is designated the *"essential"* characteristic, in that context of knowledge.

Essential characteristics are determined contextually. The characteristic(s) which most fundamentally distinguishes a certain type of entity from all other existents known at the time, may not do so within a wider field of knowledge, when more existents become known and/or more of the entity's characteristics are discovered. The characteristic(s) designated as "essential"—and the definition which expresses it—may alter as one's cognitive context expands. Thus, essences are not intrinsic to entities, in the Platonic (or Aristotelian) manner; they are epistemological, not metaphysical. A definition in terms of essential characteristics "is a device of man's method of cognition—a means of classifying, condensing and integrating an ever-growing body of knowledge."

Nor is the designation of essential characteristics a matter of arbitrary choice or subjective decree. A contextual definition can be formulated only after one has fully considered *all* the known facts pertaining to the units in question: their similarities, their differences from other existents, the causal relationships among their characteristics, etc. This knowledge determines which characteristic(s) is *objectively* essential—and, therefore, which definition is objectively correct—in a given cognitive context. Although the definition explicitly mentions only the essential characteristic(s), it implies and condenses all of this knowledge.

On the objective, contextual view of essences, a concept does *not* mean only the essential or defining characteristics of its units. To designate a certain characteristic as "essential" or "defining" is to *select,* from the total content of the concept, the characteristic that best condenses and differentiates that content in a specific cognitive context. Such a selection presupposes the relationship between the concept and its units: it presupposes that the concept is an integration of units, and that its content consists of its units, including *all* their characteristics. It is only because of this fact that the same concept can receive varying definitions in varying cognitive contexts.

When "rational animal" is selected as the definition of "man," this does not mean that the concept "man" becomes a shorthand tag for "anything whatever that has rationality and animality." It does not mean that the concept "man" is interchangeable with the phrase "rational animal," and that all of man's other characteristics are excluded from the concept. It means: A certain type of entity, including all its characteristics, is, in the present context of knowledge, most fundamentally distinguished from all other entities by the fact that it is a rational animal. All the presently available knowledge of man's *other* characteristics is required to validate this definition, and is implied by it. All these other characteristics remain part of the content of the concept "man."

The nominalist view that a concept is merely a shorthand tag for its definition, represents a profound failure to grasp the function of a definition in the process of concept-formation. The penalty for this failure is that the process of definition, in the hands of the nominalists, achieves the exact opposite of its actual purpose. The purpose of a definition is to keep a concept distinct from all others, *to keep it connected to a specific group of existents.* On the nominalist view, it is precisely this connection that is severed: as soon as a concept is defined, it ceases to designate *existents*, and designates instead only the defining characteristic.

And further: On a rational view of definitions, a definition organizes and condenses—and thus helps one to retain—a wealth of knowledge about the characteristics of a concept's units. On the nominalist view, it is precisely this knowledge that is *discarded* when one defines a concept: as soon as a defining characteristic is chosen, all the other characteristics of the units are banished from the concept, which shrivels to mean merely the definition. For instance, as long as a child's concept of "man" is retained ostensively, the child knows that man has a head, two eyes, two arms, etc.; on the nominalist view, as soon as the child defines "man," he discards all this knowledge; thereafter, "man" means to him only: "a thing with rationality and animality."

On the nominalist view, the process of defining a concept is a process of cutting the concept off from its referents, and of systematically evading what one knows about their characteristics. Definition, the very tool which is designed to promote conceptual integration, becomes an agent of its destruction, a means of *disintegration.*

The advocates of the view that a concept means its definition, cannot escape the knowledge that people actually use concepts to designate *existents*. (When a woman says: "I married a wonderful man," it is clear to most philosophers that she does not mean: "I married a wonderful combination of rationality and animality.") Having severed the connection between a concept and its referents, such philosophers sense that somehow this connection nevertheless exists and is important. To account for it, they appeal to a theory which goes back many centuries and is now commonly regarded as uncontroversial: the theory that a concept has *two kinds or dimensions* of meaning. Traditionally, these are referred to as a concept's *"extension"* (or "denotation") and its *"intension"* (or "connotation").

By the "extension" of a concept, the theory's advocates mean the concretes subsumed under that concept. By the "intension" of a concept, they mean those characteristics of the concretes which are stated in the concept's definition. (Today, this is commonly called the "conventional" intension; the distinction among various types of intension, however, merely compounds the errors of the theory, and is irrelevant in this context.) Thus, in the extensional sense, "man" means Socrates, Plato, Aristotle, Tom, Dick, Harry, etc. In the intensional sense, "man" means "rational animal."

A standard logic text summarizes the theory as follows: "The intension of a term, as we have noted, is what is usually called its definition. The extension, on the other hand, simply refers us to the set of objects to which the definition applies. . . . Extension and intension are thus intimately related, but they refer to objects in diferent ways— extension to a listing of the individuals who fall within its quantitative scope, intension to the qualities or characteristics of the individuals." (Lionel Ruby, *Logic: An Introduction.*)

This theory introduces another artificial split: between an existent and its characteristics. In the sense in which a concept means its referents (its extensional meaning), it does not mean or refer to their characteristics (its intensional meaning), and vice versa. One's choice, in effect, is: either to mean existents, apart from their characteristics—or (certain) characteristics, apart from the existents which possess them.

In fact, neither of these alleged types of meaning is metaphysically or epistemologically possible.

A concept cannot mean existents, apart from their characteristics. A thing is—what it is; its characteristics constitute its identity. An existent apart from its characteristics would be an existent apart from its identity, which means: a nothing, a non-existent. To be conscious of an existent *is* to be conscious of (some of) its characteristics. This is true on all levels of consciousness, but it is particularly obvious on the conceptual level. When one conceptualizes a group of existents, one isolates them mentally from others, *on the basis of certain of their characteristics.* A concept cannot integrate—or mean—a miscellaneous grab bag of objects; it can only integrate, designate, refer to and *mean:* existents of a certain kind, existents possessing certain characteristics.

Nor can the concept of an existent mean its characteristics (some or all), apart from the existent which possesses them. A characteristic is an aspect of an existent. It is not a disembodied, Platonic universal. Just as a concept cannot mean existents apart from their identity, so it cannot mean identities apart from that which exists. Existence *is* Identity *(Atlas Shrugged)*.

The theory that a concept means its definition, is not improved when it is combined with the view that, in another sense, a concept means its "extension." Two errors do not make a truth. They merely produce greater chaos and confusion. The truth is that a concept means the existents it integrates, including all their characteristics. It is this view of a concept's meaning that keeps man's concepts anchored to reality. On this view, the dichotomy between "analytic" and "synthetic" propositions cannot arise.

Necessity and Contingency

The theory of the analytic-synthetic dichotomy has its roots in two types of error: one epistemological, the other metaphysical. The epistemological error, as I have discussed, is an incorrect view of the nature of concepts. The metaphysical error is: the dichotomy between necessary and contingent facts.

This theory goes back to Greek philosophy, and was endorsed in some form by virtually all philosophical traditions prior to Kant. In the form in which it is here relevant, the theory holds that some facts are inherent in the nature of reality; they *must* exist; they are "necessary." Other facts, however, *happen to* exist in the world that men now observe, but they did not *have to* exist; they could have been otherwise; they are "contingent." For instance, that water is wet would be a "necessary" fact; that water turns to ice at a certain temperature, would be "contingent."

Given this dichotomy, the question arises: How does one know, in a particular case, that a certain fact is necessary? Observation, it was commonly said, is insufficient for this purpose. "Experience," wrote Kant in the *Critique of Pure Reason,* "tells us, indeed, what is, but not that it must necessarily be so, and not otherwise." To establish that something is a fact, one employs observation and the appropriate inductive procedures; but, it was claimed, to establish that something is a fact is not yet to show that the fact in question is necessary. Some warrant or guarantee, over and above the fact's existence, is required if the fact is to be necessary; and some insight, over and above that yielded by observation and induction, is required to grasp this guarantee.

In the pre-Kantian era, it was common to appeal to some form of "intellectual intuition" for this purpose. In some cases, it was said, one could just "see" that a certain fact was necessary. *How* one could see this remained a mystery. It appeared that human beings had a strange, inexplicable capacity to grasp by unspecified means that certain facts not only were, but had to be. In other cases, no such intuition operated, and the facts in question were deemed contingent.

In the post-Kantian era, appeals to "intellectual intuition" lost favor among philosophers, but the necessary-contingent dichotomy went on. Perpetuated in various forms in the nineteenth century, it was reinterpreted in the twentieth as follows: since facts are learned only by experience, and experience does not reveal necessity, the concept of "necessary facts" must be abandoned. Facts, it is now held, are one and all contingent—and the propositions describing them are "contingent truths." As for necessary truths, they are merely the products of man's linguistic or conceptual conventions. They do not refer to facts, they are empty, "analytic," "tautological." In this manner, the necessary-contingent dichotomy is used to support the alleged distinction between analytic and synthetic propositions. Today, it is a commonplace for philosophers to remark that "factual" statements are "synthetic" and "contingent," whereas "necessary" statements are "non-factual" and "analytic."

(Contemporary philosophers prefer to talk about propositions or statements, rather than about facts; they rarely say that *facts* are contingent, attributing contingency instead to *statements* about facts. There is nothing to justify this mode of speech, and I shall not adhere to it in discussing their views.)

Observe that both the traditional pre-Kantians and the contemporary conventionalists are in essential agreement: both endorse the necessary-contingent dichotomy, and both hold that necessary truths cannot be validated by experience. The difference is only this: for the traditional philosophers, necessity is a metaphysical phenomenon, grasped by an act of intuition; for the conventionalists, it is a product of man's subjective choices. The relationship between the two viewpoints is similar to the relationship between Platonists and nominalists on the issue of essences. In both cases, the moderns adopt the fundamentals of the traditionalist position; their "contribution" is merely to interpret that position in an avowedly subjectivist manner.

In the present issue, the basic error of both schools is the view that facts, some or all, are contingent. As far as metaphysical reality is concerned (omitting human actions from consideration, for the moment), there are no "facts which happen to be but could have been otherwise" as against "facts which must be." There are only: facts which *are*.

The view that facts are contingent—that the way things actually are is only one among a number of alternative possibilities, that things could have been different metaphysically—represents a failure to grasp the Law of Identity. Since things are what they are, since everything that exists possesses a specific identity, nothing in reality can occur causelessly or by chance. The nature of an entity determines what it can do and, in any given set of circumstances, dictates what it *will* do. The Law of Causality is entailed by the Law of Identity. Entities follow certain laws of action in consequence of their identity, and have no alternative to doing so.

Metaphysically, all facts are inherent in the identities of the entities that exist; i.e., all facts are "necessary." In this sense, to be *is* to be "necessary." The concept of "necessity," in a metaphysical context, is superfluous.

(The problem of epistemology is: how to discover facts, how to discover what *is*. Its task is to formulate the proper methods of induction, the methods of acquiring and validating scientific knowledge. There is no problem of grasping that a fact is necessary, after one has grasped that it is a fact.)

For many centuries, the theory of "contingent facts" was associated with a supernaturalistic metaphysics; such facts, it was said, are the products of a divine creator who could have created them differently—and who can change them at will. This view represents the metaphysics of miracles—the notion that an entity's actions are unrelated to its nature, that anything is possible to an entity regardless of its identity. On this view, an entity acts as it does, not because of its nature, but because of an omnipotent God's decree.

Contemporary advocates of the theory of "contingent facts" hold, in essence, the same metaphysics. They, too, hold that anything is possible to an entity, that its actions are unrelated to its nature, that the universe which exists is only one of a number of "possible worlds." They merely omit God, but they retain the consequences of the religious view. Once more, theirs is a secularized mysticism.

The fundamental error in all such doctrines is the failure to grasp that *existence is a self-sufficient primary*. It is not a product of a supernatural dimension, or of anything else. There is nothing antecedent to existence, nothing apart from it—*and no alternative to it*. Existence exists—and only existence exists. Its existence and its nature are irreducible and unalterable.

The climax of the "miraculous" view of existence is represented by those existentialists who echo Heidegger, demanding: "Why is there any being at all and not rather nothing?" —i.e., why does existence exist? This is the projection of a zero as an alternative to existence, with the demand that one explain why existence exists and not the zero.

Non-existentialist philosophers typically disdain Heidegger's alleged question, writing it off as normal existentialist lunacy. They do not apparently realize that in holding facts to be contingent, they are committing the same error. When they claim that facts could have been otherwise, they are claiming that *existence* could have been otherwise. They scorn the existentialists for projecting an alternative to the *existence* of existence, but spend their time projecting alternatives to the *identity* of existence.

While the existentialists clamor to know why there is something and not nothing, the non-existentialists answer them (by implication): "This is a ridiculous question. Of course, there is something. The real question is: Why is the something what it is, and not something else?"

A major source of confusion, in this issue, is the failure to distinguish *metaphysical* facts from *man-made* facts—i.e., facts which are inherent in the identities of that which exists, from facts which depend upon the exercise of human volition. Because man has free will, no human choice—and no phenomenon which is a product of human choice—is metaphysically necessary. In regard to any man-made fact, it is valid to claim that man *has* chosen thus, but it was not inherent in the nature of existence for him to have done so; he could have chosen otherwise. For instance, the U.S. did not have to consist of 50 states; men could have subdivided the larger ones or consolidated the smaller ones, etc.

Choice, however, is not chance. Volition is not an exception to the Law of Causality; it is a type of causation. Further, metaphysical facts are unalterable by man, and limit the alternatives open to his choice. Man can rearrange the materials that exist in reality, but he cannot violate their identity; he cannot escape the laws of nature. "Nature, to be commanded, must be obeyed."

Only in regard to the man-made is it valid to claim: "It happens to be, but it could have been otherwise." Even here, the term "contingent" is highly misleading. Historically, that term has been used to designate a metaphysical category of much wider scope than the realm of human action; and it has always been associated with a metaphysics which, in one form or another, denies the facts of Identity and Causality. The "necessary-contingent" terminology serves only to introduce confusion, and should be abandoned. What is required in this context is the distinction between the "metaphysical" and the "man-made."

The existence of human volition cannot be used to justify the theory that there is a dichotomy of *propositions* or of *truths*. Propositions about metaphysical facts and propositions about man-made facts do not have different characteristics *qua propositions*. They differ merely in their subject matter, but then so do the propositions of astronomy and of immunology. Truths about metaphysical and about manmade facts are learned and validated by the same process: by observation; and, *qua truths,* both are equally necessary. Some *facts* are not necessary, but all *truths* are.

Truth is the identification of a fact of reality. Whether the fact in question is metaphysical or man-made, the fact determines the truth: if the fact exists, there is no alternative in regard to what is true. For instance, the fact that the U.S. has 50 states was not metaphysically necessary—but as long as this is men's choice, the proposition that "The U.S. has 50 states" is necessarily *true*. A true proposition *must* describe the facts as they are. In this sense, a "necessary truth" is a redundancy, and a "contingent truth" a self-contradiction.

Logic and Experience

Throughout its history, philosophy has been torn by the conflict between the rationalists and the empiricists. The former stress the role of logic in man's acquisition of knowledge, while minimizing the role of experience; the latter claim that experience is the source of man's knowledge, while minimizing the role of logic. This split between logic and experience is institutionalized in the theory of the analytic-synthetic dichotomy.

Analytic statements, it is said, are independent of experience; they are "logical" propositions. Synthetic statements, on the other hand, are devoid of logical necessity; they are "empirical" propositions.

Any theory that propounds an opposition between the logical and the empirical, represents a failure to grasp the nature of logic and its role in human cognition. Man's knowledge is not acquired by logic apart from experience or by experience apart from logic, but *by the application of logic to experience.* All truths are the product of a logical identification of the facts of experience.

Man is born *tabula rasa;* all his knowledge is based on and derived from the evidence of his senses. To reach the distinctively human level of cognition, man must conceptualize his perceptual data—and conceptualization is a process which is neither automatic nor infallible. Man needs to discover a method to guide this process, if it is to yield conclusions which correspond to the facts of reality—i.e., which represent knowledge. The principle at the base of the proper method is the fundamental principle of metaphysics: the Law of Identity. In reality, contradictions cannot exist; in a cognitive process, a contradiction is the proof of an error. Hence the method man must follow: to identify the facts he observes, in a non-contradictory manner. This method is logic—"the art of non-contradictory identification." *(Atlas Shrugged.)* Logic must be employed at every step of a man's conceptual development, from the formation of his first concepts to the discovery of the most complex scientific laws and theories. Only when a conclusion is based on a noncontradictory identification and integration of all the evidence available at a given time, can it qualify as knowledge.

The failure to recognize that logic is man's method of cognition, has produced a brood of artificial splits and dichotomies which represent restatements of the analytic-synthetic dichotomy from various aspects. Three in particular are prevalent today: logical truth vs. factual truth; the logically possible vs. the empirically possible; and the a priori vs. the a posteriori.

The logical-factual dichotomy opposes truths which are validated "merely" by the use of logic (the analytic ones), to truths which describe the facts of experience (the synthetic ones). Implicit in this dichotomy is the view that logic is a subjective game, a method of manipulating arbitrary symbols, not a method of acquiring knowledge.

It is the use of logic that enables man to determine what is and what is not a fact. To introduce an opposition between the "logical" and the "factual" is to create a split between consciousness and existence, between truths in accordance with man's method of cognition and truths in accordance with the facts of reality. The result of such a dichotomy is that logic is divorced from reality ("Logical truths are empty and conventional")—and reality becomes unknowable ("Factual truths are contingent and uncertain"). This amounts to the claim that man has no method of cognition, i.e., no way of acquiring knowledge.

The acquisition of knowledge, as Ayn Rand has observed, involves two fundamental questions: *"What* do I know?" and *"How* do I know it?" The advocates of the logical-factual dichotomy tell man, in effect: "You can't know the 'what'—because there is no 'how.'" (These same philosophers claim to know the truth of their position by means of unanswerable logical argument.)

To grasp the nature of their epistemological procedure, consider a mathematician who would claim that there is a

dichotomy between two types of truth in the matter of
adding columns of figures: truths which state the actual sum
of a given column *versus* truths which are reached by adher-
ence to the laws of addition—the "summational truths" vs.
the "additive truths." The former represent the actual sums—
which, however, are unfortunately unprovable and unknowable, since they cannot be arrived at by the methods of
addition; the latter, which are perfectly certain and necessary, are unfortunately a subjective fantasy-creation, with
no relationship to actual sums in the actual world. (At this
point, a pragmatist mathematician comes along and provides
his "solution": "Adding," he tells us, "may be subjective,
but it works." Why does it? How does he know it does?
What about tomorrow? "Those questions," he replies, "aren't
fruitful.")

If mathematicians were to accept this doctrine, the destruction of mathematics would follow. When philosophers
accept such a doctrine, the same consequences may be
expected—with only this difference: the province of philosophy embraces the total of human knowledge.

Another restatement of the analytic-synthetic dichotomy
is the view that opposes the "logically" possible and the
"empirically" possible.

If the proposition that a given phenomenon exists is not
self-contradictory, then that phenomenon, it is claimed, is
"logically" possible; if the proposition *is* self-contradictory,
then the phenomenon is "logically" impossible. Certain
phenomena, however, although logically possible, are
contrary to the "contingent" laws of nature that men
discover by experience; these phenomena are "empirically"—but not "logically"—impossible. Thus, a married
bachelor is "logically" impossible; but a bachelor who can
fly to the moon by means of flapping his arms is merely
"empirically" impossible (i.e., the proposition that such
a bachelor exists is not self-contradictory, but such a
bachelor is not in accordance with the laws that happen
to govern the universe).

The metaphysical basis of this dichotomy is the premise

that a violation of the laws of nature would not involve a contradiction. But as we have seen, the laws of nature are inherent in the identities of the entities that exist. A violation of the laws of nature would require that an entity act in contradiction to its identity; i.e., it would require the existence of a contradiction. To project such a violation is to endorse the "miraculous" view of the universe, as already discussed.

The epistemological basis of this dichotomy is the view that a concept consists only of its definition. According to the dichotomy, it is logically impermissible to contradict the definition of a concept; what one asserts by this means is "logically" impossible. But to contradict any of the *non-defining* characteristics of a concept's referents, is regarded as logically permissible; what one asserts in such a case is merely "empirically" impossible.

Thus, a "married bachelor" contradicts the definition of "bachelor" and hence is regarded as "logically" impossible. But a "bachelor who can fly to the moon by means of flapping his arms" is regarded as "logically" possible, because the *definition* of "bachelor" ("an unmarried man") does not specify his means of locomotion. What is ignored here is the fact that the concept "bachelor" is a subcategory of the concept "man," that as such it includes all the characteristics of the entity "man," and that these exclude the ability to fly by flapping his arms. Only by reducing a concept to its definition and by evading all the other characteristics of its referents can one claim that such projections do not involve a self-contradiction.

Those who attempt to distinguish the "logically" possible and the "empirically" possible commonly maintain that the "logically" impossible is unimaginable or inconceivable, whereas the merely "empirically" impossible is at least imaginable or conceivable, and that this difference supports the distinction. For instance, "ice which is not solid" (a "logical" impossibility) is inconceivable; but "ice which sinks in water" (a merely "empirical" impossibility) is at least conceivable, they claim, even though it does not exist; one need merely visualize a block of ice floating on water, and suddenly plummeting straight to the bottom.

This argument confuses Walt Disney with metaphysics. That a man can project an image or draw an animated cartoon at variance with the facts of reality, does not alter the facts; it does not alter the nature or the potentialities of the entities which exist. An image of ice sinking in water does not alter the nature of ice; it does not constitute evidence that it is possible for ice to sink in water. It is evidence only of man's capacity to engage in fantasy. Fantasy is not a form of cognition.

Further: the fact that man possesses the capacity to fantasize does not mean that the opposite of demonstrated truths is "imaginable" or "conceivable." In a serious, epistemological sense of the word, a man *cannot* conceive the opposite of a proposition he knows to be true (as apart from propositions dealing with man-made facts). If a proposition asserting a metaphysical fact has been demonstrated to be true, this means that that fact has been demonstrated to be inherent in the identities of the entities in question, and that any alternative to it would require the existence of a contradiction. Only ignorance or evasion can enable a man to attempt to project such an alternative. If a man does not know that a certain fact has been demonstrated, he will not know that its denial involves a contradiction. If a man does know it, but evades his knowledge and drops his full cognitive context, there is no limit to what he can pretend to conceive. But what one can project by means of ignorance or evasion, is philosophically irrelevant. It does not constitute a basis for instituting two separate categories of possibility.

There is no distinction between the "logically" and the "empirically" possible (or impossible). All truths, as I have said, are the product of a logical identification of the facts of experience. This applies as much to the identification of possibilities as of actualities.

The same considerations invalidate the dichotomy between the a priori and the a posteriori. According to this variant, certain propositions (the analytic ones) are validated *independently of experience,* simply by an analysis of the definitions of their constituent concepts; these propositions are "a priori." Others (the synthetic ones) are dependent upon experience for their validation; they are "a posteriori."

As we have seen, definitions represent condensations of a wealth of observations, i.e., a wealth of "empirical" knowledge; definitions can be arrived at and validated only on the basis of experience. It is senseless, therefore, to contrast propositions which are true "by definition" and propositions which are true "by experience." If an "empirical" truth is one derived from, and validated by reference to, perceptual observations, then all truths are "empirical." Since truth is the identification of a fact of reality, a "non-empirical truth" would be an identification of a fact of reality which is validated independently of observation of reality. This would imply a theory of innate ideas, or some equally mystical construct.

Those who claim to distinguish a posteriori and a priori propositions commonly maintain that certain truths (the synthetic, factual ones) are *"empirically falsifiable,"* whereas others (the analytic, logical ones) are not. In the former case, it is said, one can specify experiences which, if they occurred, would invalidate the proposition; in the latter, one cannot. For instance, the proposition "Cats give birth only to kittens" is "empirically falsifiable" because one can invent experiences that would refute it such as the spectacle of tiny elephants emerging from a cat's womb. But the proposition "Cats are animals" is not "empirically falsifiable" because "cat" is *defined* as a species of animal. In the former case, the proposition remains true only as long as experience continues to bear it out; therefore, it depends on experience, i.e., it is a posteriori. In the latter case, the truth of the proposition is immune to any imaginable change in experience and, therefore, is independent of experience, i.e., is a priori.

Observe the inversion propounded by this argument: a

proposition can qualify as a *factual, empirical* truth only
if man is able to evade the facts of experience and arbitrarily
to invent a set of impossible circumstances that contradict
these facts; but a truth whose opposite is beyond man's
power of invention, is regarded as independent of and irrelevant to the nature of reality, i.e., as an arbitrary product
of human "convention."

Such is the unavoidable consequence of the attempt to
divorce logic and experience.

As I have said, knowledge cannot be acquired by experience apart from logic, nor by logic apart from experience.
Without the use of logic, man has no method of drawing
conclusions from his perceptual data; he is confined to
range-of-the-moment observations, but any perceptual fantasy that occurs to him qualifies as a future possibility
which can invalidate his "empirical" propositions. And
without reference to the facts of experience, man has no
basis for his "logical" propositions, which become mere
arbitrary products of his own invention. Divorced from
logic, the arbitrary exercise of the human imagination
systematically undercuts the "empirical"; and divorced from
the facts of experience, the same imagination arbitrarily
creates the "logical."

I challenge anyone to invent a more thorough way of
invalidating *all* of human knowledge.

Conclusion

The ultimate result of the theory of the analytic-synthetic
dichotomy is the following verdict pronounced on human
cognition: if the denial of a proposition is inconceivable, if
there is no possibility that any fact of reality can contradict
it, i.e., if the proposition represents knowledge which is
certain, then it does not represent knowledge of reality. In
other words: if a proposition cannot be wrong, it cannot be
right. A proposition qualifies as factual only when it asserts

facts which are still unknown, i.e., only when it represents a hypothesis; should a hypothesis be proved and become a certainty, it ceases to refer to facts and ceases to represent knowledge of reality. If a proposition is conclusively demonstrated—so that to deny it is obviously to endorse a logical contradiction—then, *in virtue of this fact,* the proposition is written off as a product of human convention or arbitrary whim.

This means: *a proposition is regarded as arbitrary precisely because it has been logically proved.* The fact that a proposition cannot be refuted, refutes it (i.e., removes it from reality). A proposition can retain a connection to facts only insofar as it has not been validated by man's method of cognition, i.e., by the use of logic. Thus proof is made the disqualifying element of knowledge, and knowledge is made a function of human ignorance.

This theory represents a total epistemological inversion: it penalizes cognitive success for being success. Just as the altruist mentality penalizes the good for being the good, so the analytic-synthetic mentality penalizes knowledge for being knowledge. Just as, according to altruism, a man is entitled only to what he has not earned, so, according to this theory, a man is entitled to claim as knowledge only what he has not proved. Epistemological humility becomes the prerequisite of cognition: "the meek shall inherit the truth."

The philosopher most responsible for these inversions is Kant. Kant's system secularized the mysticism of the preceding centuries and thereby gave it a new lease on life in the modern world. In the religious tradition, "necessary" truths were commonly held to be consequences of God's mode of thought. Kant substituted the "innate structure of the human mind" for God, as the source and creator of "necessary" truths (which thus became independent of the facts of reality).

The philosophers of the twentieth century merely drew the final consequences of the Kantian view. If it is man's mode of thought (independent of reality) that creates "necessary" truths, they argued, then these are not fixed or absolute; men have a choice in regard to their modes of thought; what the mind giveth, the mind taketh away. Thus, the contemporary conventionalist viewpoint.

We can know only the "phenomenal," mind-created realm, according to Kant; in regard to reality, knowledge is impossible. We can be certain only within the realm of our own conventions, according to the moderns; in regard to facts, certainty is impossible.

The moderns represent a logical, consistent development from Kant's premises. They represent Kant plus choice—a voluntaristic Kantianism, a whim-worshiping Kantianism. Kant marked the cards and made reason an agent of distortion. The moderns are playing with the same deck; their contribution is to play it deuces wild, besides.

Now observe what is left of philosophy in consequence of this neo-Kantianism.

Metaphysics has been all but obliterated: its most influential opponents have declared that metaphysical statements are neither analytic nor synthetic, and therefore are meaningless.

Ethics has been virtually banished from the province of philosophy: some groups have claimed that ethical statements are neither analytic nor synthetic, but are mere "emotive ejaculations"—and other groups have consigned ethics to the province of the man in the street, claiming that philosophers may analyze the language of ethical statements, but are not competent to prescribe ethical norms.

Politics has been discarded by virtually all philosophic schools: insofar as politics deals with values, it has been relegated to the same status as ethics.

Epistemology, the theory of knowledge, the science that defines the rules by which man is to acquire knowledge of facts, has been disintegrated by the notion that facts are the subject matter of "synthetic," "empirical" propositions and, therefore, are outside the province of philosophy—with the result that the special sciences are now left adrift in a rising tide of irrationalism.

What we are witnessing is the self-liquidation of philosophy.

To regain philosophy's realm, it is necessary to challenge and reject the fundamental premises which are responsible for today's debacle. A major step in that direction is the elimination of the death carrier known as the analytic-synthetic dichotomy.

Appendix
Excerpts from the Epistemology Workshops

*The material from this point on was not included in the edition of the book published by Ayn Rand. This appendix was made possible by a grant from the Ayn Rand Institute.

Foreword to the Second Edition

A substantial appendix has been added to this edition of *Introduction to Objectivist Epistemology*. The appendix consists of excerpts from four workshops on epistemology that Ayn Rand conducted in New York City between 1969 and 1971. The workshops were opportunities for a dozen professionals in philosophy, plus a few in physics and mathematics, to ask Miss Rand questions about her theory of concepts, which had first appeared in print in her own magazine, *The Objectivist*, in 1966–67. I myself took part in the workshops, as did Harry Binswanger, a longtime associate of Miss Rand's who has performed the complex task of editing these excerpts for publication.

The tape recordings of the workshops contain some twenty-one hours of discussion. There is much new material of philosophic interest on the tapes; what is new pertains not to the essentials of Ayn Rand's theory, but to the exact meaning, presuppositions, and/or implications of some particular aspect or formulation of the theory. Given the chance to explain some important qualifications, I am happy to make the cream of this new material available now to a wider audience.

The workshops were extended conversations. A few of the questions were submitted in writing, but most were not.

The questions generally dealt with highly technical subjects, which demand rigorous precision; Ayn Rand's answers were completely extemporaneous. She said as much or as little on a given point as the company required for its own clarity. Miss Rand did not speak with an eye to publication or consider the needs of a future audience.

No one, not even Ayn Rand, can speak extemporaneously with the precision and economy possible in written work. If she had decided to publish the workshops, Miss Rand would have edited the material extensively, weighing every word choice. The substance of her position on the issues would not have changed in such a case, but she would undoubtedly have decided to make many revisions in wording.

The questions asked in the workshops were uneven. Part of the reason is that the questioners, myself included, had not yet had the time fully to absorb so revolutionary a theory or, therefore, to know what to ask; as a rule, we were thinking aloud, groping to identify our confusions. In addition, we brought widely different cognitive contexts (and interests) to the discussions, some of us being relatively advanced in the study of Objectivism, others having only a sketchy impression. As a result, one person often needed a detailed discussion to be able to grasp a point that another considered obvious or unimportant. This kind of difference will apply, I am sure, to readers of the appendix, also.

Harry Binswanger has selected for publication the questions he regards as being of most general philosophic interest. Even these do not invariably raise issues that Ayn Rand herself regarded as critical; for the most part, she answered whatever was asked of her, regardless of her opinion of the question. I would advise a reader, therefore, to approach the appendix selectively and selfishly (in the Objectivist sense), pausing only on the material he personally finds illuminating.

The length of the appendix may not be taken as an index of its importance within the Objectivist corpus. Nor does my decision to publish this material make it "official Objectivist doctrine." Dr. Binswanger and I believe that Miss Rand would have agreed with or at least accepted our editorial decisions. But "Objectivism" is the name of Ayn Rand's achievement, and her theory of concepts is presented in the book she herself published, i.e., the present edition minus the appendix. Dr. Binswanger has done excellent, sensitive work on the appendix; he has remained as faithful as possible to the spirit and letter of the original conversations. The final result, however, is still Ayn Rand in an edited version that she herself had no opportunity to see or approve.

Aside from its new epistemological content, the appendix offers the reader another value: a glimpse of Ayn Rand's mind at work in the heat of philosophical give and take. I had hundreds of such conversations with Miss Rand and always found her method of approach fascinating in its own right, regardless of the subject being discussed.

Here is a chance not only to learn further details of her theory of concepts, but also to see Ayn Rand herself in philosophic action.

—Leonard Peikoff
Executor, Estate of Ayn Rand
South Laguna, CA
April 1989

Preface

The purpose of these workshops, Miss Rand says in her opening remarks, was to "chew" the Objectivist theory of concepts. "Chewing" was her metaphor for a broad range of mental activities which, by analogy with physical chewing, break down a complex whole so that it can be digested. Such "chewing" includes: defining terms, checking the meaning of key formulations, concretizing points by means of examples, drawing implications, and integrating the topic with related material.

Since what follows is not a verbatim transcript of the workshops, and since Ayn Rand never reviewed this material in any form, the reader has a right to know what editing has been done and what measures were taken to ensure that the result is a faithful version of the intellectual content of the sessions in general and of Ayn Rand's statements in particular. The editing consisted of cutting, reorganizing, and line-editing.

Cutting. A full transcript of the workshops would run to triple the length of this appendix. I have selected what I consider the most interesting and illuminating of the discussions and have condensed further by eliminating, within the sections selected, some of the repetitions and digressions that are endemic to oral exchanges. But when in doubt about including a somewhat repetitious passage, I left it in, on the grounds that "chewing" requires looking at the same point from slightly different perspectives. My general policy was to err on the side of over-inclusiveness in regard to Miss Rand's answers, as this may well be the last opportunity for her statements on these topics to be published.

I was more liberal in condensing the participants' questions. Some of the questions were considerably longer, wordier, and more roundabout than they appear here. Sometimes a question was rephrased several times, with exchanges among several of the participants, before its meaning became clear, and much of that circling around has been eliminated. But I stuck closely to the professors' formulations when Miss Rand's response was to express agreement with what they said.

Reorganizing. The workshops proceeded through the book in sequence, chapter by chapter. But that order did not apply on the smaller scale: within each chapter, the order of topics was determined by what each questioner, in turn, chose to ask. Consequently, some rearrangement of topics was called for in order to create a more logical sequence. I have collected into one location questions on related topics, irrespective of when in the twenty-one hours they actually occurred. For instance, the question I have placed first here actually occurred about three hours into the first session. In one or two cases I have inserted into a continuous discussion a few paragraphs from a separate discussion, but otherwise, in changing the order of topics, I have kept separate discussions separate rather than joining or merging them.

In its present form, the discussion begins with questions dealing with the heart of the process of concept-formation— abstraction through measurement-omission—then moves to concepts and words, then returns to take up some of the more technical aspects of measurement and related quasi-mathematical issues. After that, the progression conforms to the order of the chapters in the book, followed by a more metaphysically oriented section centering on the concept of "entity." The appendix concludes with a section on some issues in the philosophy of science, plus a historical postscript. (The table of contents given here is entirely my own.)

Line-editing. Even though her remarks were extemporaneous, little alteration of Miss Rand's statements was needed.

Of the changes that have been made, the vast majority consisted merely in innocuous alterations for the sake of grammar and smoothness, such as rearranging the order of clauses within a sentence, changing the tense of verbs, and specifying antecedents for pronouns that would be ambiguous in written form.

There were a few instances where Leonard Peikoff and I jointly believed that a given statement might be confusing or misleading without further elaboration. In these cases I either deleted the statement outright or used square brackets to insert my own clarifying term or remark. (Please note: square brackets, not parentheses, signal my insertions.)

Since the whole process required editing in several layers over a period of months, at its completion I went back through the entire manuscript, checking word by word against the corresponding sections of the tapes.

I am satisfied that the result is a fair and accurate rendering of the discussions.

—Harry Binswanger
New York City
April 1989

Appendix Contents

131

Concepts as Mental Existents (p. 153)
>   Are concepts products or processes?
>   Can the same mental entity be in different minds?
>   Are concepts less determinate than concretes?

Implicit Concepts (p. 159)
>   What does "implicit" mean?
>   Why "implicit concept" is not a contradiction.
>   Do animals have implicit concepts?
>   When may one call a concept "implicit"?

The Role of Words (p. 163)
> Words and Concepts
>>   Words as standing for concepts.
>>   Do words precede concepts?
>>   Concepts vs. perceptual groups.
>>   Concepts, words, and meaning.
>>   Concepts vs. qualified instances of concepts: words versus phrases.
> Words and Propositions (p. 177)
>>   Are concepts prior to propositions?
>>   The "dilemma" of understanding long sentences.

Measurement, Unit, and Mathematics (p. 184)
> Measurement (p. 184)
>>   What is the unit for measuring entities (e.g., triangles)? "Unit" vs. "standard."
>>   Does measurability imply reductionism?
>>   The error of confusing methods of measurement with metaphysical facts ("extensive" vs. "intensive" qualities).
> Exact Measurement and Continuity (p. 190)
>>   Bergsonian continuity vs. contextually exact measurements.
> Numbers (p. 196)
>>   How do we form concepts of numbers? Is "one" more metaphysical than other numbers?
>>   "One" vs. "unit"—does perception give us quantitative information?
>>   When do children learn numbers?

Philosophy of Science (p. 289)

Philosophic vs. Scientific Issues

Is "matter" a scientific or a philosophical concept? Is the mind-brain relation a philosophical issue?

Properties of the Ultimate Constituents (p. 290)

What can philosophers say about the ultimate con-stituents of matter?

Induction (p. 295)

On induction in general.

Causal explanation and the integration of knowledge.

Scientific Methodology (p. 301)

Does predictive success guarantee the validity of a hypothesis?

Imaginary numbers and other concepts of method.

Concluding Historical Postscript (p. 307)

How did Ayn Rand arrive at her theory?

Opening Remarks by Ayn Rand

I am very glad to see you all here. I have a definite purpose in mind for these sessions—namely, to make as clear as possible the nature of the Objectivist theory of concepts. My purpose here will not be to talk about Objectivism generally, but to discuss in detail—or, as we call it, to "chew"—this particular book. I regard it as very important; I hope you do too. I think this is a foundation which will help us to understand anything else about Objectivism.

I do not want to discuss my Foreword; I assume that everybody here understands what the problem of universals is. The only other issue left open in the Foreword is the question of the validity of sensory data. I indicated that any argument against the validity of sensory data commits what we call the fallacy of the "stolen concept" by relying on the validity of the senses in the attempt to deny them. And I assume that everyone here, if he is in any agreement with us at all, does accept the fact that sensory data are valid.

I also would like to add that the study of sensations as such is much more the province of science than of philosophy, since we are not consciously aware of single, isolated sensations. Therefore, we can start where we in fact do start: on the level of percepts.

I will ask everyone, to the best of his ability, to consider the subject from scratch—that is, from the beginning, as if we know nothing about concepts. Start from that, as near as one can, and avoid questions based on a different context, on some philosophical theory which is false. In framing your questions, please try to observe whether they are based on and imply some premise improperly accepted as an axiom. Or, in other words, please check your premises.

Abstraction as
Measurement-Omission

Overview of the Process

Prof. A: I want to check my understanding of your theory of concept-formation. What I would like to do is give a brief summary of the process and ask you to comment as to whether I understand it correctly.

AR: All right.

Prof. A: First of all, I'd like to distinguish the Objectivist position on concept-formation from the Aristotelian position. According to the Aristotelians, there is some common element, or essence, which is identical in all the concretes of a given kind, and concept-formation is simply the selective awareness of that element. So for Aristotle, the "manness" of men would be something that you would merely focus on selectively; and the "manness" of each man is the same.

The Objectivist position is that the "manness" of each man is specific—or not the "manness," but the characteristic of rationality. As I understand it, each person's form of rationality has specific measurements, and my rationality or "manness" would not be literally identical to someone else's. But what we do in concept-formation, through a process of measurement-omission, is integrate the concretes according to their common attributes.

Now, as I understand it, the measurement-omission is accomplished by means of differentiation. Take the concept of "blue." You begin as a child with two blue objects of different shades perhaps (so their specific color measurements differ), and, say, one red object. And then you are able to see that the two blues belong together as opposed to the red; whereas if you just consider the two blues by themselves, you would only be aware of the differences between them; you wouldn't see them as similar until you contrasted them to the red.

AR: That's right.

Prof. A: Now, the heart of the matter that I want to check on is this. Is it that by means of this differentiation you see blueness as a range or category of measurements within the Conceptual Common Denominator: color? That is the way I understand it. You see the blue of this object and the somewhat different blue of that other object; both have specific measurements, but those measurements fall into one category, as opposed to the measurements of some red object, which fall outside that category. So that the omission of measurements is seeing the measurements as falling within a given range or category of measurements—

AR: Yes.

Prof. A: —within the Conceptual Common Denominator.

AR: Yes, that's right. Now, the essential thing there is that you cannot form a concept by integration alone or by differentiation alone. You need both, always. You need to observe similarities in a certain group of objects and differences from some other group of objects within the common standard or kind of measurement. So that you could differentiate a red cup from two blue cups, but you couldn't differentiate a blue cup from a heavy stone—there is no Conceptual Common Denominator in that kind of distinction. Does that answer your question?

Prof. A: Yes.

AR: There is one thing that I want to correct you on, unless it was just foreshortening. You said that "manness" consists of rationality. Don't ever forget the full definition is "rational animal." Otherwise you may give the impression that rationality is the equivalent of the concept "man."

Prof. A: No, that was just an offhand way of speaking.

AR: Merely foreshortening. Okay.

Prof. A: So the Aristotelians thought there really was an attribute of blueness as such—like a kind of little banner sticking up from blue objects saying "blue." Whereas the Objectivist position is that there is a Conceptual Common Denominator uniting a red and two blues, and that the two blues are close together on the measurement range within that Conceptual Common Denominator, and that all the different shades of blue can be integrated because they fall within that range.

AR: Exactly.

Similarity and Measurement-Omission

Prof. B: In forming the concept "blue," a child would perceive that two blue things, with respect to color, are similar and are different from some red thing. And he places the blues in a range of measurements within the broader category, red being somewhere else on the scale.

AR: Right.

Prof. B: Now, in fact, he doesn't have a category of measurements explicitly, so what actually goes on, as you indicate, is that he perceives similarities and differences directly.

AR: That's right.

Prof. B: Then is what enables him to classify the blue things as blue the fact that he experiences them as belonging together, as against the red one?

AR: If you are trying to project what his psychological state actually is, I think the better way to say it would be: he would feel "these things are similar and these things are different," rather than "they belong together," because the second is a more sophisticated concept.

If you want to know what the nature of the process is, it would be more useful to try to remember how you, as an adult, learn new concepts. Because we learn new concepts constantly—for instance, concepts for new inventions, such

as television or radar. Ask yourself how you learned that
these objects are called by such-and-such name, and how
you learned to distinguish television from radio, or radar
from other forms of wireless communication. Observe that
you would first have to grasp that there is such an entity,
and then you would have to grasp in what way it is different
from the class of objects which it resembles most. You
would immediately have to establish a relationship of genus
and differentia. Now, it never occurred to you to measure
television, and it wouldn't be necessary to do so. You simply grasped what it has in common with radio and in what
ways it is different.

Prof. B: Regarding similarity, is it correct to say that
similarity is the form in which we perceive certain quantitative differences within a range?

AR: That's right.

Prof. B: So, "similarity" is an epistemological concept,
and a formulation of the metaphysical base of that would
be: quantitative differences within a range.

AR: That's right.

*   *   *

Prof. B: To describe the process of concept-formation on
a conscious level, one wouldn't have to refer to omitting
measurements. Is the purpose then of discussing it in terms
of omitting measurements to stress the metaphysical basis of
the process?

AR: No, not only to stress the metaphysical basis, but to
explain both the metaphysical and the epistemological aspects. Because, in modern philosophy, they dismiss similarity practically as if it were ineffable; the whole nominalist
school rests on that in various ways. The nominalists claim
that we form concepts on the ground of vague similarities,
and then they go into infinite wasted discussions about what
we mean by similarity, and they arrive at the conclusion that
nobody can define similarity. So that one of the important
issues here, and the reason for going into the process in
detail, is to indicate the metaphysical base of similarity *and*

the fact that it is grasped perceptually, that it is not a vague, arbitrary abstraction, that similarity is perceptually given, but the understanding of what similarity means has to be arrived at philosophically or scientifically. And similarity, when analyzed, amounts to: measurements omitted.

*   *   *

Prof. C: I understand how one grasps similarity on the perceptual level. Aristotle, presumably, was unable to identify how we grasp similarity beyond that point. He held that we grasp the essence of things—namely, how they are similar—intuitively. What in addition to that is the Objectivist theory stating?

AR: He didn't say you grasp *similarities* intuitively. He said you grasp the essence of things intuitively.

Prof. C: Yes, the essence as the fundamental similarity.

AR: But that isn't the way he saw it. Aristotle proceeded from a certain erroneous metaphysics. He assumed that there are such things as essences—and that's the Platonism in him. But he didn't agree with Plato's theory that essences are in a separate world. He held that essences do exist, but only in concretes. And the process of concept-formation, in his view, is the process of grasping that essence, and therefore grouping concretes in certain categories because they have that essence in common. It is the same essence, but in different concretes.

You see, he approaches the subject from that perspective. He isn't concerned with perceived similarities and differences. And since he can't explain how it is that we grasp these essences, which are not perceived by our senses, he would have to treat that grasp as a direct intuition, a form of direct awareness like percepts, but of a different order and therefore apprehending different objects.

Measurement-Omission and Generality

Prof. D: This is meant to be a counterexample to a very important part of your thesis: the role of measurement-

omission in concept-formation. In general, I agree with what
you say, but here is the problem I have. I take it that a
concept's generality of reference is achieved by leaving out
the specific measurements of the objects referred to.

AR: Right.

Prof. D: But now take the following case. I have a concept of a specific kind of tire, "710-15 tires." This concept
specifies all of the significant measurements of the tire (its
width and diameter). So what measurements have I left out
in forming the concept to achieve the generality?

AR: The measurements relevant to the concept "tire."
When you say that this is a particular kind of tire, and you
specify the measurements, you are talking about a subcategory of the wider category "tire." In order to identify it as a
710-15 tire, you first had to know that it is possible to have
620-15 tires (or whatever the figures might be), which you
would also subsume under the concept "tire."

What you have omitted in classifying a particular group
by its measurements is the fact that those measurements
may be altered and the object would still be a tire, but not a
tire of this subgrouping. You have merely isolated a subcategory of the wider concept "tire."

I think it is exactly the same process as I described in
subdividing "table" into "dining table," "coffee table," etc.
[page 23] Those are subcategories, with more restricted
measurements, of the wider category, whose measurements
are also limited within a certain range.

Prof. D: But if it is the omission of the exact measurements that provides a generality of reference, then if you
reintroduce the exact measurements wouldn't you dissolve
the generality?

AR: You merely narrow it down. You merely form a
subcategory.

Prof. D: But I would find that all of these particular tires
measure exactly 710 by 15.

Prof. E: There would still be many respects in which the
measurements of those tires would vary, even if the physical

dimensions that you specify remain constant. For instance, they could be whitewall tires or ordinary black ones, presumably they could be made out of somewhat different types of material, etc. Therefore, even though a certain range of measurements was fixed, there would still be variations along other dimensions.

AR: But also there is the ultimate variation which you mustn't forget: they are individual tires. Suppose, theoretically, that you could with the finest instruments produce a set of tires of exactly the same measurable aspects in every respect. This wouldn't make them blend into one super-tire. You would still say, "I have one hundred tires of this particular kind."

But in order even to make that observation, you first have to have the concept "tire." You first have to know that the issue involved here is the issue of measurements. And if this particular group of tires is identical in all their measurements, it is a subgroup; in this respect they are different from other tires, which may have different measurements.

Prof. D: But if the essence of generality was the omission of the specific measurement of the individuals, then by reintroducing the specific measurement of individuals the generality would be lost.

AR: Except for one very important element that you omit here and that can't be omitted: the Conceptual Common Denominator. Even if all tires, [not just one subgroup], were absolutely alike in every measurement (which is not really possible, but assuming that for the sake of argument), you couldn't form the concept "tire" unless there was something that you could isolate that grouping from. Let us suppose it is the concept of the wheel or some other part of an automobile. Unless you differentiate this particular grouping from another one with which it has something in common but differs in measurement, you couldn't have a concept. Because you forget there are two aspects of the process—one is integration, but the first one is separation [i.e., differentiation].

Prof. D: But does the separation give you the generality, or is it the type of integration that operates that gives you the generality?

AR: Both. One is not possible without the other. You could not integrate a given set of concretes unless you could first differentiate it from other concretes. You have to isolate it first, and then you can integrate it into a particular grouping and form a concept. But if you can't isolate it, you can't abstract.

Prof. D: Then you are maintaining that the generality remains in the case of the subcategory where measurements are specified; the generality isn't lost because it was originally obtained in the concept of "tire" by leaving out measurements, and bringing back in the measurements now doesn't affect the generality of the notion of tires.

AR: Not only was the generality present originally, but you are using and introducing it when you say these are 710-15 *tires*. The generality is present in the classification of these objects as tires. By identifying them in that form you are introducing the issue of measurement-omission by classifying them still as tires. If you didn't do that, then you couldn't call them tires. Then they would be sui generis objects; but they are not, they are tires. Why do you classify them as that? Because their submeasurements, which you are now specifying, are different from the measurements of others which you call "tires"; yet you subsume them in the same concept, in the same category. So you are using measurement-omission even in the classification.

The Conceptual Common Denominator

Prof. E: In the process of concept-formation in childhood, am I correct that it is impossible for a mind to mistakenly choose a Conceptual Common Denominator? That is, if in fact the two groups were incommensurable, the child's mind would just stop. He couldn't actually form a concept in this case mistakenly, could he?

AR: I don't think so. Here, frankly, I have not considered it, but as an offhand answer, I don't quite see how that would be possible.

Prof. A: On the perceptual level, you wouldn't then be aware of similarities and differences.

AR: Yes. Now in the case of abstractions from abstractions that sort of mistake is unfortunately made constantly. Only the result isn't really a concept. It usually comes out as one of those "anti-concepts." [See page 71.]

*   *   *

Prof. D: I can think of some cases that seem to present a difficulty for the statement: "All conceptual differentiations are made in terms of commensurable characteristics." What would you say about the case of distinguishing mental entities from physical entities? You have the concept of "mental entity" vs. the concept of "physical entity," and there you are distinguishing objects which presumably possess no commensurable characteristic.

AR: But you don't form those concepts directly. You form the concept "mental entity" only after you have formed the following concepts: the concept "man," the concept "consciousness," then you identify certain mental states or events in your own mind, such as thoughts, let's say, which you call "mental entities." Then you infer that other human beings also possess the ability to have mental entities in their minds. Therefore you have gone through a long conceptual chain, making differentiations as you went along. You didn't start by looking at reality from scratch so to speak, and as a first-level concept form the concept "mental entity" as distinguished from "physical entity." That would not be possible. They would be incommensurable.

Now remember, I said here that you cannot form a concept, a specific concept, by differentiating objects through an incommensurable characteristic. But, [once formed], you can relate such objects in a wider sense. And the commensurable characteristic between physical objects and consciousness is the content of consciousness, as I discuss in Chapter

4. There is a commensurable link [between concepts of consciousness and existential concepts], but that link will be
found after you have established the fact of consciousness.
Then you consider, "What do I have inside my mind?" and
you see that it is exclusively made up of content derived
from the outside world, from existence. (It may be indirectly
derived, such as you may have thoughts about other thoughts,
or you may think about your memories. But ultimately the
content of your consciousness, since it begins tabula rasa,
consists entirely of your awareness of the outside world.)
And there you have the commensurable attribute, or one
of the commensurable attributes, which is essential in forming concepts of consciousness.

*   *   *

Prof. A: Isn't what is commensurable or incommensurable an issue of one's context of knowledge? Between length
and color, for instance, there is actually a commensurable
characteristic in a wider context of knowledge—both are
attributes—but in order to reach that wider characteristic,
you have to begin by making differentiations which you can
grasp as commensurable. Or else, you would never get to
that later stage.

AR: That's right. Even in the wider context, however, it
isn't that characteristics which appeared at the first level to
be incommensurable suddenly become commensurable.

Here we are talking particularly about the process of
concept-formation. In that process, you cannot form a concept to unify concretes into one category except by means of
a commensurable characteristic. And two characteristics that
appear to you, on the perceptual level, as incommensurable
(like length and green) will not be commensurable at any
stage. But you will be able to establish certain relationships
between them through many other intermediate concepts.
But by themselves those two will remain incommensurable.
If we take just the referents of the concepts "length" and
"green," there is nothing that you can establish as a commensurable characteristic between them.

Prof. A: If you differentiated length and green from man, at a sophisticated level of knowledge, on the basis of the fact that man is an entity, while length and green are both attributes, there you have found a Conceptual Common Denominator, but you couldn't reach that stage without the earlier abstractions.

AR: That's right. But between those two, if you were to consider only those two attributes, apart from "man" or any other concepts, just those two, they won't become commensurable. But when you establish the category "attributes of physical objects," then you see they have that in common.

Concepts as Open-ended

Prof. A: Concepts are open-ended in the sense that every new concrete of the same type is to be subsumed under the concept. Can you say anything about the process by which a child moves from a limited group from which he forms the concept to making it open-ended? How does he get beyond the concretes from which he starts?

AR: In order to grasp a concept he has to grasp that it applies to all entities of that particular kind. If he doesn't, he's merely repeating a word. If you ever watch how a child learns to speak, he may first grasp only that "nose" applies to his own nose and, let's say, his mother's. But he hasn't grasped the concept until he can point to any face and say "nose." And that is what children usually do; that is exactly how they learn words. First they have to grasp the word as standing for a particular concrete, then they begin to apply it to other concretes of that kind. Until they have done that, they haven't got it yet. But once they begin to apply the word to new concretes of the same kind, they've made it open-ended.

Prof. A: So to make the classification open-ended is part of the integration itself?

AR: Yes.

Prof. A: To see that there is a *kind* of thing.

AR: Yes.

Three "Hard Cases"

Prof. D: Here are some concepts that present a difficulty with respect to leaving out differing specific measurements and abstracting a common feature. What measurements of what particulars do we leave out and what common features do we retain in the case of the following three concepts: (1) "God"; (2) "infinity"; (3) "nothing"?

AR: What measurements do we omit?

Prof. A: Yes. And what common features of particulars are retained in order to get the concept "God"—

AR: I would have to refer you to a brief passage about invalid concepts [page 49]. This is precisely one, if not the essential one, of the epistemological objections to the concept "God." It is not a concept. At best, one could say it is a concept in the sense in which a dramatist uses concepts to create a character. It is an isolation of actual characteristics of man combined with the projection of impossible, irrational characteristics which do not arise from reality—such as omnipotence and omniscience.

Besides, God isn't even supposed to be a concept: he is sui generis, so that nothing relevant to man or the rest of nature is supposed, by the proponents of that viewpoint, to apply to God. A concept has to involve two or more similar concretes, and there is nothing like God. He is supposed to be unique. Therefore, by their own terms of setting up the problem, they have taken God out of the conceptual realm. And quite properly, because he is out of reality.

The same applies to the concept "infinity," taken metaphysically. The concept of "infinity" has a very definite purpose in mathematical calculation, and there it is a concept of method. But that isn't what is meant by the term "infinity" as such. "Infinity" in the metaphysical sense, as something existing in reality, is another invalid concept. The concept "infinity," in that sense, means something without identity, something not limited by anything, not definable.

Therefore, the measurements omitted here are all measurements and all reality. Now, what was the third one?

Prof. A: "Nothing."

AR: That is strictly a relative concept. It pertains to the absence of some kind of concrete. The concept "nothing" is not possible except in relation to "something." Therefore, to have the concept "nothing," you mentally specify—in parenthesis, in effect—the absence of a something, and you conceive of "nothing" only in relation to concretes which no longer exist or which do not exist at present.

You can say "I have nothing in my pocket." That doesn't mean you have an entity called "nothing" in your pocket. You do not have any of the objects that could conceivably be there, such as handkerchiefs, money, gloves, or whatever. "Nothing" is strictly a concept relative to some existent concretes whose absence you denote in this form.

It is very important to grasp that "nothing" cannot be a primary concept. You cannot start with it in the absence of, or prior to, the existence of some object. That is the great trouble with Existentialism, as I discuss in the book [page 60]. There is no such concept as "nothing," except as a relational concept denoting the absence of some things. The measurements omitted are the measurements of those things.

Prof. A: Does the concept of "non-existence" refer only to an absence? Is there no valid concept of sheer non-being, of something that never was and never will be?

AR: That's right. Non-existence as such—particularly in the same generalized sense in which I use the term "existence" in saying "existence exists," that is, as the widest abstraction without yet specifying any content, or applying to all content—you cannot have the concept "non-existence" in that same fundamental way. In other words, you can't say: this is something pertaining to the whole universe, to everything I know, and I don't say what. In other words, without specifying content.

You see, the concept of "existence" integrates all of the

existents that you have perceived, without knowing all their characteristics. Whereas the concept of "non-existence" in that same psycho-epistemological position would be literally a blank. Non-existence—apart from what it is that doesn't exist—is an impossible concept. It's a hole—a literal blank, a zero.

It is precisely on the fundamental level of equating existence and non-existence as some kind of opposites that the greatest mistakes occur, as in Existentialism.

Abstraction as Volitional

Prof. A: Abstraction is a volitional act. Is that right?

AR: Oh yes.

Prof. D: Then how do I go about abstracting the very first time? How do I know what to do, volitionally? Unless I first had the idea of abstraction, how could I proceed to will to abstract?

AR: No, you do something else volitionally. That is, you abstract volitionally, but you don't will it directly the first time. Do you know what you will? You will to observe. You use your senses, you look around, and your will is to grasp, to understand. And you observe similarities. Now, you don't know yet that this is the process of abstraction, and a great many people never grasp consciously that that's what the process is. But you are engaged in it once you begin to observe similarities.

And although I hesitate to talk about volition on the preconceptual level—because the subject isn't aware of it in those terms—even a preconceptual infant has the power to look around or not look, to listen or not listen. He has a certain minimal, primitive form of volition over the function of his senses. But volition in the full sense of a conscious choice, and a choice which he can observe by introspection, begins when he forms concepts—at the stage where he has a sufficient conceptual vocabulary to begin to form sentences and draw conclusions, when he can say consciously, in effect, "This table is larger than that one"—*that* he has to do volitionally. If he doesn't want to, he can skip that necessity, and you can observe empirically that too many people do, on too wide a scale.

Prof. D: This very first time, or these first times, the child makes observations, and then he finds he has done something which is *fait accompli*, as it were. And what he was doing, although he didn't have a name or concept for it, was abstracting.

AR: That's right. He was talking prose and he didn't know it. That joke [from Molière] really is very important. In a certain sense, it names a great many psychological processes.

Assuming we give words to what goes on in his preverbal consciousness, all he has to will is: "I will look. I will see what things are like." And in that process he makes a discovery: some things have similarities with others and are different from still other things. Now that is a discovery. He doesn't will it at first. Later the process becomes more conscious, but at first it is a discovery. What does he use? His senses. His sensory apparatus at that stage functions automatically. As he discovers certain things, he begins to direct his sensory apparatus, and that is volitional.

Prof. D: So he doesn't will to abstract; he looks and then he finds he has done something that is useful to him. Then he does it again and again, but how does he get to the fully conceptual stage?

AR: He expands the process. He would say, "By observing, I have seen differences between papers, cups, and tables." Now some strange, nasty relatives enter the room, and he could say, "I will now direct my attention to learning what the difference is between them and my parents." That he would have to do consciously.

What would be the subverbal process? It would be as follows: "By observing distinctions and similarities, I have learned a great many things about inanimate objects in my room. I can handle them better because I have observed them. I know that I can drink from a cup but I can't drink from the table. I can deal with these objects if I observe

their characteristics—what they have in common and in
what ways they are different from each other. Now, I am up
against a bewildering experience—people—and there are
differences among people, differences which are not so easy
to perceive. If I merely look at my mother and my aunt, I
won't see differences—at least none that tell me something
about the two entities. I have to do something else. I have
to consciously direct my attention to observe. If I don't like
this aunt, what is it about her? But I like my mother. Why
do I? In what respects are they similar? They are both
women. In what respects are they different, since I like one
and not the other?

And then he might observe: "My mother is gentle and
understanding, but this new creature yells at me or talks
baby talk, and I don't like it." He might observe that much;
but his senses won't do it automatically. Here he had to
decide: "I want to understand the difference." All his
senses gave him is a generalized impression. To differentiate
it, he has to do something by conscious decision.

And you can observe that, unfortunately, very few people
carry that method through life—particularly with regard to
such a complex subject as human character. They do not
conceptualize why they like one person and not another—
what the meaning is of their own reaction. It is in that field,
particularly, that they stop—and stop very early. And that is
very unfortunate.

Concepts as Mental Existents

Prof. F: In your definition of concept, you use the word "integration." You say: "A concept is a mental integration of two or more units which are isolated according to a specific characteristic(s) and united by a specific definition."

AR: That's the generalized definition. The exact definition is the one at the bottom of page 13. ["A concept is a mental integration of two or more units possessing the same distinguishing characteristic(s), with their particular measurements omitted."]

Prof. F: Yes, there again the word "integration" is used. Do you mean that a concept is a process of integration or, alternatively, that a concept is the product of a process of integration?

AR: The second. Here I refer to the fact that the result of a process of concept-formation is a mental entity, a mental unit, which is an integration of the various elements involved in that process. The reason why I used the word "integration" is to indicate that it is not a mere sum but an inseparable sum forming a new mental unit.

*　　*　　*

Prof. F: If you and I have the same concept, does that mean that the same entity is in both of our minds?

AR: If we are both careful and rational thinkers, yes. Or rather, put it this way: the same entity *should be* in both of our minds.

153

Prof. F: Okay, taking concepts, therefore, as entities: they do not have spatial location, do they?

AR: No, I have said they are *mental* entities.

Prof. A: When you say a concept is a mental entity, you don't mean "entity" in the sense that a man is an entity, do you?

AR: I mean it in the same sense in which I mean a thought, an emotion, or a memory is an entity, a mental entity—or put it this way: a phenomenon of consciousness.

Prof. A: Wouldn't you say that consciousness is itself an attribute of man?

AR: Right. A faculty of man. And of animals, or at least the middle and higher animals.

*   *   *

Prof. F: When you form a concept, the concept itself is perfectly determinate, right?

AR: In which sense?

Prof. F: Even though the concept has been formed by leaving out measurements, the concept is still determinate in the sense that it is subject to the Law of Identity.

AR: Oh yes.

Prof. F: So therefore, in the case of a concept, you have a determinacy which is non-quantified.

AR: Except that a certain category of measurements is retained. Therefore it is quantified to that extent. When you form a concept, you determine what kind of measurements are appropriate. For instance, in the case of the concept "table," a certain range of measurements is included, but the particular measurements are omitted. So the table may be of any shape or any size, provided it has a flat surface and supports. You here set a range of measurements of shape to determine your concept, but you omit the individual measurements.

Prof. F: So the difference between the concept and the concrete is that the concrete has a greater determinacy, right?

AR: Are you going from this to the idea that matter is the principle of individuation, that everything is one as a kind of Platonic form, but that matter constitutes individuals?

Prof. F: I'm saying that I'm confused about this particular point.

AR: I see. I think the nearest relationship is the relationship of algebraic symbols to arithmetical numbers. Could you say that arithmetical numbers have a greater determinacy or individuation? Not really.

Prof. F: Yes. The algebraic symbol is a variable, and the number which we finally substitute for the algebraic symbol at the end of the equation is what we speak of as the value of that variable. And it is more determinate. The variable must be at some place, and yet the specific place is not given.

AR: No, a variable can be at any given number of places within the specified range. And to say the number is more determinate introduces a certain kind of confusion. Because in a metaphysical sense only concretes exist. Therefore, when we form a concept, we cannot say that we have removed it in a certain sense from individuality or the existence of concretes. Isn't there a Platonic element in the question?

The basic overall point would be always to keep in mind that this is a cognitive process, not an arbitrary process; it's a process of perceiving reality and is governed by the rules of reality. Nevertheless, it's our way of grasping reality; it isn't reality itself; it's only a method of acquiring knowledge, a method of cognition.

Prof. B: I see another confusion here. The concept as a mental entity is determinate. It's individual, it has identity, you can measure it in the way that you discuss in Chapter 4. The concept, if it is formed correctly, has a determinate reference, which means that it refers to a determinate aspect of reality. To say that the concept is less determinate than the concrete is to treat the concept as if it were a concrete in reality—

AR: Of a different kind, yes. That's right. That's the element that is somewhat Platonic here.

Prof. D: It was said that a concept is not a concrete, it is a determinate result with a determinate reference. Now we do have a concept of "concept," but I don't find any concretes that it is relating. Or if I do find concretes, they are things, existents.

AR: No, the referents of the concept "concept" are other concepts. For instance, let's say you form the concepts "table," "chair," "man," and a few other concepts of perceptually given concretes. Then at a certain level you can form the concept of "concept," the concretes of which are all your other specific, earlier-formed concepts.

Prof. D: But they aren't concretes, though.

AR: They are mental concretes. You are now discussing an integration of mental entities. "Concept" refers to mental entities. The referents of the concept of "concept" are all the concepts which you have learned [and will ever learn].

Prof. D: Then a mental entity is a concrete?

AR: As a mental entity, yes. It is a concrete in relation to the wider abstraction which is the concept of "concept." Take another, similar case: the concept of "emotion." What are its concretes? The various emotions which you observe introspectively, which you are able to conceptualize. And first you conceptualize them individually. You would form the concepts "love," "hate," "anger," "fear," and then you arrive at the concept "emotion," the units of which will be these various emotions that you have identified.

Prof. D: I misunderstood, then, something that Professor B said. I thought that he was maintaining that these weren't really concretes, not even concretes with holes in them, so to speak—not even vague concretes.

Prof. B: No, that was the *content* of the concept. The concept as a mental entity would have measurements; it would be a certain mental product.

AR: A mental entity standing for a certain number of concretes—a concept—is not the same as the concretes in vague form. Because some schools of philosophy did hold just that—that a concept is a memory of a concrete, only very vague. You see a concept is not a vague concrete, it is a mental entity—which means an entity of a different kind, bearing a certain specific relationship to the physical concretes.

Prof. D: But metaphysically, though, the concept is a concrete; it's a mental entity. You have a concept of "emotion." The referents are these various mental entities, this particular emotion and that particular one. And then the concept of "emotion" itself is a mental entity in actual being.

AR: Yes, you can call it that.

Prof. D: So metaphysically, not epistemologically, all we have here are concretes.

AR: If you mean: does such a thing as the concept of "emotion" in a mind really exist? Yes, it exists—mentally. And only mentally.

Prof. E: Would it be fair to say that a concept qua concept is not a concrete but an integration of concretes, but qua existent it is a concrete integration, a specific mental entity in a particular mind?

AR: That's right. But I kept saying, incidentally, that we can call them "mental entities" only metaphorically or for convenience. It is a "something." For instance, before you have a certain concept, that particular something doesn't exist in your mind. When you have formed the concept of "concept," that is a mental something; it isn't a nothing. But anything pertaining to the content of a mind always has to be treated metaphysically not as a separate existent, but only with this precondition, in effect: that it is a mental state, a mental concrete, a mental something. Actually, "mental something" is the nearest to an exact identification. Because "entity" does imply a physical thing. Nevertheless, since "something" is too vague a term, one can use the word "entity," but only to say that it is a mental something as distinguished from other mental somethings (or from nothing). But it isn't an entity in the primary, Aristotelian sense in which a primary substance exists.

We have to agree here on the terminology, because we

are dealing with a very difficult subject for which no clear definitions have been established. I personally would like to have a new word for it, but I am against neologisms. Therefore I think the term "mental unit" or "mental entity" can be used, provided we understand by that: "a mental something."

Prof. A: I think I can give an analogy to clarify the two perspectives on "concept" that had been confused. Suppose you have a map of a city. In relation to that city, the map is generalized: it doesn't include the shape of specific houses, every little curve in the street, etc. But if you look at the map not insofar as it refers to the city, but just as a piece of paper with lines and colors on it, it is entirely specific. It doesn't have any little regions of vagueness or non-identity.

AR: That's a very good comparison. Yes, that is correct.

Implicit Concepts

Prof. G: The question I have deals with the concept "implicit." I want first to get at the general notion of "implicit" and then its meaning in the notions of "implicit concept," "implicit measurement," etc.

AR: Well, I would like to state my general definition, and then let's examine it.

The "implicit" is that which is available to your consciousness but which you have not conceptualized. For instance, if you state a certain proposition, implicit in it are certain conclusions, but you may not necessarily be aware of them, because a special, separate act of consciousness is required to draw these consequences and grasp conceptually what is implied in your original statement. The implicit is that which is available to you but which you have not conceptualized.

Prof. G: This is one of the points I want to get at. In both Chapter 1 and other parts of your book, you use the concept "implicit" to talk about "implicit concepts," "implicit knowledge," and "implicit measurement-omission." Now, I thought I could observe that there were several senses of "implicit," both as it is actually used in ordinary discussions and in your own discussions. What I would like to understand is in what sense or senses you were using the term in each of the above cases.

AR: Remember, we are not linguistic analysts here.

Prof. G: I don't think there is any assumption of that. I am not a linguistic analyst.

AR: Okay.

Prof. G: Take the notion of "implicit measurement-omission." There seem to be two senses of "implicit" here. One sense could be that there is some form of awareness or recognition, but not an explicit formulation, of the process of measurement-omission. I know you don't hold that. But, for example, you could say that when concepts are formed, there is a certain form of awareness or recognition that something like measurement-omission is involved, but one can't explicitly state the fact that the concepts are formed through measurement-omission.

The other sense of "implicit" would be not that there is some form of awareness or recognition—that might not be present at all—but the sense of "implicit" in which something is presupposed by, or is a condition for, something else. I think this might be present in axiomatic concepts, for example. When you say that axiomatic concepts are implicit in all knowledge, the sense of "implicit" there might also include the notion that axiomatic concepts have a relationship to other concepts in a hierarchy—there is a logical connection between axiomatic concepts and other concepts. And I think that the nature of the relationship here would be that axiomatic concepts are presupposed in higher concepts.

AR: I would have to ask you what you mean by "presuppose." Normally, "presuppose" means that you cannot hold concept A unless you have first grasped concept B. There is an almost chronological projection here—if you do not grasp B, you cannot grasp A. That is what "presuppose" means. That isn't the same thing as "implicit."

Prof. G: Then I was just wrong on that.

AR: You are wrong on the second but, as near as I understand you, you are right on the first: "implicit" is a knowledge which is available to you but which you have not yet grasped consciously. And by "grasped consciously" I mean: brought into conceptual terms. You have not identified it conceptually. So that, if I say that "existence" is implicit in the first awareness, I mean the material from which the concept "existence" will come is present, but the child just learning concepts would not be able to form the concept "existence" until he has formed a sufficient number of concepts of particular existents.

Prof. G: What I would like to do is to get a better understanding of the nature of that awareness. Let's consider the notion of "implicit concept." You state, on page 6, that when one has an implicit concept, one grasps the constituents of what may later be integrated into a concept.

AR: Yes.

Prof. G: Now, I take it that, in this sense of "implicit," there is a form of awareness here which is below the level of the explicit. There is no formulation on the part of the person involved.

AR: It simply means just what I said. It is not yet conceptualized, but it is available. Therefore, if you substitute the definition "conceptualized or not" for "explicit and implicit," it will be perfectly clear.

Prof. G: Why do you identify this type of awareness as an implicit *concept*? There seems to be an obvious objection that the notion of "implicit concept" is a contradiction in terms. For you to have a concept, there must be some form of integration, and you are speaking here only of an awareness which is avowedly not integrated; it is just an awareness of the units themselves.

Prof. E: May I make one brief observation? If I follow the drift of your comment, you would also say that it is a self-contradiction to describe a fertilized egg in the womb as a "potential man," because a man is defined as a rational animal and the egg is not yet a rational animal; so we are applying an adjective to a noun where the adjective, out of context, doesn't allow for the defining characteristic of the noun. Is that the drift of your argument? Because on the face of it that seems awfully linguistic-analytical to me. That is, you just observe the conjunction of an adjective and a noun, and divorce it altogether from the content of the two concepts.

AR: I am afraid so.

Prof. G: It would be like saying that calling a fertilized egg a "potential man" is a contradiction in terms. That's helpful. Let me ask a related question. Would you want to maintain that animals, which do have an awareness of the units, would have implicit concepts?

AR: No, because conceptualization as such is not possible to them.

Prof. G: So the notion of implicit concept presupposes the awareness of a conceptual being.

AR: It presupposes a consciousness capable of conceptualization.

*   *   *

Prof. B: Would you say that a child has an implicit concept of "table" at the stage when he has isolated the differentiating characteristics of tables but has not yet integrated them?

AR: At any stage before he is ready to grasp the word "table." An implicit concept is the stage of an integration when one is in the process of forming that integration and until it is completed.

Prof. B: Any time after he detects the similarities and differences?

AR: Right. What has to be clearly delimited is only this: not everything that is around you is an implicit concept. For instance, subatomic physics is operative there in the room which the infant first observes, but you can't say that its concepts are implicit merely because when he reaches college age he will grasp them. They are not implicit concepts. An implicit concept is the stage, that period of time whatever it might be, when a child is actually focusing on a certain group of concretes, isolating them from the rest of his field, and/or integrating them. And that's not all done instantaneously: it is a process. It is in that process that the future concept is implicit.

The Role of Words

Words and Concepts

Prof. F: On page 16, you refer to words as being themselves concepts. Do you mean that literally? For instance, you say that prepositions are concepts. Do you mean that prepositions stand for concepts? Is this a shorthand way of saying that?

AR: Oh yes, certainly. I have stated that words are perceptual symbols which stand for these products of the mental integrations.

And in case this isn't clear, I would like to add one thing. Why did I say "perceptual"? Because words are available to us either visually or auditorially. They are given to us in sensory, perceptual form. And by means of grasping them, on the perceptual level, we are able to operate with concepts as single mental units. In other words, every time we think of the concept "table," we don't have to add up the sum of all the tables we have seen or visualize them. "Table" as a sound or a visual image is on the perceptual level. Mentally, it stands for that particular integration of concretes which we have called "table."

So the word is not the concept, but the word is the auditory or visual symbol which stands for a concept. And a concept is a mental entity; it cannot be perceived perceptually. That's the role played by words.

Prof. D: On page 19, you say: "The process of forming a concept is not complete until its constituent units have been integrated into a single mental unit by means of a specific word." Now this seems to imply that words precede concepts—that without the word there wouldn't be the concept. But you also speak of words "designating" concepts and words "symbolizing" concepts—which seems to imply that the word does not precede the concept. Again, you say on page 10: "Every word . . . is a symbol which denotes a concept." This passage seems to have the same implication: a denial that the word is first and the concept second.

AR: Most emphatically, I did not mean that words precede concepts. And I would like to know what gave you that impression—because even the sentence you quoted from page 19 made clear, I thought, that the word comes at the end of a process of conceptualization, not at the beginning. One's mind first has to grasp the isolation and the integration which represents the formation of a concept; but to complete that process—and particularly to retain it, and later to automatize it—a man needs a verbal symbol. But as far as the process of concept-formation is concerned, the word is the result of the process.

Prof. D: So the concept would be formed prior to the introduction of the word, and the word would be used as a device for retaining the concept?

AR: That is a word's main function, but its function is not merely that. I meant exactly what I said: to *complete* the process. Let me make this a little clearer. Suppose a child is forming the concept "table." First, he has to isolate a table from the rest of his perceptual concretes, then integrate it with other tables. Now, in this process words are not present yet, because he is merely observing, and performing a certain mental process. It is after he has fully grasped that these particular objects (tables) are special and different in some way from all the other objects he perceives—it is then that he has to firm up, in effect, his mental activity in his own mind by designating that special status of these particular objects in some sensory form [i.e., by means of a word].

It is for the purpose not only of retaining the concept but also of making and completing the process of concept-formation that he has to designate the tables by some kind of sensory symbol. The main function of doing so is to enable him to retain the concept and be able to use it subsequently. But even apart from the future, in the process of forming that concept, in order for it not to remain a momentary impression or observation which then vanishes—in order to make it in a *concept-forming* process—he has to identify what he has just observed in some one, concrete, specific, sensory form.

This probably becomes somewhat clearer in the chapter on the cognitive role of concepts, but I would ask you all to keep in mind that a very important part of my entire theory is what I call unit-economy: the substitution of one mental unit for an indefinite number of concretes of a certain kind. That is the essence of why we need concepts—that is the essence of what concepts do for us. Therefore, the substitution of one unit which refers to x number of possible units is the essence of concept-formation. The process is not complete without that substitution.

Prof. D: So until the word was interposed, there would not in the strict sense be a concept?

AR: Right.

Prof. D: Then I take it that the process is as follows. An integration occurs which cannot yet be said to be a concept. And a sound, a sensuous concrete, is introduced to hold down, so to speak, this integration. And at that point the sound, as being used to hold down this integration, becomes a word whose meaning is the integration.

AR: Oh no. The meaning is not the integration. The integration is the process. The meaning is the objects which are being isolated and integrated. The meaning of the word is always metaphysical, in the sense of its referents, not psychological. The meaning of the word is out there in existence, in reality. The process that one had to perform in order to arrive at that meaning, and at that integration, is psychological.

I want to stress this; it is a very important distinction. A great number of philosophical errors and confusions are created by failing to distinguish between consciousness and existence—between the process of consciousness and the reality of the world outside, between the perceiver and the perceived. Therefore, it's very important here, if the issue arises at all, to stress emphatically that a concept and its symbol, the word, stands for certain objective referents—for existents outside, in reality. And in the case of concepts of consciousness, one's own consciousness serves as the observer and the processes of consciousness as the observed, as the object which one observes and integrates. But in either case, whether it is concepts of outside existents or of one's own consciousness, the concepts always refer to some facts which one is conceptualizing, and never to one's method or process.

Prof. D: Then would this do as the statement of the process? One integrates, then introduces a sensuous concrete holding the integration. At that point the sound or the sensuous concrete becomes a word whose meaning is the objects integrated.

AR: That's right.

Prof. D: And at the same time one has for the first time a concept.

AR: That's right. I also want to stress what I said earlier: the essential nature and purpose of the process of concept-formation is unit-economy. And therefore when a great number of concretes, an indefinitely large number, has been transformed into one unit, then the process is completed.

Now, it has to be a specific unit; and it cannot be specific, it cannot be concrete, unless it is sensuous. Because reality is concrete, and we perceive by means of our senses. Suppose we attempted to have a concept which was symbolized by a certain feeling. Let's say that I have a feeling of combined pleasure and disgust at the concept "table" —suppose I tried to hold that concept by means of such a feeling. Needless to say, that would not be a concept. It would not last beyond the mood of the moment. And I would not have performed the most important part of the process—namely, the substitution of one handleable, perceivable, firm, objective unit for the enormity which I want to subsume under this concept.

*   *   *

Prof. D: There's still some puzzlement concerning the difference between "unit" and "concept." Take the stage of concept-formation where a child regards certain entities as resembling each other. A child is observing these three notepads, and they are just entities so long as he does not show that he is treating them as distinct from other objects.

AR: Okay.

Prof. D: But now he notices similarities and differences, and treats these as related together and distinguished from some other things. So these three objects are at this point units. But has he thereby arrived at the point of conceptualizing them? As far as I can see there is one more step involved in this unification, according to the definition given of "concept" on page 10: "A concept is a mental integration of two or more units which are isolated according to specific characteristics and united by a specific definition."

AR: Aren't you confusing two aspects here? The definition on page 10 refers to what a concept *is*—it refers to the product of the process. But now you are describing the process. Well now, as a process yes, you first have to separate them as you described. And in the process of deciding that these three have something in common and are different from others, you are treating them as a unit. You are now looking at them not only as three blue objects, but three units of one group that have something in common as against everything else.

Prof. D: I've described the process, but I have arrived also at a product which is: these regarded as units. Now at that point do I have the concept of "pad," or do I still have something further to do, a further integration to make, before the product would be a concept?

AR: Yes. You have to give it a name.

Prof. D: Oh, give it a name—not "united by a specific definition"?

AR: A definition would be involved in more complex subjects, but on the first level, you don't have to have a definition. None of us would use a definition of "table," but in fact a definition is possible. In regard to a higher complexity of concepts, however, you couldn't possibly hold it in mind beyond a moment, without giving it a definition.

But here, as you described the process of forming a concept of three perceptual entities, when you've reached the point you described—that is, you now regard them as units of one group—that knowledge as such is not going to be a concept in your mind, for the following reason. In order to hold the group, you still have to mentally project, visualize, or deal with three entities. Therefore you are not yet mentally out of the stage of perceptual awareness.

Prof. D: In other words, at this stage there would be just this perceptual group.

AR: That's exactly what you would have: a perceptual group.

Prof. D: Now suppose I hadn't given them a name yet, and I go to another room. And there are some more of these notepads on a table. Would it mean that I wouldn't identify these, just automatically, as related?—that I would have to go through this integration over again, and then that integration would again be just at the perceptual level?

AR: No, it depends on how bright a child you are. I suspect—strictly by empirical observation—that a child does precisely this before he's ready to learn to speak. That is, to grasp that a word identifies a certain group of objects, he would probably be doing exactly what you describe. He would observe something in common in these pads, and then he goes into another room and he sees two more. He might connect them in his mind, so that if he could state his mental process, it would amount to: "Oh, these are something like the three I saw in the other room." Only he wouldn't have any of these words nor the concept "three." But it would be precisely by observing certain objects more than once and not necessarily only in one room—it's precisely by learning to differentiate, which I believe takes quite a period of time—that a child becomes ready to form the concept fully, which happens when he finds a word for it.

Prof. D: Now suppose this child tasted these, but he still doesn't have any words. And he tastes them and he likes them. But later when there aren't any in the room, he starts squalling. And his mother runs around wondering how to quiet him. She tries bringing him different objects, but nothing quiets him. And then she brings him one of these pads, and that quiets him, and he starts eating it. And so she says, "Why, he was crying for the pad all along." But he still doesn't have a name for these things. Isn't this behavior indicative of his approaching these now open-endedly? There wasn't even one in the room, and he was crying for it. And so one would have to say that even without a name these are being treated in an open-ended way rather than a purely perceptual way?

AR: Only to this extent: what you are describing is exactly the preconceptual stage. That is the mind in process. At the end of that process, he will be ready to grasp that a word names these objects.

Otherwise, observe the following. Infants in the first weeks of life are not able to learn words. Before they begin to speak, you observe that they are beginning to make sounds, inarticulate sounds, as if they were trying to communicate something. Therefore some enormous amount of information is already in their mind—perceptual information on its way to becoming conceptualized or brought into conceptual order. But in order for it to become a concept, the infant has to acquire some method of identifying the total of these objects conceptually. That's the purpose that a word serves. Because if he doesn't have a word, he will be tied to his perceptual material.

So assuming for a moment that he could learn to speak but without concepts, he would have to say to his mother the equivalent of: "I want another one of those blue objects which I saw day before yesterday." But he can't say any of that, nor can he hold it in his mind that way for very long.

Therefore, if your question is: at what point does this preliminary mental activity become a full-fledged concept? I say it becomes that when the child learns that a *perceptual* symbol—remember that a sound or the visual shape of a word is a percept—when he learns that that percept stands for all those concretes that he's trying to integrate.

Prof. D: The word takes him beyond the perceptual level because now he's not limited to the five pads he saw. But even without the word, though, in the case of the child I was referring to, isn't he already beyond the five pads he saw? He might have eaten the five.

AR: He wouldn't be there to ask for the sixth if he did.

Prof. D: But suppose he does the next day, though. He knows they are gone, and he's howling, and when he's brought a new one he's satisfied. And he smiles when he sees it being brought. Let's suppose that the presence of a word is necessary for the existence of a concept. Is it because the word open-ends the unification going on?

AR: It ends the process.

Prof. D: Didn't he already have it open-ended without the word? He went on to new ones.

AR: He has an open-ended identification from memory. He might remember that there were blue pads, and he would like more blue pads. But he couldn't hold more than, well, let's say five identifications of that kind. Maybe he'll remember the five pads and two ashtrays and three pens. But if each time he has to hold it by a visual type of memory, or by taste if he's eaten it, without any other form of identification, it would be impossible for him to progress beyond that stage.

Prof. D: You say that the word, then, permits him to let go, as it were, of visual memory. The word, though, is a sound that is denoting the concept, i.e., this group of things in an open-ended way.

AR: Right.

Prof. D: But now the meaning of the sound, then, is what it denotes.

AR: Right.

Prof. D: But what it denotes will have to be present to his mind.

AR: Well, certainly. But not every instance of it.

Prof. D: No, but what will be present to his mind again would be perceptual memories, wouldn't it?

AR: At first just the memory of one blue pad; as his conceptual development goes higher: the essential characteristics of the concretes which form the units of a given concept. It isn't that he lets go of concretes in the sense that he no longer has to know what his concept refers to. But he doesn't have to carry in mind the specific memory of all the different concretes of that kind which he has observed.

Prof. D: Now every entity, mental and otherwise, is a concrete existent.

AR: That's right.

Prof. D: So that related to the sound can only be some concrete existents that are present to his mind.

AR: Not if it's a sound which he accepts as standing for an unlimited class of specific, concrete existents. The sound has a crucial distinction from just a noise in nature. He learns to understand its meaning as: the word—the concrete, if you wish—that names an unlimited number of existents.

Prof. D: Could I pursue my question from a slightly different angle? Suppose we now have a sound which supplies us with a perceptual concrete, and we relate this sound to this open-ended group—to these things and things like it.

AR: That's right.

Prof. D: And the sound is just a perceptual concrete that serves for my making this relation. Why would a word, a sound, be needed? Why couldn't I use, say, just one of the perceptual concretes of this kind and respond to it as representing "that and anything like it"? It's not a word, it's just one of the perceptual concretes held visually.

AR: Then I would ask you: how long could you continue this process? Assuming now that you have no words at all, but you are able to hold it by this kind of method. Instead of a sound, you deal with a visual memory of a pad plus the

parenthetical implication "and other objects like this." Now
how would you proceed beyond the level of identifying
objects?

Prof. D: Isn't that all I'd have to do at the most basic
level of conceptualization—just be able to identify in my
mind such and such pads and things like the pads that I
consider concretely? And why couldn't I use simply a non-
verbal concrete to hang these relations on?

AR: You could, up to a certain point. And I'm sure that
that's what children begin with. But after you have identified a certain number of perceptually given objects, then
you want to establish relationships, let us say. Well, how
would you do it? By the equivalent of what? You would
have to say "length" is that attribute which I see in—then
visual image: table, visual image: pad, visual image: street—
and you'd stop right there.

The principle involved here is unit-economy. The proper
answer to your question comes in the book where I discuss
what I call the "crow-epistemology": the fact that any
consciousness—animal or human—can deal mentally with
only so many units [in one frame of awareness]. And observe on an adult level: you know that you could not deal
with all of your knowledge in any one instant of time, that
you can handle only so many aspects of a subject, you can
hold it in the focus of your attention only so long and no
more. In other words, no human mind has the capacity to
hold all of its knowledge simultaneously.

Therefore, the question becomes: how much can a mind
handle if one has to constantly carry images of concretes?
How much if, when you identify or try to analyze any aspect
or attribute of these concretes, you have to do it by holding
these mental images? From the aspect of the capacity of a
human consciousness, it would be enormously restricted.
Whereas what the substitution of words for images does is
enable you to handle a total as a single unit.

That's probably the most important aspect of why human
beings have concepts. What purpose do they serve? Why
can we learn and do much more than animals can? Precisely

because by conceptual means we substitute one concrete for an unlimited number of concretes. If you want to concentrate on the concept "table," you can learn an enormous amount about how to build a table, how to use it, what you can do with it, how to change and make variations on tables. What makes that type of thinking possible? Only the fact that you do not have to carry in mind a concrete image.

Otherwise, you'd have to have a concrete image of table, of length, of weight, of color, of shape, and I don't know how many other things would be involved. That cannot be done, simply because a mind cannot hold that much together.

And more than that; the fact that Aristotle is right and not Plato is very relevant here: abstractions, as such, do not exist. Only concretes exist. We could not deal with a sum of concrete objects constantly without losing our grasp of them. But what do we do conceptually? We substitute a concrete—a visual or auditory concrete—for the unlimited, open-ended number of concretes which that new concrete subsumes.

Now observe an interesting issue: a case like Helen Keller. She couldn't use either auditory or visual symbols. She had to be taught tactile symbols. She had to learn some mental condensation, some form of perceptual substitution or perceptual shorthand in order to be able to grasp the perceptual world at all. She had only tactile means. And she learned, and she was able to communicate, even to think and write. But prior to the time of learning this type of physical symbol, she was not able to grasp or deal with anything [conceptually], as far as could be observed. Therefore I wouldn't say the symbol has to be auditory or visual. If a mind is born handicapped in a certain way, there can be a substitute. Assuming a healthy child, the auditory and visual symbols are the easiest and the most productive. You can do more by that method. But some other method has to do if a person is handicapped.

The principle here is that in order to deal with a wide range of knowledge, you have to reduce the concretes to a single concrete, a concrete of a different order, a symbolic concrete. But that symbolic concrete has to be perceptual; it cannot be held in some undefined terms. It can be held that way just long enough for you to grasp the concept but not beyond it.

Prof. E: If you tried to represent the whole class by means of the image of one of the particular concretes in the class, wouldn't you be forced to the position that every time you wanted to employ the concept you'd have to re-form it?

AR: In a way.

Prof. E: He suggested, for instance, that you could say, "It's this or anything like it." But you obviously imply: like it *in some respects*. Because there are many things like it in other respects which wouldn't represent *that* class. So you'd have to remind yourself of the particular respect. Which would require you to say, "Well, I mean the sort of thing it has in common with those." So you'd have to recall those concretes and re-perform the abstracting process. Whereas, when you use a word, you retain the essence of what's in common without being tied to one concrete and without being required to ignore its particular concreteness in order to use it as a symbol.

AR: That's right. That's absolutely true.

*   *   *

Prof. D: There are some questions that arise in my mind concerning the denotation of words and the denotation of concepts in this connection. On page 13, one reads that, "The first words a child learns are words denoting visual objects."

AR: The first ones, yes.

Prof. D: If the essential function of words is to denote concepts, and if the expression "words denote visual objects" states their essential function, it would look as if one could deduce that concepts are visual objects.

AR: Well, one could do that, if one dropped the context. But, you see, I do not think that any information can be conveyed by any one sentence out of context. If it could be, we wouldn't need to write a book. Therefore, when you read a particular sentence, you have to take cognizance of the context which has been established.

Now here the context has been established that the word denotes a concept which in turn denotes the objects it subsumes. There can be no such thing as a concept without the objects to which it refers. And conversely, a sound, if it is to be a word, cannot denote objects directly, without representing a concept. (A word which did that would be a proper name.) But a concept is only a mental unit, a symbol, for a number of concretes of a certain kind. Therefore, when I say words denote visual objects, I do not have to repeat: "Don't forget that the visual objects have been conceptualized, and the word is the result of that process and names all those visual objects." Otherwise, I would have to repeat every preceding sentence in every sentence I write.

Prof. D: Granted, then, that concepts denote objects in reality and that the concept is a mental unit, I wonder whether it isn't in some kind of indirect sense that words denote objects—indirectly, via the concept—with the direct meaning of the word being the concept, the integration.

AR: I don't think we can make that distinction. A word which is not a proper name does refer directly to an indefinite number of concrete objects. A concept, in the form of a word, refers to them directly, not indirectly.

Prof. D: The word refers to the objects directly so that the objects directly constitute the meaning of the word?

AR: That's right.

Prof. D: Then suppose Descartes' evil demon waved his wand and those objects were put out of existence, would this mean that the word wouldn't have any meaning?

AR: If Descartes' evil demon existed, nothing would have any meaning, and we couldn't have a science of epistemology. We have to deal with reality as it is. If we project a different kind of reality, then nothing we say or do would be applicable.

Prof. D: But if the objects themselves are the word's meaning, then if you do away with the objects, you would find that the word has become just a meaningless sound.

AR: What do you mean, "do away with"? Do you mean that the objects cease to exist, or that they vanish as if they had never existed?

Prof. D: Suppose that these cups on this table are all of the cups that exist in the world. Then they constitute the meaning of the word "cup." And now I shut my eyes. While my eyes are shut, somebody waves a magic wand or whatever and actually destroys the cups. Then the meaning of the word "cup" has been destroyed. So as I shut my eyes the word "cup" will become simply a sound.

AR: Now wait. To continue on the terms of your example, the important question here would be: what happens to your memory under these conditions? If you remember that there were cups, and now somehow they have disappeared, the concept still has meaning—as a memory. The person waving the wand would also have to erase your memory of such existents. If he could do that, then of course the concept and the meaning would disappear.

Prof. D: But then suddenly the meaning of "cup" would change from these cups to cups past. And then you have to suppose that past cups are objects in reality.

AR: Consider all the people born in the eighteenth century, let us say—men who couldn't possibly be alive today. When you use the word "man" in reference to them, the concept "man" stands for existing men, even though they do not exist *now*. The meaning of a concept includes, as I have said repeatedly, not only all the present referents but also all the future ones that anyone might consider, and all the past instances. The meaning remains the same, the nature of the referents remains the same, that which they have in common with present men (and which made you include them in the concept "man") remains the same, even though the particular physical concretes are not there any longer.

Prof. D: Well, I certainly agree to that. But if you equate the meaning of the word with the existents, if you make that theoretic move—

AR: The meaning of the word includes all the instances of that existent. Specifically and emphatically not only the presently existing referents, but all the referents of that kind, past, present, and future. If a concept did not do that, it would not be a concept—you could form it today, but you could not use it tomorrow, and you could not use it to think about yesterday.

*   *   *

Prof. B: I want to get clearer on the distinction between a concept and what you call a "qualified instance" of a concept. How would you classify "stationery supplies" in that regard?

AR: That is a qualified instance of a concept; it is used as if it were a concept, but it is a compound concept.

Prof. B: What would turn it into a concept?

AR: If we had a special word for it.

Prof. B: Just as the phrase "Conceptual Common Denominator" became a concept by reducing it to "CCD"?

AR: Yes, that's right.

Prof. B: If the phrase "stationery supplies" became, in effect, one unit—if you hyphenated it, so to speak, then it would become a concept?

AR: That's right.

Words and Propositions

Prof. F: My question is about the relationship between concepts and propositions. Concepts are logically prior, aren't they?

AR: Yes.

Prof. F: If every concept is based upon a definition, isn't that definition itself a proposition?

AR: Oh yes.

Prof. F: Well then, the concept is in this case based on a proposition.

AR: No, but the first concepts are not. First-level concepts, concepts of perceptual concretes, are held without definitions. And I even mentioned in the book that most people would find it very difficult to define the commonplace, easy, first-level concepts for that very reason. They are held first without any definitions, mainly in visual form, or through other sensory images. By the time you accumulate enough of them, you can progress to propositions, to making use of your concepts, organizing them into sentences which communicate something. And the concepts you form from then on, which are abstractions from abstractions, those you couldn't hold visually; they require formal definitions. But by the time you get to them, you are already capable of forming propositions.

And observe that that's true even by simple empirical verification: if you see how a child learns to speak, he doesn't start by uttering sentences. He first utters single words, and then after a while, when he has enough of them, he begins to try to communicate in sentences.

Prof. F: Most concepts, then, involve definitions which are propositions. But don't definitions, in turn, come down to simple, ostensive—

AR: At the start, to ostensive definitions, yes.

Prof. B: It is still true that every concept is prior to any proposition that contains that concept. You have to have the concept before you can use it in a proposition. You can't utter a proposition with the word "man" unless you have already formed the concept of "man." Putting it that way, doesn't it remove whatever question you had?

Prof. F: Yes.

AR: There is something I would like to add. There is a passage in the book where I said every concept stands for a number of implicit propositions. And even so, chronologically we have to acquire concepts first, and then we begin to learn propositions. Logically implicit in a concept is a proposition, only a child couldn't possibly think of it. He doesn't have the means yet to say, "By the word 'table' I mean such and such category of existents [with all their characteristics]." But that is implicit in the process. And that is important when you get to Kant—and to the whole analytic-synthetic dichotomy—that every concept represents such an implicit proposition, logically. But that doesn't mean that a child has to learn simultaneously concepts and propositions.

Take, for instance, a simple concept of the first, perceptual level, like "table." Implicit in the use of the word "table," and in the grasping or forming of that concept, is the [definitional] proposition: "By the sound 'table,' I mean objects whose distinguishing characteristic is a flat surface and supports." Now, a child doesn't have any of those concepts, but what does he do? Implicitly, he uses the word "table," once he has learned it, in that manner.

Prof. B: When you say the proposition is implicit, you mean implicit in the way you use it, that is: the material is available. And doesn't the relevant material include facts such as that the table is flat? That fact is implicit—meaning: you have to grasp that fact perceptually before you can form "table," and isn't that part of the concept?

AR: Yes. But here it isn't only a matter of what is involved in the concept, but also in the way the child uses the concept before he can form propositions, or the way an adult uses it in a fully conscious way. Implicit in every concept is "By this sound I mean such and such category of existents."

Prof. B: But wouldn't you agree that implicit in every concept are all the propositions stating all the facts he needed to form that concept?

AR: That's right.

Prof. F: But isn't a proposition by its very nature complex, that is, made up of two or more concepts?

AR: Oh yes.

Prof. F: But then how can you say that every concept expresses a proposition?

AR: Implicitly. The material is there but a child cannot yet form it, precisely because he needs to form each concept separately before he can unite them.

Prof. E: In other words, you can hold complex information, sufficiently complex to generate a proposition, in a *perceptual* form.

Prof. F: But if every concept is based upon a complex operation like this, then in the very process of forming a concept you must have gone through this complex experience.

AR: Well, of course.

Prof. E: But you only identify the elements of what you are doing when you reach the stage of epistemology.

AR: I think I've indicated that in the book, when I say the following: a child first has to grasp the concept of entities before he can grasp actions or attributes; yet, to separate entities from each other he has to be aware of attributes. He has to separate tables from chairs, let's say, by seeing that they have different shapes. Now he is aware of attributes, *perceptually*. He has not yet conceptualized why he thinks tables are different from chairs. He merely observes that, and he says, in effect, "This is table; this is chair." Then when he has learned such abstractions as "shape," and "difference," and a great many others, he can consciously, in conceptual terms, identify the things which at first were observed perceptually.

All our knowledge, you see, begins perceptually, and the whole process of concept-formation rests on isolating, one step at a time, objects from an enormous field. We are aware, let's say, of a whole room, but we can't form all the concepts involved at the same time. It has to be done one at a time.

Incidentally, what is also very important here is that since reality is not a collection of discrete concretes which have nothing to do with each other, since it is actually an integrated, interrelated whole, the same is true of our conceptual equipment. We cannot begin to use it until we have enough interrelated concepts to permit us, beginning with a small vocabulary, to reach higher and higher distinctions. Observe that all concepts on the first, perceptual level are enormously interrelated. And it would be impossible to say that we have to conceptualize tables first or chairs first. Or inanimate objects in the room before persons. There would be no rule about it.

Everything is interrelated, and for a concept to become fully and consciously clear to a child, to a mind just starting, he needs several other concepts. He is in an accelerating period of transition now. At first he might be able to say just "table" and "Mama." But very quickly his vocabulary enlarges, because everything is connected in some way or related to everything else in his field of knowledge, and as he clarifies his first concepts, the process of forming others becomes easier. But before he begins to speak he has to acquire a great many of them because they are all interrelated.

And the difficulty there is that before he can form propositions, he needs adjectives and verbs—particularly verbs—and that is a very difficult mental feat, really, to go from nouns, which are fairly easy, to verbs, which stand for actions, and then to qualities (i.e., adjectives).

*   *   *

Prof. D: You say that one's mind is able to encompass only so many units—five or six. What then happens when we are discussing something, as we are now? I am talking in sentences, and there are a lot of concepts that must be evoked in order for you to understand what I am saying. Now, as I go from word to word, does a concept come into being and then go out of existence? And if so, how do you understand the first part of my sentence when I am at the end? How do you keep so many things in mind?

AR: What's the problem here? How much we can hold at one time?

Prof. D: I present it as a kind of dilemma.

AR: As a dilemma?!

Prof. D: I am speaking in sentences, and each sentence contains various words which are denoting concepts. This means that as I speak now, in order for you to understand what I am saying, each word has to evoke a particular concept. And that concept will either continue to exist in time or it will cease to exist, say, when the next word comes. Now, in the latter case, I wonder how anyone understands a sentence, because the first part of the sentence with all its concepts is long over and gone at the end. On the other hand, if all these concepts continue to exist, one after the other, so that they are all there together finally at the end, I would have so many entities present in my mind I couldn't hold them.

AR: Isn't the issue here an equivocation on "the existence of a concept"? In your example, you are assuming that the concept exists only for the specific split second when it is invoked. You are assuming that a concept does not exist prior to the moment of your uttering it and stops existing the moment you go to the next word, which empirically is not true. If we talk of the existence of a concept, we have to say that it exists in a man's mind so long as he is able to bring it into his full conscious attention.

Certainly your entire vocabulary is not constantly in the focus of your conscious attention. But it is available to you the moment you need it. It is certainly clear that when you are uttering a sentence, you are using concepts which do exist in our minds, and we are able to recognize and hold them for the length of your sentence—particularly if the sentence is grammatical.

You know that we do communicate, and that we are able to follow an argument, and that you cannot tell us everything at once. That is what we have words for, first, then words organized in sentences, then paragraphs, and then sequences and volumes. We have to focus gradually and in installments, if you are presenting a very complex issue.

Therefore there is no dilemma at all about the fact that we are able to read a book and understand what it's about. Or that we are able to hear an entire speech or a single sentence. How can it be a dilemma, when we know that it's a fact? It can be a dilemma only on the basis of our arbitrarily rewriting reality.

Prof. D: Well I didn't mean that the fact was a dilemma, but if I have presented a certain theory concerning the fact, I could very well be in a dilemma if my theory had some defect in it.

AR: That's right.

Prof. D: So what I am attempting to do is to see how in terms of the Objectivist theory of concepts one would explain the fact that we do, of course, understand the sentence. Now, you said that as I utter my sentence, these existents called "concepts" do not cease to exist the moment the word is uttered and gone, but that they are held throughout the sentence. But then I was wondering whether one wouldn't be confronted with an overloading of one's capacity to consider items.

Suppose I utter the following sentence: "A child is not and does not have to be aware of all these complexities when he forms the concept 'table.' " Well, there are twenty-one concepts I'm holding in my mind by the time I get to the end of the sentence—twenty-one mental entities are present in my mind. And that would seem to be a kind of overloading of my capacity to view things.

AR: The answer to how we are able to understand a whole sentence, let alone a whole book, lies in the nature of concepts. Which part of their nature? Automatization. When a concept automatically stands in your mind for a certain kind of concrete, when you don't have to take the time to remind yourself what you mean by the word "table," by the word "child," etc., it's that speed of lightning-like integration of the referents of your concepts to your words that permits you to understand a sentence.

Prof. B: Isn't this question really about the theory of propositions, not of concepts? There are twenty-one concepts, but the first five of them, say, are integrated into one clause, and the various clauses are integrated into one proposition, and that's how we hold it.

AR: Yes.

Prof. E: If you just strung out twenty-one words at random from the dictionary, you couldn't hold them all.

AR: Yes.

Prof. A: Or if you read that same sentence backward, you wouldn't be able to hold them either.

AR: That's right.

Prof. A: So there's something going on, when you read the sentence forward, that enables you to grasp it.

Prof. E: The proposition, in effect, becomes a unit itself.

AR: Yes.

Measurement, Unit, and Mathematics

Measurement

Prof. F: I would like to raise a question about the measurability of attributes. Length is obviously an attribute and it is measurable. And I am sure that everyone agrees that hardness and temperature are measurable. But now let's take the example of triangularity. And let's ask if there are such things as degrees of triangularity. It seems to me that a given entity either is a triangle or it is not a triangle.

And there's a related question that you might want to treat at the same time. Sometimes you speak as if every individual, every concrete, is a unit. Did you mean to say that?

AR: No. Every concrete is a unit *when* regarded as a separate member of a group of two or more similar concretes. A unit is a concrete, an existent, regarded in a certain manner, regarded in a certain relationship. Every concrete is a unit when it is so regarded. But that doesn't mean that every concrete can serve as a standard of measurement. Because "unit" here has two different meanings. A unit selected as a standard of measurement [e.g., the inch] has to be a given quantity of a given *attribute*, not of an *entity*.

But now what do you mean by "degrees of triangularity"?—because there is no such thing.

Prof. F: It follows then that for this attribute, triangularity, there is no unit in terms of which it can be measured.

184

AR: No, it does not. Triangularity is one form of two-dimensional shape, and shape can be measured. Triangularity isn't a special attribute; the attribute is shape. In the case of triangles it is a triangular shape; in the case of squares it is something else. And all of them have to be measured in terms of linear measurement. I even referred to that as an example.

Prof. E: It's interesting that you asked that, because it's the identical question that I once asked, and I remember what Miss Rand's answer was at the time, which made it perfectly clear. Now please correct me, Miss Rand, if my formulation is not one you would endorse.

At the time, she distinguished between a simple and a complex attribute. She said that there are things, such as triangularity, which are attributes, in the sense that they can't exist independently, but which nevertheless have more than one measurable aspect. And that to measure a complex attribute is not to take a unit of that attribute in itself as the standard of measurement, but to measure the various distinguishable aspects of that attribute. So that for triangles, you'd have to measure the number of sides, the length of the sides, the angular relations between them—which sum of aspects constitutes the triangularity. So to measure a triangle is no more than to measure the distinguishable aspects of the attribute.

In effect, there's such a thing as a complex attribute, which is still an attribute metaphysically, but is measurable by a different procedure than a simple attribute like length. Would you agree?

AR: In a sense. Is that the question about whether you take "little triangles" to measure every triangle?

Prof. E: That's right.

Prof F: So there are complex attributes and simple attributes.

AR: Well, put it in a somewhat more relevant way. All attributes, in order to be measured, have to be reduced to the kind of unit which we can perceive and by means of which we can establish a [quantitative] relationship. So if we perceive two triangles, by means of measuring them qua triangles we will never get anywhere. It is not possible to measure shapes that way. What would we have to do? Reduce them to linear measurement.

But, a point I want to make very clearly: let us not make metaphysical distinctions on the basis of our methods of cognition. In other words, to say that you have to measure shape, for instance, in terms of, ultimately, reducing it to linear measurement is not to say that various shapes possess different attributes metaphysically. That's only creating confusion. And to tell you the truth, I do not quite understand the relevance or the consequences of distinctions of this kind—such as simple attributes versus complex ones. The attributes are what they are; *our methods* of measuring them may be simple or complex.

Prof. F: All right. What we called a "complex attribute" is merely due to a complex method of measurement, right? Would that be correct, to leave it just as an epistemological distinction?

AR: I think that, for precision, we'd better say "complex method," not "complex attribute." Because "attribute" relates to the existent, "method" relates to our form of measurement.

Prof. F: So can we then conclude this: not every concrete is a unit?

AR: Units serving as standards of measurement? Or concretes regarded as units? Which do you mean? Not every concrete can be taken as a standard of measurement qua concrete. A triangle cannot be taken as a standard of measurement for triangles. But a triangle can be regarded as a unit when we form the concept "triangle."

If we observe various shapes and find a difference between triangles and squares, how do we separate the two categories? By regarding all triangles as units of one group and observing that they have a characteristic in common—a certain kind of shape—that distinguishes them from another group which are squares. In that sense we do regard triangles as units. And in that sense every existent—not only every concrete, but also every attribute, every action, every relationship—is regarded as a unit when it is unified into a concept.

But if I understand you correctly, your question was more pertaining to methods of measurement. And in that sense, you are correct when you say not every concrete can serve as a unit of measurement. And I have indicated that it isn't a concrete entity that one has to use [as the standard], but an attribute. We can't measure by means of concrete entities; we measure only by relating attributes of certain entities to a selected standard of measurement which is the concrete unit selected as this standard—like an inch or a meter or a mile. That's a concrete unit of measurement, which represents an attribute, not an entity. Is that your question?

Prof. F: Essentially, yes. I just wonder why the term "unit" should be used at all, except in those cases where the thing can be used as a unit of measurement. I'm suggesting that it might be best to simply use the term "concrete" and not the term "unit."

AR: But the [implicit] concept "unit" is essential to concept-formation. The essence of the first two pages of the book is to point out that only when we learn, in infancy, to regard concretes as units—only then can we begin to form concepts. So if there is any verbal confusion, I would say it would be better not to use the word "unit" for "standard of measurement." There's only one difficulty that would occur there: that which we select as a standard of measurement has to be a unit.

Prof. F: Yes. It may be a verbal problem here. You see, what I'm trying to say is this. A triangle cannot be regarded as a unit of triangularity, but ultimately it must be analyzed in terms of extension, length, and so forth.

AR: Right.

Prof. F: And some of the words that you use led me to think that you might want to say that a given triangle, because of the fact that it is a unit, is therefore a potential standard of measurement. And this seemed to me obviously wrong, and that's why I raised it.

AR: But in cases like this, I think we have to rely on the context to establish the meaning. Because it isn't arbitrary or purely linguistic that I use such a term as "unit of measurement." The mental relationship involved is the same as in regarding individual existents—concretes—as units when we form a concept. The relationship, the aspect from which we regard it, is the same. But that doesn't necessarily imply that every concrete existent can be a unit [of measurement]. If we say that only units of attributes can serve as units of measurement, need there be any confusion? I don't believe so really.

A "unit of measurement" means one concrete, belonging under a concept, which is taken as the standard compared to which you then measure all the other concretes belonging under that concept. If you take an inch as a unit of measurement of length, an inch is a specified unit of length when regarded against other lengths. But once you have selected the standard of measurement, thereafter you determine, you actually denote, the length of other objects in relation to that object whose length you have chosen to be one inch long.

Prof. H: So in both senses "unit" is used as one of a group.

AR: Yes, but this time it is chosen as a standard by which you measure.

Prof. F: You just used the phrase "unit chosen as a standard." I want to call your attention to the sentence, on page 7, where I expected you to use that phrase, but where you used the opposite: "Measurement is the identification of a relationship—a quantitative relationship established by means of a standard that serves as a unit." Why didn't you say there "unit that serves as a standard"?

AR: That's purely verbal. I did not intend any different meaning. I think it was because my emphasis here was on the fact that the standard chosen will be a unit of the measurement which has to be performed.

*   *   *

Prof. F: Your statement that all entities are measurable in terms of their attributes raises this question in my mind: do you think all measurements in the last analysis come down to things like measurements of length, velocity, and so on, in a reductionistic sort of way? For instance, you stated that colors can be measured in terms of wavelengths of light. And if we do that with all attributes, it seems to me that ultimately we will come down to a few fundamental measurements—measurements, say, of velocity, of gravity perhaps, electromagnetic measurements—

AR: You mean reductionism in the materialistic sense?

Prof. F: No, I am not going that far at the moment. I am merely suggesting that all *material* measurements may come down to a small list of measurements, ultimately.

AR: But isn't that a scientific question more than a philosophical one? Whether everything in nature is ultimately reducible to subatomic particles and [whether measurement is reducible] to counting them—isn't that a question for science to determine? Philosophy cannot answer it one way or another. I would never attempt to say—because it would be completely arbitrary—whether all measurements are ultimately relatable to only one set. That would be a scientific issue in regard to the nature of the universe. I would claim that all existents—since they are part of one universe—are measurable. But I have never said that all standards of measurement are ultimately translatable one into another or reducible one to another. That would be a claim for which nobody has any evidence one way or the other.

*   *   *

[In response to a question about Norman Campbell's dichotomy of "intensive qualities" and "extensive qualities"—the two requiring, he claimed, different systems of measurement:]

AR: I object in principle to the idea of making metaphysical distinctions of any kind on the basis of our ignorance. The fact that we can measure certain attributes but cannot be as precise in regard to others does not justify the idea of saying that entities possess two different categories of attributes, some of which are "extensive," others "intensive."

Campbell's standard here is not the nature of the entities but our capacity to measure—which means our state of knowledge, which is greater in one case than in another. That is what I mean by taking our ignorance as a metaphysical standard.

What would one say properly about the situation? Merely that some attributes are easily related to one another quantitatively, and others, are harder to relate, and we have not yet learned how to measure them. I don't see how that has any metaphysical significance. By "metaphysical" I mean: in the nature of these entities. Are we to say these entities have attributes essentially different from one another—with the standard of difference being our ability to measure them? I don't think that is the proper methodology for establishing the nature of entities.

Exact Measurement and Continuity

Prof. D: Your definition of "measurement" involves a realist conception of the relationship of measurement to the world. And measurement involves not only some quantity but also a standard of measurement, a quantitative standard of measurement, involving a unit that can be repeated over and over.

AR: That's right. But don't leave out the rest of it. I said "some quantity, but may exist in any quantity." I specifically never said what kind of quantity, expressed in what mathematical figures, or achieved by what method.

Prof. D: But what if we suppose that any numerical system is going to be discrete in nature and rest upon discrete items?

AR: It has to.

Prof. D: Whereas suppose someone maintained that reality is continuous. For instance, Bergson wanted to maintain that. If Bergson is right, then there is this gap between any numerical system and reality: reality is continuous, numerical systems are discontinuous, discrete. Then it would be the case that in a strict sense there wasn't any exact measurement possible, because your discrete units would never be able to handle this continuum. You would always have those little infinitesimals left over.

AR: Bergson wasn't the first to argue that. Zeno did the same thing. Would you answer for Bergson if you can, since he can't be called upon: how did we get to the moon? Without measurement?

Prof. D: Oh, I am not denying the practicality of measurement.

AR: How can it be practical if it doesn't relate to or correspond to the metaphysical nature of reality? How can we achieve fantastic things in regard to the material world and yet suppose for one minute that what we are doing is arbitrary and has no absolute, unquestionable relationship to the facts of reality? Because the Bergsonian position amounts to denying the validity and the existence of measurement. Now, are we going to argue on that point?

Prof. D: Not on the practical value of measurement.

AR: What is the distinction between the practical and the theoretical? That's a distinction which I do not recognize. "Practical" means acting in this world, in reality. If what we do works, how is that possible if it doesn't correspond to reality?

Prof. D: Well, suppose the correspondence were just a gross one. For instance, I can approximate, and my approximations are not terribly gross ones. I use a ruler, and I say that this room is fifteen feet long and ten feet wide. And if I order lumber to build another room of this size, I will get approximately enough lumber. So someone could maintain that the measurements are practical enough, even though metaphysically there isn't a correspondence.

AR: But I would not know, and I wish you would explain to me, what is meant by "metaphysically" in this kind of context. There are two different things involved here. If what we do is only approximate—which I do not grant, but let's assume it is—that reflects merely on our capacity to perform exact measurements. How do we assign our incapacity to the metaphysical nature of reality? And more than that, if you say that we cannot, with a simple ruler at home, measure invisible submicroscopic lengths, will that invalidate the measurements which we are able to perform?

And more than that, my main point is this. I would like somebody to explain to me, and I am not being just rhetorical, what is meant by "a continuous reality." And in that context, what does Bergson think, if that is not a contradiction in terms, about the process of measurement?—about the discrete vs. the continuous? I have made it clear—and this is really only common sense—that when you perform a process of measurement you take a ruler and you decide this is the standard you are going to use. Now, does it mean that, if you then proceed to measure a mile by means of that ruler, there is some kind of "discontinuity" in the mere fact that you have to move that ruler over and over and take your measurement in installments? It merely means that you cannot measure the whole mile at once. Now expand the same principle to interplanetary distances and it still applies.

The fact that we *isolate* a unit is precisely the point I had in mind when I wrote—let me quote this because it is relevant—"A unit is an existent regarded as a separate member of a group of two or more similar members. Two stones are two units; so are two square feet of ground if regarded as distinct parts of a continuous stretch of ground." The mere fact that we cannot encompass the whole of the universe at a glance does not mean that, when we attempt to measure it or to establish relationships one step at a time, we somehow destroy the "continuity of existence." You would not say that, if we measure this table in so many motions of moving the ruler, we have broken it up, whereas in reality it is a continuous table.

Prof. D: No, but one could say that if reality, space, and so on, are continuous, then no discrete unit of measurement would ever be able to take care completely of measurement. Because no matter how small you made your unit, there could still be a little bit left over or short. And if then you make even a smaller unit of measurement to take care of that little bit left over, still there would be a little left over or short. You could carry out the decimals as far as you wanted to and there'd still be a discrepancy.

AR: From the viewpoint of whom? Let me now go mystical, like Bergson, and suppose we were a different size, the size of little beings inhabiting an atom (you know the metaphor that the atom is like a solar system). If we were that size, we could with the naked eye perform minute measurements which we cannot do with our instruments now.

Prof. D: It wouldn't be exact though, if space is continuous.

AR: Now, we have to define terms. What is the standard of exactness here? What is the standard of exactness that Bergson was discussing? That is the crux of the issue. We use the term "exact," and now Bergson challenges it. What did he mean by "exact"? And what did he mean by "continuous"?

Prof. D: He would mean by "exact" I think this: it would involve what existed in reality, and an exact measurement would be one which corresponded, without any more or less, to what existed in reality.

AR: Now, since it is an exact measurement, it presupposes a consciousness that is doing this. Whose consciousness?

Prof. D: Well, say mine.

AR: All right. And if you are able to measure it, and you are able to grasp relationships by means of measurement which you didn't invent, that is exactness. And if you are able to grasp that maybe some milli-milli-parts of a millimeter are not correct and you are not able to bring it to a greater precision, who grasped that? You did. Therefore, your concept is correct, does correspond to reality, and it is reality that you have been consulting in discovering that perhaps you can't measure submicroscopic quantities.

Prof. F: So the very concept of "exactness" is a contextual concept. Suppose I say to you that I will meet you in this room exactly one year from now. If when you arrive I take out a stopwatch and say you are a tenth of a second late, this is dropping the context.

AR: Exactly. Everything that we discuss, *everything*, is done from the human viewpoint and has to be, because there is no such thing as "reality in itself." That is one of the concepts of Kant's that we have to be very careful of. If we were omniscient like God, we would still have to perceive reality by our God-like means of perception, and we would have to speak of exactitude from that viewpoint. But "things in themselves"—as separated from consciousness and yet discussed in terms of a consciousness—is an invalid equivocation. That would be my widest metaphysical answer to any construct à la Kant and Bergson.

Prof. D: So you answer this question by saying that contextually, for our purposes, the measurement will do. In saying that the sides of this right triangle are each 1 foot long and the hypotenuse is 1.414 feet long, that will do.

AR: What is inexact about it?

Prof. D: Well, geometrically it is inexact but it will do for building a platform.

AR: No, that is not what I am saying. I am saying that when we speak of measurement, we begin with a perceptually given unit, and that unit is absolute and exact [within the context of our means of perception]. Then conceptually we may refine our methods and we may measure such things as milliseconds and a part of a subatomic particle, which we can't do perceptually. But the standard of these measurements, the base from which conceptual complications may later be derived, is that which we perceive directly on the perceptual level; that is what measurement means, that is its base. Therefore, when I say that for measurement there has to be a unit of measurement, I mean that even when you take a submicroscopic, conceptual type of measurement, that type ultimately has to be reduced back to our standard of measurement, which is the perceptually given, and nothing more or less.

With scientific development you might discover that, microscopically, the edge of this piece of paper is ragged and has tiny mountain peaks and valleys. That is not relevant to your [macroscopic] process of measurement, because you had to use the perceptual method as a start in order to get to your microscopic instruments of measurement.

Prof. I: On the exactitude of measurement, is this chain of reasoning correct? We measure this book first, say, in inches. And we find that it is six inches long, plus a little bit. Then we subdivide the unit "inch" into sixteen equal subdivisions, measure it again, and find that it is six and three-sixteenths inches long. Then we fix up some fancy apparatus by which we can measure it by means of light waves, and we get accuracy to twenty decimal places. Then we ask, well, what is the relationship to the unit "inch" *really*? Well, it is what it is, but if we want to say that it is really six plus the square root of two inches long, we are saying this independent of any possible measurement that we can actually perform. As such, we are attempting to abstract consciousness away from a concept of consciousness, and therefore it is invalid. In short, isn't it meaningless to ask, "What is the relationship to the inch really, out of context of a given instance of measuring?"

AR: Yes, in the sense of going beyond the point where more minute measurement is possible. Because then you would say that under any circumstances there will be sub-subquantities which you can't measure by the same ruler. In that sense it would be an improper switch of the term "measurement." When you speak of measurement, you always have to define contextually your method of measurement. So that if you say it is so much measured by a ruler, or it is something else measured by some fancy apparatus, you have complied with the requirement of absolute correspondence to reality. You have said it measures so much by such and such means.

But to talk about what it would measure without any consciousness there to measure it, that would be improper.

Prof. E: Every measurement is made within certain specifiable limits of accuracy. There is no such thing as infinity in precision, because you are using some measuring instrument which is calibrated with certain smallest subdivisions. So therefore there is always a plus or minus, within the limits of accuracy of the instrument. And that's inherent in the fact that everything that exists has identity. Now if that's so, you can measure up to any specifiable degree of precision by an appropriately calibrated measuring rod.

If exactness in measurement is defined in such a way that you have to get the last decimal of an infinite series, by that definition no measurement can be exact. The concept of "exact measurement" as such becomes unknowable and meaningless, and therefore what would it mean to say a measurement is inexact? Exactness has to be specified in a human context, involving certain limits of accuracy. Is that valid?

AR: Yes, in a general way. But more than that, isn't there a very simple solution to the problem of accuracy? Which is this: let us say that you cannot go into infinity, but in the finite you can always be absolutely precise simply by saying, for instance: "Its length is no less than one millimeter and no more than two millimeters."

Prof. E: And that's perfectly exact.

AR: It's exact. If an issue of precision is involved, you can make it precise even in non-microscopic terms, even in terms of a plain ruler. You can define your length—that is, establish your measurement—with absolute precision.

Numbers

Prof. J: What measurements are omitted in forming concepts of particular numbers, for example, the concept of "seven"?

AR: In a certain sense the measurements omitted from the concept of numbers are the easiest to perceive. What you omit are the measurements of any existents which you count. The concept "number" pertains to a relationship of existents viewed as units—that is, existents which have certain similarities and which you classify as members of one group. So when you form the concept of a number, you form an abstraction which you implicitly declare to be applicable to any existents which you care to consider as units. It can be actual existents, or it can be parts of an existent, as an inch is a part of a certain length. You can measure things by regarding certain attributes as broken up into units—of length, for instance, or of weight. Or you can count entities. You can count ten oranges, ten bananas, ten automobiles, or ten men; the abstraction "ten" remains the same, denoting a certain number of entities viewed as members of a certain group according to certain similarities.

Therefore, what is it that you retain? The relationship. What do you omit? All the measurements of whichever units you are denoting or counting by means of the concept of any given number.

Here the omission of measurements is perceived almost at its clearest. And I even give the example in the book—it's an expression I have heard, I did not originate it—that an animal can perceive two oranges and two potatoes but cannot conceive of the concept "two." And right there you can see what the mechanics are: the abstraction retains the numerical relationship, but omits the measurements of the particulars, of the kind of entities which you are counting.

Prof. B: Does that mean that the referents of numerical concepts are not the entities as such, but entities regarded a certain way? In reality, each entity is one—that's metaphysical. For you to have two, three, or four requires an act of consciousness to view them in a certain way?

AR: That's almost correct, except that you can't say that in reality there's only one. As entities, each one is only one, but when you view them as seven, let's say seven men, in reality there *are* seven men. This is the important thing, otherwise it becomes subjective. In reality there *are* seven men. Why do you identify them as seven men, and you don't include in that four men, two potatoes, and one streetcar? In order to count them, you have to classify them as having something in common. It's from that aspect that you can count them.

Prof. B: The Greeks used to say that two is the first number, that one had a kind of special status. Entities in reality, apart from consciousness, are individual entities, and a group doesn't have any higher metaphysical status.

AR: None whatever.

Prof. B: But it's as if the numbers higher than one are

tools of integration and not direct designators of—I can't say it without making a mistake!

AR: That means you are on the wrong track. The number "two" is crucially important epistemologically, because to form concepts you need two or more existents between which you observe similarities. It's in that sense that the number two is very important, epistemologically. Metaphysically, it is all equal—there is no *metaphysical* hierarchy between one and a million.

Prof. B: The reason it comes up is that any object that you choose in reality can be viewed objectively as two of one kind of units or four of another kind of units or whatever, depending on how you divide it up or how you view it. For instance, we can view this book as one entity, as two halves, as one hundred pages, etc.

AR: That's right.

Prof. B: But isn't there some special metaphysical status to the fact that it is one entity? To say that this is one is somehow a more metaphysical statement, and it is that distinction that I'm trying to pin down.

AR: More metaphysical than what? Than saying that it is one hundred pages, or that it is two halves of one book?

Prof. B: But to say that this is one book and to say I have . . . no, it remains metaphysically the same.

AR: It remains the same. But you know where you might sense a distinction? It's that the term "one" is the concept "entity." And the concept "entity" is the base of your entire development. It has that great epistemological significance.

*   *   *

Prof. E: Is there a distinction in meaning or referent between the concept "unit" and the concept "one," in the sense, for instance, that you grasp that this is one ashtray, or one book? To regard it as a unit is to regard it, as you say, as a member of a class of similar things. Is that same perspective involved in grasping that it is one?

AR: Before you have a concept of numbers?

Prof. E: Yes.

AR: You will perceive that it is one, as an animal would, but you couldn't grasp the concept "one" without a concept of more than one—without a concept of numbers.

Prof. E: Perception gives you directly a certain kind of quantitative information.

AR: Yes.

Prof. E: Even prior to either implicit or explicit concepts.

AR: That's right.

Prof. E: And is it true that that quantitative information is presupposed, before you form even the implicit concept "unit"? In other words, a young child would have to perceive that this is one, even though it has no implicit concept of that, before it could even form the implicit concept "unit."

AR: Of course, and here is where we have to be Aristotelian: everything that exists is one. "Entity" means "one." But we couldn't have the distinction between what we mean by "one" vs. what we mean by "entity" if we didn't have the concept of numbers more than one which, after all, are only multiplied ones or divided ones.

Prof. E: So you get quantitative information by perception; then, via the process of grasping similarities and differences, you form the implicit concept "unit." You then rise to the general conceptual level, at which point you are able to form conceptually for the first time the concept of various numbers, including "one."

AR: Right.

Prof. E: Am I correct in saying that "one" and "many," as concepts, are metaphysical, while "unit," as a concept, is epistemological?

AR: That's right.

Prof. E: Is it correct to say that "quantity" is a metaphysical concept and "measurement" an epistemological one, in the sense that if human beings and consciousness were erased, there would still be quantities, but there would no longer be such a thing as measurement. Measurement involves a human act of establishing relationships.

AR: Of establishing quantity, that's right.

Prof. E: And is that why you formulate the nature of

concept-formation in terms of omitting measurements rather than omitting quantities?

AR: Right.

Prof. E: Because you omit the relationships that you could establish?

AR: Yes. But the quantities continue to exist whether you measure them or not.

*   *   *

Prof. H: This is related to the issue of forming number concepts. On page 9, you say that the stage at which a child learns to count is when he is learning his first words.

AR: It comes a little later, as a matter of observation. It is almost simultaneous but not quite. Before a child can be taught to count, he has to have the beginnings or the rudiments of the vocabulary.

Prof. H: You meant counting explicitly, as in counting how many people are in this room, not just in the sense of perceiving the quantity.

AR: No, literally to count, as a conscious activity. He perceives the quantities, but he has to first form some concepts identifying objects, and then he can begin to count the objects explicitly.

Prof. H: You say that it occurs shortly afterward. From what I have observed, it seems to occur quite a bit later, so that it seems to be a much higher-level process.

AR: It isn't so much higher-level, but the fact is that you cannot begin to count objects until you have learned to distinguish them, and you cannot distinguish them firmly until you have learned some words—i.e., formed some concepts. Therefore, it is part of the same general development. But a child does have to acquire some conceptual vocabulary, meaning: learn to identify some concretes in reality, before he can begin to count.

Prof. H: I was taking it too literally.

AR: No, if I said "when he is learning his first words," I meant in the same general period of development.

Mathematics

Prof. B: You have said [in a section here omitted] two things about the mathematical field. One was that once the base has been established, one can proceed without direct reference to perceptual reality. The second point was that the mathematical field was more precise than the conceptual. Would both of those facts be due to the particular nature of mathematics—that it is a science of method?

AR: In part. Also it is a science that defines the entities it deals with very simply. For instance, all you have as the basis of your operation is the arithmetical series. You don't need any further definitions as a base. From then on you work with that base. Whereas in other conceptual knowledge you deal with such a complexity of phenomena that your definitions can change as your knowledge expands, and your definitions may be very imprecise indeed. That's one of the differences.

Prof. B: In other words, you have all of the material before you from the beginning in mathematics. There's no new information which you are going to integrate into your concepts. Rather you are going to build up abstractions from abstractions, such as "function," "limit," and so on.

AR: That's right. This is not to imply that non-mathematical concepts necessarily have to be in some way less exact than mathematical concepts. No. The ideal to aim at is to bring your concepts into exactly that kind of precision. At least those concepts you know—you cannot have omniscience, and you cannot guarantee that you will not expand your knowledge (as I explain in Chapter 5) and change a concept's defining characteristic.

But the proper epistemological ideal is to have your conceptual knowledge, as far as it extends,in as precise a form as mathematics. Or as mathematics used to be, prior to Russell. When I say "mathematics," I really don't mean the modern status of the science, but proper mathematics, rational mathematics.

Prof. B: In other words, it is not in the nature of the two fields that one must be more precise than the other. You are talking journalistically.

AR: I am talking not journalistically, but empirically, of the difficulty of the job involved. But this is one of the very vague suggestions of why I think that mathematics has something to do with the essential pattern of concept-formation— that it serves as an ideal.

But I don't want to sound Platonic here. It is simply that the kind of perfection which mathematics used to have (and applied mathematics still seems to have) is the pattern for concept-formation and concept-use. That is the way our conceptual equipment should be. But it's much harder; more is involved.

Prof. B: When you say it is the pattern, are you saying it is just an illustration or in some sense it serves that role? That's not mathematics' function—you wouldn't define mathematics in those terms if you ever worked this out.

AR: Oh no. It's simply that mathematics, being a science that deals predominantly with concepts, and clearly defined concepts whose definitions do not change, gives you the pattern of precision that you have to bring into your conceptual equipment; which latter, dealing with a much more complex field of knowledge, is much more prone to error or ignorance or change, change on the basis of newly discovered and relevant knowledge. So that mathematics as a science which deals with firmly defined entities can serve as a model.

*   *   *

Prof. C: Don't the definitions of mathematical concepts change with the growth of our knowledge?

AR: No. Philosophically, you may have much better definitions of mathematical terms than they have today. But that's merely due to the fact that there's been no real philosophy of mathematics to speak of. But the actual definitions do not change.

Prof. C: I don't see why you say that. For example, in the case of "number," first there were natural numbers (1, 2, 3,

4, etc.), then fractions were included under the concept "number," because they were similar. Then they invented imaginary numbers and other numbers which have even a more dubious status, like trans-finite numbers, etc. But in any case, the definition of the concepts would change in this wider context.

AR: Well, not of the concept "number," for instance.

Prof. C: Why?

AR: Because look right in your presentation: first you have natural numbers. And then you have fractions. Well, that's not the same concept, it's a subdivision. It's a new elaboration of what you know about the science of numbering. But the addition of fractions, for instance, hasn't altered in any way your understanding of the basic number series. "One," "two," "three," etc. remain the same. But then you might have new combinations or new relationships numerically which you identify as fractions, and then powers or roots. But your knowledge of "number" hasn't changed. [Just as forming subdivisions of "man"—such as "farmer" or "brother"—does not change the concept of "man" or its definition.] What you can do with numbers, or what type of measurements you can discover, that's a development in your use of numbers, but not a change in the definition of "number" itself, in the way that the definition of "man" can change.

Prof. B: Take "seven." You don't learn more information about "seven" which leads you to change the definition of "seven."

Prof. E: You don't discover new phenomena previously unencountered which require you to distinguish "number" in a new way, the way you do in the case of the child's expanding definitions of "man."

Abstraction from Abstractions

First-Level Concepts

Prof. F: I have a fundamental question about the hierarchy of concepts. On page 22 you say, "The meaning of 'furniture' cannot be grasped unless one has first grasped the meaning of its constituent concepts; these are its link to reality." Now, what about the meaning of "table": can we say that the meaning of "table" cannot be grasped unless one has first grasped the meaning of "dining table," "conference table," "writing table," and so forth? Are these its constituent concepts? Or is the concept "table" a kind of privileged concept that comes at a kind of absolute bottom in the hierarchy of concepts and has a direct relationship to reality?

Or would you say that where a concept comes is determined by the context of one's own learning? For instance, might a person form the concept of "furniture" without having formed the concept of "table" before? Might he form the concept of "living being" before he has formed the concept of "animal"?

AR: In a sense, yes. There is a big problem here, however, whether this applies all the way through the conceptual chain—which I would claim cannot be the case. But, on the level we are discussing, there is a certain element of the optional. Because when you first form your concepts, you might conceivably first form in a very loose way the

204

concepts "living entity" versus "inanimate object," and later subdivide into "man," "animals," "plants," etc. (and "tables," "rocks," "houses," on the other hand). In a loose way, that can be done, but only up to a certain level. Because, suppose you started with the concept "living being." You would then find that that is too generalized a category, and you would have to say, in effect, "By living beings I mean men, animals, and plants."

Therefore, understanding what your original semi-concept "living being" meant would depend on what you mean by the constituents, such as "man," "animal," and "plant."

What then is the ultimate determinant here? What I call the "first level" of concepts are existential concretes—that to which you can *point* as if it were an ostensive definition and say: "I mean *this*." Now, you can point to a table. You cannot point to furniture. You have to say, "By furniture I mean . . ." and you would have to include all kinds of objects.

Prof. F: Why wouldn't one have an equal difficulty when one came, let's say, to the concept of "bird"? Why wouldn't one have to say, "By bird, I mean eagles, penguins, and hummingbirds"?

AR: Because, in fact, one doesn't. And that is the difference between subcategories of concepts and first-level concepts. Because, you see, you could not arrive at the differences between eagles, hummingbirds, etc., unless you had first separated birds from other animals.

Even if chronologically you may learn those concepts in different orders, ultimately when you organize your concepts to determine which are basic-level concepts and which are derivatives (in both directions, wider integration or narrower subdivision), the test will be: which objects you perceive directly in reality and can point to, and which you have to differentiate by means of other concepts.

Prof. F: Then you are suggesting that metaphysically there are certain lowest species or infima species: certain concepts that are directly tied to concretes. Whereas, on top of them, we continually build higher-order concepts, which refer, in turn, to the lower.

AR: Yes, if you mean, by "metaphysical," existential objects—entities which exist qua entities.

Prof. E: I'd like to ask a follow-up question. This is the kind of question I get all the time, which I do not fully know how to answer. I will give the example: "table" is first-level, and then you can go up to "furniture" or down to "living-room table," etc.

AR: That's right.

Prof. E: Then I get this kind of question: Is it theoretically possible for someone to start by first conceptualizing living-room tables (he wouldn't, of course, be able to call it "living-room *table*" since he wouldn't yet have the concept "table") and then "desk," etc. and have separate concepts for all of what *we* call subcategories of "table," and then one day, in effect, grasp in an act of higher integration that they have something uniting them all, and reach the concept "table"?

AR: Theoretically, maybe; existentially, no. By which I mean that in order to do that, if that is how a child starts, he would have to live in a furniture store. He would have to have observed an enormous number of certain kinds of tables so that he isolates them first and then arrives at the overall category, which is "table."

Here, the process is directed by what is available to the child's observation when he begins to form the concept.

Prof. E: Would the state of his ability to discriminate also be relevant to defining what is a first-level concept? In other words, he couldn't perhaps discriminate subtler distinctions before he had the gross category.

AR: Exactly. And he has to have, and this is very essential, a sufficient number of examples of a given category differentiated from other dissimilar entities before he can form a concept.

Prof. E: What do you say about this objection? People say you can't point to table, all you can point to is living-room table, or dining-room table, etc., and, therefore, how do you distinguish "table" from "furniture" in this respect?

AR: The answer is in the Conceptual Common Denominator. If you point to table and you say, "I mean this," what do you differentiate it from? From chairs, cabinets, beds, etc. You do not mean only a dining-room table but not an end table. What is involved here, in the act of pointing, as in everything about concepts, is: from what are you differentiating it?

Prof. B: Isn't the issue then what similarities and differences you are able to be aware of? And wouldn't that be a function of two things: the actual properties of the objects plus the context that you are in?

AR: That's right.

Prof. B: Take the earlier question of whether you could form the concept of "furniture" before the concept "table." In order to do that, you would have to perceive the similarities uniting all items of furniture before you perceived the difference between a table and, say, a bed. And the question is: how could that ever come up?

AR: The difficulty here is that the infant or child would have to have a much wider range of perception than is normal to a beginning consciousness. He would have to consider objects outside of the room, objects moving in the street, and then conclude: by "furniture" I mean the objects in this room. Even subverbally, if this is what he observes, he has already made an enormously wide range of observations, which is not likely as a beginning. In logic, there would be objections to that, because how would he differentiate furniture from, let's say, moving vehicles in the street? How did he get to that wide a range without first observing the immediate differences and similarities around him?

Prof. B: If he looked at a bed and a dresser, let's say, he would have to see them as different before he saw them as similar.

AR: That's right. Also, remember that we use "table" as an example because that is the object most likely to be one of the first perceived by a child in our civilization. But now suppose a child has to grasp the concept "coconut." In our civilization that would be a much later development. He would probably first grasp "food," then maybe "apple" and "pear," until some day he discovers an unusual food—a coconut. But now take a child in a primitive society, in a jungle. He never heard of tables, and he might be bewildered when he first sees a table in the home of the local missionary. But "coconut" might be one of the first concepts he forms because coconuts are all around him.

The overall rule for what is first-level is: those existential concretes which are first available to your consciousness. But they have to be concretes. A first-level concept cannot be one which, in order to indicate what you mean by it, requires other concepts, as is the case with "furniture." "Furniture" is not a term designating concretes directly. It is a term designating different kinds of concretes which all have to be conceptualized, as against another very broad category, such as moving vehicles, let us say.

In other words, if, after you have acquired a conceptual vocabulary, a given concept cannot be understood by you or communicated by you without reference to other concepts, then it is a higher-level concept, even if maybe somehow you grasped it first (and I question the issue of whether you could grasp it first). But the hierarchy that you will establish eventually when you are in the realm of a developed language, the hierarchy of which concept depends on the other, will not be determined by the accidental order in which *you* learned them, because that can have a great deal of the optional element and depends on what is available in your immediate surroundings.

It is after you are in the realm of language, when you can organize your concepts and say what you mean by "table," what you mean by "furniture"—it is at this level, logically and not chronologically, that you can determine which are concepts of the first order and which are derivatives.

*   *   *

Prof. C: I have a follow-up on this same issue. You state,

"Observe that the concept 'furniture' is an abstraction one step further removed from perceptual reality . . ." What I would like to get at is: what is that "one step"? It seems to be the fact that to identify the units subsumed by "furniture," you need to grasp the objects' function, which is something that one does not perceive directly. The function is a more abstract characteristic.

AR: May I point out something here? I said, in this sentence, an abstraction one step further removed from *perceptual* reality. Now, remember, abstractions also are real. Abstraction itself is only our epistemological process, but that which it refers to exists in reality; but it would not be available to us by direct perceptual means. And, therefore, the term "perceptual reality" is very important here. I don't mean that higher abstractions are a step removed from reality. I mean they cannot be perceived by perceptual means; in order to grasp them, we need concepts.

A child *can* observe perceptually the function of an item of furniture. But it cannot be the *first* thing that he observes, because, before he can observe a function, he has to isolate the objects of which this function is a characteristic. In order to observe that a table is something on which you put objects, a bed is something on which you lie down, he first has to conceptualize those objects; then he conceptualizes what he can do with those objects—what their function is.

Prof. C: But how does one focus on the function of a thing? Just looking at a chair or a bed, for instance, doesn't tell you what its function is. So how does a child recognize the similarity in this case when there isn't some perceivable characteristic like color that tells him that those things go together?

AR: What do you mean here by the function? The use which you can make of it, in the case of furniture. Well, you can observe that directly, after you have conceptualized or isolated those objects. How does a child discover what a table is for? Suppose he tries to lie down on the table and finds he is uncomfortable, but he lies down on the bed and he is comfortable. He observes that he is put on the bed at night, but dishes are put on the table for dinner. That is observed perceptually. But to conceptualize it, he would first have to isolate and grasp such a thing as table versus bed.

The function itself is observable directly, but to conceptualize it he first has to conceptualize the objects as objects. Because here the function is an action-concept. It is either what the thing can do or what you can do with it. And an action-concept cannot precede an entity-concept. He first has to conceptualize the objects—the entities—then, the kinds of action they can perform or he can perform with them.

Prof. C: So you don't agree with my distinction that there are characteristics like color and shape that are directly given in perception, as opposed to a set of other characteristics for which one must have a vaster amount of knowledge or data?

AR: I thought I agreed in a certain sense, if I understood you correctly. If your question pertains to the order in which it is possible to form concepts, then I would agree with you that certain concepts, such as concepts of function or action, even though perceptually observable, cannot be conceptualized without a prior conceptualization of the acting or functioning entities. So, if you are asking, "Can concepts of function be formed ahead of the necessary antecedent concepts?" I would say "no." In that sense I agree with you. When you say there is something extra that is required—the something extra is the conceptualization of the entities involved, which is required before you can take the next step of conceptualizing the functions.

But we are referring here to the order of concept-formation. The fact that functions can be observed perceptually is not the essential issue here. A child can see a moving object directly, but he cannot form the concept "motion" until he has formed the concept "object." Therefore, it is the order of possible conceptualization that is different here. This is what makes concept-formation hierarchical. This is what forms the dependence of certain concepts on certain others in human conceptual development.

But as to which part of this conceptual hierarchy involves direct, perceptual observation and which is purely conceptual—that is a somewhat different question. On the lower levels of conceptualization—lower in the sense of first to be conceptualized—all that first material is available to direct perception but cannot be conceptualized indiscriminately, although certain optional elements exist on the lower level.

The higher concepts, the abstractions from abstractions, come when you have to integrate perceptual concretes with concepts of consciousness or concepts of human action. For instance, such a concept as "marriage" cannot be grasped perceptually. Even if you observed all the actions of a couple, that wouldn't give you the concept "marriage," because here certain relationships, actions, and processes of consciousness are involved.

So the distinction regarding the hierarchy in concept-formation is not what can or cannot be perceived perceptually, even though it is true that on the higher levels the referents cannot be perceived by exclusively perceptual means. The issue here is: which concepts can be formed first and which depend on other concepts that had to come before you reached that level. And the distinction between an object and its function or action is one of those. You cannot grasp the function before you have conceptualized the object.

* * *

Prof. D: On the question about "furniture" versus "table" versus "coffee table," I'm not clear as to the answer you gave to the question of whether or not it was contextual.

AR: My answer is that although there is an element of the optional for certain first-level concepts, the logical determination of which concept is primary, or first, and which is derivative depends on whether that second concept required the conceptualization of the first, before it could be conceptualized.

The hierarchy here refers to your concept-forming process —in other words, it's a hierarchy of epistemology, not of metaphysics. Furniture exists on the same level as tables and chairs. But the question is, which *concept* depends on which? And the answer here is: that concept is second-level which, to be grasped, requires prior conceptualization of its constituents.

So even if we suppose that some child grasped "furniture" before he grasped "tables" and "chairs" (which is highly unlikely), in organizing his concepts later, he would have to place "furniture" second, and "tables" and "chairs" first. But he wouldn't include "dining tables" and "coffee tables," etc., as first-level, because those are subdivisions; he would have to form the concept "table" before he could subdivide it into particular classes of tables.

Prof. E: Then is it true that while there is a certain area of option, chronologically speaking, as to which concept is formed first and which is formed by derivation, either by subdivision or as a wider integration, it is nevertheless true that once the conceptual apparatus has been developed and you establish a logical hierarchy, that hierarchy is invariant for human beings, being dictated by the nature of the concepts, with no option as to which concept is higher-level and which is lower-level?

AR: Correct.

Prof. E: Now to distinguish your view here from Aristotle's. Aristotle would also say that you could arrange concepts on a hierarchical level, in effect from "table" on up or "man" on up. But he would say that what qualifies as a first-level concept is exclusively dictated by metaphysical considerations, and that subtypes of "man" or subtypes of "table" have, in effect, a lesser metaphysical status.

AR: Correct. We do not say that.

Prof. E: Whereas, would it be correct to say that, for Objectivism, once we have the logical hierarchy, the designation of concepts as first-level within the logical hierarchy is dictated by a combination of metaphysical and epistemological considerations, and are in that sense objectively first-level, if I can use that terminology, as against intrinsically, in the Aristotelian system?

AR: Exactly right.

Prof. B: I don't understand the difference between the chronological and the logical order. In establishing the logical order, you consider whether the second concept requires the first one in order to be formed. But if it is possible to form the concept of "furniture" before "table"—I don't think that is possible, but if it is—then why, in your logical hierarchy, would "furniture" be derivative?

AR: Yes, but if chronologically you form "furniture" first, you would have only a very approximate, very woozy lumping together of certain objects as against something else, say moving objects. Therefore, your concept at that stage would be enormously imprecise, and one could say almost tentative. Before it can become a fully clear concept in your mind, so that you know what you mean by "furniture" fully, you would have to know which objects you call furniture as against vehicles, architectural features, etc.

Therefore, it is the precision of your concept, which you need in order to firmly differentiate it from everything else in your context of knowledge, that determines the hierarchical status of your concepts. So, you can form a vague approximation, but that is not yet a concept.

Prof. D: Well, someone might say you can't form the concept "flower" clearly unless you know the specific kinds of flowers. I must say "flower" is a kind of woozy concept in my mind because I don't know peonies from roses, etc.

AR: No, that isn't wooziness. The issue is: can you tell a flower from an animal or a man? You see, the clarity depends on whether you are able to differentiate and draw clear lines of demarcation, within the context of your knowledge, between one concept and another. If you can, that is conceptually valid. If not, then it is approximate or at a preconceptual stage.

May I ask one general question? Is it of great importance what happens on the first levels of concept-formation? That is not important. The order in which we can or cannot form

concepts and which we can do first is really more psychological than cognitive.

Prof. E: I think it is a question of preserving the objectivity of the logical hierarchy that is the crucial question.

AR: But the logical hierarchy depends on which categories you regard as depending on which. Do you know where
it would have importance? Only in regard to issues such as
the "stolen concept," where somebody will claim that some
concept exists while denying the concepts on which it depends. But aside from that, I don't think it is significant
which concepts we form in what order, except that when we
have reached the full conceptual level, when we can form
sentences and can differentiate concepts consciously, when
the process has become self-conscious, then it is important
to organize the relationships.

Prof. F: I am very disturbed by this, because it seems to
me that you either are or are not asserting that there are
some concepts whose formation does not require lower-level
concepts. I think this is a major position. You either are or
are not saying that there are some concepts whose formation requires no lower-level concepts. Which is it?

AR: All the things which you can perceive directly [and
conceptualize] without presupposing in that concept some
other conceptual material, those are the first-level concepts.
And if you want to form "animal" first and species later or
vice versa, that is optional. But you couldn't have the concepts "love," "truth," "justice" as first-level concepts. You
don't perceive them perceptually, directly.

Prof. F: So Objectivism holds that there are first-level
concepts?

AR: Epistemologically, not metaphysically.

Regardless of what a given man did chronologically, once
he has his full conceptual development, a very important
test of whether a concept is first-level would be whether,
within the context of his own knowledge, he would be able to
hold or explain or communicate a certain concept without
referring to preceding concepts. For instance, if a man formed
the concept "furniture" directly from perception and then

found that in communication he had to say, "Well by 'furniture' I mean tables, chairs, and other objects," he's classified it as second-level.

Prof. B: But you can give a definition of "furniture" without referring to types of furniture. Take the man who formed "furniture" directly from the perceptual level. If you ask him what he means by "furniture" he can answer: "movable man-made objects within a human habitation . . ."

AR: Oh, that he couldn't do. That I can say with assurance. Because he couldn't arrive at that kind of definition while bypassing the identification of the objects he means. He could conceivably memorize that definition if he's heard it, but he couldn't form it himself. Because you'd have to ask him, "Well, which objects do you mean?"

Prof. B: But then he'd just point to items of furniture without having to use the classification—

AR: While seeing no distinction between tables, beds, chairs, etc.? Seeing only their distinction from architectural features or small objects, but no distinction between them?

Prof. B: He'd have to point to more than one. He couldn't point to just this table.

AR: No, if he means "furniture" he'd have to point to several different items of furniture. And then the question arises, psychologically, is it possible to form that kind of differentiation while never conceptualizing the particular things? The answer would be "no," because he cannot point to those objects if he hasn't conceptualized them.

Prof. B: Can you say why that is? It has to do with similarities and differences, doesn't it?

AR: It has also to do with what is more immediately and easily available to his consciousness, when he's starting to conceptualize, as against that which is much harder to identify and separate, and requires a wider context. To separate furniture from architectural features is a much more complex issue of observations and requires a certain subtlety, which is why I say it is not likely—if a man has that much subtlety, he would certainly not fail to observe the differences between tables and chairs.

Lower-level Concepts as Units in Relation to Higher-level Concepts

Prof. C: You say that one forms wider concepts by taking lower-level concepts as units. I was somewhat perplexed; I would have liked to see a different phrase used, namely that the wider concepts are formed from *the knowledge of* the lower concepts. Because some people, in mathematics for example, take a certain level of abstraction and quit referring to reality thereafter and deal with nothing but the concepts.

AR: That would be psychology, or psychopathology, and I couldn't go into that. That some people would take language improperly—there's no protection against that.

Prof. C: But there's another, more reasonable, objection. On occasion, in the development of science, or any particular area of learning, one makes incorrect, invalid conceptualizations, and it is later recognized that this is the case and one would reclassify the knowledge that one had based on this error. So my point is, would it not be more precise to say that it's the knowledge held by the lower-level concepts that is used?

AR: No, it would not. It is not possible to summarize the preceding in making a statement. My statement has to be taken in the context of the material where it appears. And if I have explained that concepts represent a certain kind of knowledge, derived by a certain method from reality, I do not repeat that every time I use the word "concept." Remember, when you are dealing with the irrational, there are no limits to it. Because then every time I use the word "knowledge," I would have to answer the questions: "What is knowledge?" "What is reality?" "What do you mean by 'What do you mean?' " And then you are in the middle of logical positivism or linguistic analysis. It cannot be done that way.

Prof. A: Is it even true that higher-level concepts could be defined that way? First-level concepts don't stand for your knowledge of the existents, they stand for the existents themselves.

AR: Right.

Prof. A: Wouldn't the higher-level concepts, too, stand not just for the knowledge contained in the lower-level concepts, but also for all the knowledge ever to be obtained about their units?

AR: That's right. That's a very good addition; thank you for noticing it. Because every concept stands for present knowledge *and* future knowledge. That's brought out later in the book, but it's a very important point. Because if a concept stood only for your knowledge, the next time that somebody discovered something new it would invalidate your entire conceptual chain.

Subdividing by New Characteristics

Prof. B: I would like to ask about the CCD in subdivision. Suppose you are subdividing "man" into "bachelor" and "married." The essential characteristic of man is rationality. But "bachelor" and "married" are ranges of measurements of another characteristic, not the essential one.

AR: Yes, but you retain the essential characteristic, and then subdivide the two types of men according to the characteristic: relationship to the opposite sex—a characteristic implicit in the basic concept "man" but which, in fact, is not essential to that concept.

The concept "man" retains its full power, so to speak; it remains in effect, but the characteristic according to which you now subdivide is the relationship to the opposite sex.

Prof. B: And that is the CCD for the subdivision?

AR: Yes, because every member of the concept "man" would have some relationship, which would be either married or single—or indifferent.

Conceptual-level Similarities

Prof. C: I understand the point that a child's first concepts are based on perceptual similarities, like similarities of color and of shape. But later, when he is dealing with more complex issues, the similarities seem to be more abstract. At what point in his conceptual development does grasping similarities depend on some mental operation beyond mere sense perception?

AR: At the point where he has to deal with concepts that involve more than just perceptual knowledge. When he begins to deal with concepts of actions—and above all concepts of consciousness—at that point he can deal with them only by means of abstractions from abstractions.

For instance, if his mother tells him, "Don't steal the cookies or you will be a bad boy," he cannot possibly understand that without grasping what is "bad." There is no referent in perceptual reality to which he could point and say, "This is bad[ness]." He would have to say, "The action of stealing the cookies is bad. But what does Mother mean by 'bad'?" If he merely says, "Well, she will beat me if I steal the cookies and will kiss me if I don't"—his thinking is still on the perceptual level. It's when he grasps that some principle is involved here wider than the mere action of stealing the cookies and of reward and punishment as direct perceptual consequences—it's at that point that he's entered the realm of abstraction from abstractions.

Prof. E: Wouldn't even "stealing" be an example of that?

AR: Exactly.

Prof. E: All you grasp perceptually is taking.

AR: That's right. Exactly. He is dealing with things which are distinguishable—as "stealing" is a different concept from "taking"—but he can't point to something in reality and say, "This is ownership, and therefore these cookies belong to my mother and not to me." There's no perceptual evidence of that, because even if he observes that his mother made the cookies, that doesn't give him the concept of "property."

"Similarity" is not exclusively a perceptual concept; there is conceptual similarity. For example, suppose he has grasped the idea of stealing the cookies, and then he concludes, "If I take money from my mother's purse, or if I take the toys of the child next door, I'm stealing. Any time I take something which belongs to somebody else without their consent, that means the abstraction 'stealing.' " He has observed the similarities among all these actions. What's the similarity? Some object doesn't belong to him, yet he appropriates it. That's a very complex abstraction from abstractions, yet that is the similarity among all the instances of that principle.

Prof. C: But looking from the perspective of invalid concepts, when people claim that they see similarities, how would I dispute their claim when the issue is not perceptual?

AR: Are you looking for a formulation of what it is that one does [in grasping conceptual similarities]?

Prof. C: Yes, so that the criticism of subjectivity is not applicable.

AR: Well, what would you do on the perceptual level? You simply point. If you say that these two colors are similar, but that this color and that one are different, you simply point. Well, you do the same thing on the conceptual level by means of identifying what concepts you are dealing with.

In other words, if you claim that Descartes and Kant are similar in their metaphysics, but some Kantian tells you, "No, they are entirely different, because Kant was really an apostle of reason and Descartes was not," you would ask him to define what he means by "reason," and by "metaphysics," then you give him your definitions. Then you say, "I claim that they are similar in respects A, B, and C, which are essential to the question under discussion: the similarities or differences of their metaphysics."

And if he answers you, "Yes, but Descartes was French and Kant was German," you dismiss that as not relevant to the subject under discussion. Your definition of the concepts, your pointing out exactly what it is that you are discussing, substitutes for the perceptual evidence on the first level, where you merely point and say, "I mean *this*."

On the conceptual level, you define your terms, and if anyone disagrees and is subjectivist about it, you make him define his. And that may take a long time in a complex issue. But you will be able to prove your case, if you are taking the right position about what is similar and what is different. You will have to specify what you are discussing and by what attributes or characteristics you establish your claim that these are similar and those are different.

Prof. C: I know that I see similarities not only at an elementary level but between theories and so on. But my question is: can you identify the mental steps that one takes in grasping, intuitively, more abstract similarities? For the perceptual level, I find the answer satisfactory that to look is to see, but I'd like to know the process for the more advanced stages.

AR: The answer is the same: to look is to see—but what constitutes a "look" on the conceptual level? Your grasp of the referents of the concepts you are dealing with. All that you need to do is to look—remembering what a look means on the conceptual level: identify what you mean by your concepts not only definitionally, but by reducing them to the facts of reality, to the perceptual level. Identify what kind of things your concept refers to in reality. And by defining and concretizing that, you will see the differences and similarities as easily as on the perceptual level.

If you want to know why, with regard to abstractions from abstractions, you can "intuitively" know which are similar and which are different, that's really a psycho-epistemological question. Your ability to see abstract similarities "intuitively" simply stems from the fact that you have automatized that knowledge. For a human being's purposes of dealing with an ever larger amount of knowledge, a great deal of automatization is required. You would never get very far if you had to constantly and consciously retrace all the steps of how you formed each concept and then compare each concept from scratch with each new one.

What is automatized is your understanding of what you mean by those concepts. And if you go very high in the conceptual chain, you may be unable to identify instantly why a certain high-level concept seems to you to have similarities with another. You will say, "I know it intuitively."

What do you mean by that? That the knowledge has been automatized in your mind. Then what's needed, if you want to prove it to somebody who doesn't see it, is to break down that automatization—that is, to identify exactly the defining characteristic, and even some of the lesser characteristics, if necessary, of the concept. You give an exact statement of what you are dealing with and where you see the similarity and the difference.

Prof. E: If the question is: how do you objectively validate a claim to similarity? I would do it by following the definition of "similarity": the same characteristic, varying in measurement or degree or intensity.

Take the example of the primacy of consciousness in Descartes and Kant. They obviously are not identical in degree or intensity, because they vary in measurement. Take just the primacy of consciousness in those two: Descartes is semi-apologetic, and Kant is vehement about it. For Descartes, there are several aspects of his philosophy exempt from it, and in Kant it's all-embracing. So it's the same characteristic but differing in various measurements. You can establish the similarity objectively simply by showing that the variations in that characteristic are variations in measurement.

But now there's a second issue. Identifying and even validating the similarity does not yet establish that it is a fundamental similarity. For instance, both Descartes and Kant had royal patrons. That's not a fundamental similarity. So you'd have to use the test of fundamentality: how much of the rest of their philosophy does it explain? Now, clearly the primacy of consciousness explains a great deal; the fact that they had royal patrons explains little or nothing.

So you'd have two different tasks: (a) to establish the similarity by showing the characteristic is the same and only the measurements vary; and, (b) if you claim that it is a fundamental similarity, to show that a significant number of the rest of the subject-matter's characteristics follows from this similarity. Would you agree with that?

AR: Yes.

Prof. B: I understood the question to be not how you

validate similarity, but what is the pattern of the process of grasping it. If I had never thought about the question of Kant and Descartes before, I'd define to myself what is the respect in which I'm asked to show they are similar. And the answer is: metaphysics. So I'd ask: what is the real fundamental in metaphysics? And the answer to that would guide me in gradually abstracting from all the metaphysical statements in those two philosophers where they stand on that fundamental issue.

In other words, I would use my knowledge of the fundamental characteristic in metaphysics to guide me in abstracting their position on that fundamental. And then I would compare them directly.

And in a good psycho-epistemology, that process is automated. The interesting question would be: "Why is it automated?" And isn't the reason this: in a good psycho-epistemology you originally hold the issue in terms of fundamentals, and therefore it's stored away in a form—I don't know how to say it—where the wires cross more easily?

AR: That's right. It's a good metaphor.

Prof. B: It's your point that the conscious mind sets the purpose for the subconscious. If you give yourself the question: "Are Descartes and Kant similar?" what your mind immediately feeds you depends on what you've stored and held as the fundamentals of Descartes and Kant.

AR: Right. That's a very important observation, psycho-epistemologically. That's one of the worst consequences of faulty definitions: you will be confused every time you have to use these concepts, precisely in a case like this. If you haven't filed by the fundamentals of the issue, but by some accidental characteristic, when you need to compare them you'll be in real trouble.

Concepts of Consciousness

"Thought" vs. "Emotion"

Prof. B: What is the CCD uniting thinking and emotion? The CCD would have to be a characteristic of both for which there is one unit of measurement applicable to thinking and emotion, and I don't see that they have the same unit of measurement.

AR: I mentioned in Chapter 4 that the CCD for all concepts of consciousness is: action of consciousness. That is the common denominator.

Prof. B: Is there a unit of measurement for that characteristic which holds for both thinking and evaluation?

AR: All measurements in regard to concepts of consciousness are only approximations. With that in mind, the common denominator would be intensity—the intensity of a given mental state and its hierarchical importance to you, measured by the ordinal numbers. Therefore, you could compare thought to an emotion by the process which your consciousness performs in either, and by its value or importance to you.

Prof. B: I experience it introspectively, but I can't name what is the common process.

AR: Do you mean that you are looking for a common unit of measurement for each process of consciousness, like between thought and emotion, and between emotions and memory?

Prof. B: Yes.

AR: What makes you assume that is necessary? Here you don't differentiate each separately from the others. You keep the total context, which is: your mental actions, the content of your consciousness. And then you isolate them from all the others, not one from the other.

Prof. B: I think that is the key, but what is puzzling me is a comparison that I am making to the other abstractions. For instance, for "table" the CCD would be the shape—

AR: The shape of the table versus the shape of the chair, let's say.

Prof. B: And the point is that tables and chairs are both measured by the same unit of measurement, that is, a unit of measurement of shape.

AR: Right.

Prof. B: Now, if we draw the parallel, the CCD for thinking and for emotion would be conscious action, both measured by the same unit—the unit of conscious action— only I can't find any.

AR: Here you don't need a unit; you need first the demarcation of the field. All of the concepts of consciousness have one thing in common: that it is a process or an action of consciousness and it is internal, it is your psychological process versus the outside world. Therefore, you have already separated all of these particular phenomena which you want to conceptualize, and have separated them in a radical way from existential concepts.

In existential concepts you don't start by saying, "Well, all of this is existential, now what is the difference between tables and chairs?" Because you don't even have the distinction yet of existential versus psychological. As to concepts of consciousness, however, since consciousness consists of processes and their content, you cannot become aware of it until it has some kind of content. But there the range of what you have to conceptualize is infinitely smaller than in concepts of existential objects. You have already classified them: they concern that which takes place in your mind, as distinguished from the objects which your mind observes. That is your first line of demarcation. Thereafter, all your concepts of consciousness have as their Conceptual Common Denominator that it is a state of consciousness.

But now how do we find a measuring unit for a state of consciousness—is that really relevant? Once you have identified different processes—you say, "I know what my mind does when I think, when I feel, when I remember"—isn't that sufficient for conceptualizing purposes? Since the overall category is already very clearly defined and delimited.

Prof. B: But what enables me to differentiate thinking from emotion is that introspectively they are different perceptually, directly.

AR: No, that they are different actions. Now, would this help you? I mentioned that what they have in common is the object.

Prof. B: Right.

AR: For instance, what you think about a given event and what you feel about it are two different things. In what way are they different? The event is the same, but you observe that your mind does something different. Your consciousness is in a different state according to whether you think about this event or have feelings about it. Well, that is sufficient differentiation.

Prof. B: Just as in the case of conceptualizing colors.

AR: Yes.

[The reference is to the statement on page 15: "Centuries passed before science discovered the unit by which colors could actually be measured: the wavelengths of light—a discovery that supported, in terms of mathematical proof, the differentiations that men were and are making in terms of visual similarities." The point seems to be that just as we didn't need to find a unit of color in order to distinguish blue from red, so we don't need to find a unit of conscious action in order to distinguish thinking from feeling.]

Intentions

Prof. D: According to your statement on page 29, every

act of consciousness has a content. But this relationship seems to be of a special kind. For instance, if I truly say, "I intend to go home," it would seem to be absurd to say, "Well, maybe you're wrong, you are not intending that at all." It would seem, in short, as if there were a necessary connection between the action and the content.

AR: Will you tell me in your example which you classify as the content and which is the action of consciousness?

Prof. D: This is, perhaps, more a part of the question I am asking you. I say, "I intend to go home." According to your analysis, there would be an action of consciousness and an object or a content connected with it.

AR: That's right. The action of consciousness is a consideration and a conclusion drawn. You have considered the subject of your going home and you have decided that you will. The expression of that is, "I intend to go home" —meaning that you have given consideration and reached a certain intention or conclusion. That is the action of your consciousness.

Now, what is the content of that action? The question of the trip home. The subject here is the issue of going home or not, the contemplating of a certain journey. The action is the consideration of that subject and a certain conclusion reached, which you then announce as, "I intend to go home." Those are the two elements. What is missing?

Prof. D: Suppose I say, in a dark room, "I am hitting a dog." But then I turn on the light and it turns out I was hitting a pillow. Here there is a contingent relationship between the action and the object.

Prof. E: I think he is trying to suggest that in connection with at least certain actions of consciousness you have a kind of infallibility about them—you can't be mistaken in your view of what they consist of—whereas in physical actions you can be mistaken about the object.

AR: I would say, quite as an aside, that the exact opposite is true.

Prof. E: I don't think that is an aside, I think that is the point.

Prof. D: Based upon this notion that I couldn't be mistaken, one would want to say there is some kind of necessary connection between the action and the object of the action. There would be some kind of absurdity in someone saying, "You must be mistaken, you don't really intend that."

AR: Now we are talking about the action of your consciousness, aren't we? Not about whether you really will go home or not.

Prof. D: Yes.

AR: If it were true [that men couldn't be mistaken about the actions of their consciousness in this way], we would be living in Atlantis. If men identified introspectively their inner states one tenth as correctly as they identify objective reality, we would be a race of ideal giants. I ascribe ninety-five percent or more of all psychological trouble and personal tragedies to the fact that in the realm of introspection we are on the level where savages were (or lower) in regard to extrospection. Men are not only not taught to introspect, they are actively discouraged from engaging in introspection, and yet their lives depend on it. Without that, nothing is possible to them, including [proper] concept-formation.

Prof. D: How do you mean that they are mistaken? Are most people mistaken when they say they are thinking of going home?

AR: Make it a little more complicated than that and I would say most people do not even report their inner states correctly—and I don't mean now anything like lying; it is an issue of personal identification, or lying to yourself. They could tell you, "I hate my mother-in-law," when in fact they are secretly in love with her (I don't mean in the Freudian sense). It is possible, because of the human capacity for evasions, repressions, and above all, rationalizations and other defense-mechanisms. This is a field of which we are merely glimpsing the first stages, and yet look at the enormity of the disasters possible to man in that realm.

The Base of Introspective Concepts

Prof. E: In the case of extrospective knowledge, we are fallible, we can make errors. But we know that we can, in principle, arrive at the correct answer to any question given two facts: the use of a rational method combined with certain incontestable data on which we base all of our reasoning—namely, the direct evidence of the senses, about which we can't be wrong, as apart from errors in conceptualizing it or reasoning about it.

AR: Right.

Prof. E: The question is: insofar as we are to arrive at knowledge of the content of consciousness, what is the stand-in for the evidence of the senses—the incontestable, infallible data which are the foundation for all subsequent inference?

AR: That's an interesting question. I would say the foundation there is the same as in extrospective knowledge. In other words, the base is that which you can conceptualize directly and which corresponds to that same level of conceptual development in the extrospective world. Everything else has to be built on that.

Prof. D: That would be something like, "I am thinking."

AR: Oh no. First it would be your understanding of your mental state when you say "table," "chair," "dog," "cat," etc. It's your understanding of the difference between consciousness and existence, and of knowing: here are simple concepts I can perceive, and I know what my mind is doing when I identify "This is a table," "This is a chair." That's the base.

Above that base, a more complex level would be: "And what is it to me?" It's when you enter the evaluative realm that you are in the greatest complexity. And the base there, the equivalent of the first-level concepts in extrospection, would be any simple evaluation which you can identify with certainty. If you can say, "By 'love' I mean what I feel for my mother"—or simpler: for ice cream—and you know that

that's what you mean by "love," that's your base for the evaluative realm.

[In sum, the base is] your conceptualization of the simplest, first-level [extrospective] concepts available to you, and your first conceptualizations of your values, in the simplest terms. That is the base of your introspective conceptual hierarchy. If we can be mistaken about introspection as much as about extrospection—perhaps more—to what do we refer when we have to correct an error of introspection? Well, we would refer to those simplest beginnings of a consciousness, that which we can conceptualize in most direct terms.

For instance, it might be terribly difficult to know what you feel about your mother-in-law, let's say (she's supposed to be the object always of mixed feelings), so it might be hard to decide fully what you really feel about this person. It would be a little easier if you then ask, "Well, how do I really evaluate that person?" Then you might find that you don't really know. If you want to check, you bring your mental attention, your chain, down to determining what kind of inner states you know for sure, in the simplest terms. And from that, try to rebuild, step by step, your evaluation of this particular, complex problem.

Definitions

Essential Characteristics as Fundamentals

Prof. C: On page 45, you state, "Metaphysically, a fundamental characteristic is that distinctive characteristic which makes the greatest number of others possible; epistemologically, it is the one that explains the greatest number of others." Could you explain how that applies to the sequence through which a child progresses in his definition of "man"? For instance, in the child's first definition: "a thing that moves and makes sounds," I don't see how the essential characteristic there is also a fundamental one. I don't see that the definition explains much about man. It merely distinguishes him from other things that the child sees.

AR: But first of all, are you clear on why I put this statement in this form—why the distinction between "metaphysical" and "epistemological"? I'd like to pause on that for a moment.

"Metaphysically" here refers to that characteristic which, in the nature of the thing, makes other characteristics possible. "Epistemologically" means the way we would proceed to discover a causal explanation. You see, I could not put the second into a metaphysical category, because nature as such doesn't explain. A thing just *is*, and certain characteristics are the causes of other characteristics. But metaphysically—that is, apart from human observation or knowledge—it doesn't constitute an explanation, it's just a fact. Epistemologically, the process of determining a defining characteristic will proceed by means of the question: which characteristic explains the others? Metaphysically, this means: which characteristic makes the others possible? Which is the cause?

Now, let's apply it to a child's development. There the question doesn't yet enter, because he doesn't have to select a fundamental characteristic from among a great many different observed characteristics. On that level of development, he has observed only two characteristics distinguishing man from inanimate objects: these objects are motionless and silent, man moves and makes noises. Here he doesn't yet choose a fundamental from among many characteristics which distinguish man from inanimate objects, because he doesn't have that knowledge. The only distinctions he can observe are the defining characteristics. They are essential by default, in effect—because he can't observe everything at once.

It's only with the development of his knowledge, when he observes more things than merely movement and noise, when he observes that inanimate objects like automobiles also move and make noises—it's when he has to make a choice among man's distinctive characteristics and he has to decide which one is essential that this process begins. Then choosing the fundamental is a necessity. But on the first steps, to discover even one characteristic that distinguishes one group of existents from others is sufficient.

The Expansion of a Definition

Prof. C: You state that: "All definitions are contextual, and a primitive definition does not contradict a more advanced one: the latter merely expands the former." Now I don't understand why you say that the latter expands the former, as opposed to "narrows it down." Take, for example, your sequence of implicit definitions, for a child, of the concept "man." The first definition is: "a thing that moves and makes sounds." Now I agree that to form the next definition his knowledge has to expand, but it seems to me that the definition itself narrows, in that it no longer includes all the concretes which move and make sounds.

AR: But you are making an equivocation here. Bear in mind that all definitions are contextual and that the purpose of a definition is to distinguish a given group of existents from all others. Now, if a child forms the implicit definition of "man" as "something that moves and makes sounds," this means that all he has so far observed are motionless, inanimate objects and men. And this is only his first differentiation. He, in effect, says: there are things that do not move and are silent and then there are things which move and make noises. And by the things which move and make noises, he means men.

Well now, he doesn't *contract* his definition of "man" when he later changes it to: "a thing that walks on two legs and has no fur." He has now expanded it, because he has observed more distinguishing characteristics of men, which distinguish man from a wider field of knowledge. You see, by the time he needs to define "man" in a more specific way, he knows that the definition "moves and makes noises" includes much more than man, and therefore as a definition of man it is no longer valid. Therefore it is not a contracted definition, it's expanded in the sense of his having observed more characteristics of man.

Prof. C: I see where I was making an error. I was thinking, in line with modern philosophy, that a concept is equal to its definition, and assuming that all the concretes that fit the formula "moves and makes noises"—even the new ones that he later discovers—were therefore part of his original concept of "man." And that's wrong.

AR: Yes. That's precisely why the definition now has to be expanded.

Prof. A: Isn't it also true that, since the later definition is more fundamental, it's expanded in the sense that it contains or implies the earlier defining characteristics?

AR: Plus others, yes.

Prof. A: So a rational animal is also something that moves and makes noises.

AR: Exactly. Each later definition subsumes the earlier ones.

Prof. A: The definition has expanded in the sense that whatever knowledge is contained in "moves and makes noises" is also contained in "a rational animal" and more as well. Because a rational animal is also an animal that moves and makes noises.

Prof. E: The issue is only which characteristics are explicit in the definition versus which are implicit.

Prof. H: It is easy to assume that when the definition changes, the concept changes.

AR: No, the context of your knowledge changes. When you know more, you select a different essential characteristic by which to define the object, because you now have to differentiate it more precisely. Your knowledge has expanded, but the concept doesn't change.

The similarities and differences according to which you originally formed the concept still remain. So you haven't changed your concept. Your old distinction remains the same; the concept refers to the same entity. Only now you know more, your field of knowledge is wider, and therefore you have to define your concept by a different essential characteristic.

Prof. H: I was falling into the old trap of thinking that the concept refers to the—

AR: To the definition only.

Prof. B: Or only to the similarities and differences known at a given time.

AR: Yes. But if you keep in mind that your concept refers to referents, to things, you will see that it doesn't change, but your knowledge changes.

Philosophical vs. Specialized Definitions

Prof. B: This question pertains to the discussion of definitions on page 44. You say that the ultimate definition of man is "a rational animal." I take it then that it would be wrong to define man as "a rational primate."

AR: Oh yes.

Prof. B: Is that because man's distinctive form of consciousness makes him a basic subdivision of "animal" rather than just a minor subcategory? In a sense, all other animals are limited to sensory forms of consciousness, but man is rational. That means you can make a basic subdivision of "animal" into "man" and "non-man" on the grounds of whether the consciousness is rational or just perceptual.

AR: Yes, but what would be the purpose of this? Here you have an evaluative consideration entering. Is the distinction by type of consciousness more important then, let's say, the distinction between animal and bird, by feathers and ability to fly? You see, it wouldn't necessarily be important formally, as you formed the concept, whether the characteristic by which you subdivide is of a tremendous, momentous kind or merely the only one you can observe that is at all significant. After you have formed the concept, it is a separate intellectual pursuit to find out whether that distinction is really enormously important, which [in the case of man versus animals] it is. But that fact is not of significance to the subdivision, to the classification of man as a rational animal.

Prof. E: I was wondering whether you would agree with the following, which is my understanding of why the genus of man for a general definition would remain "animal."

Definitions and conceptualization always have to take into account the cognitive context. The normal adult does not deal with subdivisions like "primate." And, therefore, for a general literate adult, "rational animal" would be appropriate, even if for a more specialized degree of knowledge you need the further subdivision.

I can give this parallel: suppose a normal adult were defining "amnesia." I think a valid definition would have as its genus something like "mental illness" or "mental disorder" (with the differentia indicating loss of memory). Whereas the psychiatrist, who subclassifies mental ailments, could say its genus was something narrower, I think they call it a "dissociative reaction" or something of the sort. But that would not affect the validity of the genus "mental disorder" for a generally educated adult.

AR: Yes, that is correct. I would add one thing of a more general nature. Philosophical problems have to be solved on a level of knowledge available to a normal adult at *any* period of human development; so that philosophical concepts are really not dependent on the development of individual sciences. And "primate" or "mammal" would be a very specialized subdivision of a concept according to a particular science.

Prof. A: Then would it be wrong for a biologist to define man as "a rational primate," or would that be correct in his context?

AR: It would be correct in his context, if he remembers that he is speaking here from a professional context. And, as you know, they subdivide even further. Any subdivision within a given science is proper provided it is not substituted for the basic philosophical definition which is valid for all men in all stages of knowledge.

Meaning and Referent

Prof. B: Someone once raised the following objection to the idea that the meaning of a concept is its referents. Take the concept "glass," meaning drinking glasses. Suppose one person has seen millions of glasses in his life, but only those of one particular type. A second person has seen only a few dozen glasses, but of a wide variety of different types. The question is: who would know more of the meaning of the concept "glass"? Even though the first man has seen many more *referents* of the concept "glass," it seems that the second man, who has seen fewer of the referents, knows more of the *meaning*.

AR: When you ask, "Who knows better the meaning of the concept?"—the answer is: both equally, because the concept doesn't include the non-essential variations. To have the concept "glass" means you can differentiate a glass from all other objects. Therefore their knowledge is exactly the same.

Prof. B: But the meaning isn't just the essential characteristic.

AR: The essential characteristic and lesser characteristics also. But now if one man has observed more characteristics than another, he knows more about the referents of the concept, which doesn't mean that he understands the meaning of the concept better.

Prof. B: The meaning of the concept is the entities which it integrates, and you know the meaning when you know which entities it integrates.

AR: That's right.

Prof. B: So if they both have the same standards for integration, they both know the meaning equally.

AR: Exactly.

Prof. B: So, the meaning is the referents; the form in which we hold our knowledge of the meaning is the essential characteristics.

AR: That's right. But the important distinction here is understanding the meaning of a concept versus knowing more about its referents. A simpler example of the same kind would be: who knows more about the concept "man," a layman or a doctor? Well, they both understand the concept equally, but the doctor may know more about the referents of the concept "man"—namely, about his physiology. Or a psychologist will know more about the type of consciousness of the referent.

Prof. B: So "knowing more about the meaning" is equivocal. It could mean knowing more about the objects or knowing more about what makes those objects glasses.

AR: Exactly. About what differentiates those objects from all others.

Prof. A: Now I'm totally confused. Because I thought the meaning *is* the referent.

AR: The meaning is the referent, but your understanding of the meaning of a concept and your knowledge about the referent aren't the same thing.

Prof. A: By "understanding the meaning of the concept" you mean understanding what a concept means?

AR: Yes, understanding which existents it refers to in reality. So that if you can distinguish the referents from all other existents in your knowledge, you have fully understood the meaning of the concept. But then if you study various aspects of these referents, you may come to know more about them than someone else, but that is an issue irrelevant to understanding the meaning of the concept.

Prof. A: Then would it be correct to describe the person who goes into more intensive study as learning more about—

AR: About the referents. Not about the meaning of the concept. That's the important thing. He knows more about the units, but not about the concept.

Understanding the meaning of a concept is an epistemological issue. It is understanding to what in reality that concept refers. It's being able to distinguish the referents from all other existents. That's understanding the meaning of a concept. How much you know about the referents is something that varies from man to man. But the understanding of the *concept* is the same once you can distinguish the referents from all other things.

In that sense the understanding of the concept "man" was the same a hundred years ago as it is today, or is the same today for a savage and a scientist. They both understand the concept, but one knows more about the referents than does the other.

And, incidentally, the concept subsumes all the characteristics of the referents, known or yet to be discovered. And in that sense, what we know today—if we took the total sum of knowledge about a given concept, like "man"—would still apply a hundred years from now, when, let's assume, men will know much more. But they won't know more about the concept, they will know more about the referent of the concept.

Prof. A: So in the argument against the analytic-synthetic dichotomy, when you say that newly discovered characteristics are included in the concept's meaning, you mean they belong to the same units.

AR: Yes. But it doesn't change the concept.

Prof. A: Some philosophers raise this objection: how could you mean by a concept more than you know at a given time? So the answer is: well, you don't know every aspect of the referents, but you do know fully *which* referents you are talking about.

AR: And you know what you do know about these referents and by what characteristic you distinguish them from other referents, which is all that concerns you in regard to concept-formation.

Prof. B: You do know fully now what you mean.

AR: Exactly.

Prof. A: The concept is fully meaningful if you can isolate validly a group of referents—

AR: From all other referents, yes.

Definition by Non-essentials

Prof. K: In Chapter 7 you discuss the error of "definition by non-essentials," and you distinguish between the cognitive and the epistemological results of that error. Would you explain how these two categories are differentiated?

AR: The distinction is between the content of knowledge and the method of acquiring it. It's really explained right in the text. I say, "Cognitively, such an attempt would produce nothing but a bad hash of equivocations, shoddy metaphors, and unacknowledged 'stolen' concepts." Now that refers to the content of your knowledge. Then I say, "Epistemologically, it would produce the atrophy of the capacity to discriminate"—which is an issue of the method of functioning of your consciousness.

Therefore, cognitively, a definition by non-essentials will wreck the content of your knowledge; and, epistemologically, it will incapacitate or greatly hamper your capacity, because it will be impossible to proceed with that kind of error in your method. All extension of knowledge is contextual: you build new knowledge on the basis of the old. And if you have undefined terms, patches of vagueness, or invalid concepts, it will affect all your subsequent cognitive steps. It hampers and ultimately destroys the method of acquiring knowledge.

Contextual Reclassification

Prof. E: This question is a request for an example. On page 66 you say, "The definitions of concepts may change with the changes in the designation of essential characteristics, and conceptual reclassifications may occur with the growth of knowledge." Could you give an example of a conceptual reclassification?

AR: That really refers to derivative concepts. For instance, in a primitive state of knowledge of medicine they subdivided "man" according to certain characteristics which were predominantly invented, and then with the growth of knowledge they reclassified—you know, like "the choleric"—

Prof. E: The four humors—"the melancholy"—

AR: —etc. Well, that proved to be invalid, and therefore the classification is no longer used.

Prof. A: Would another example of that be the whale, which was originally thought of as a fish but is now, in a wider context of knowledge, classified as a mammal?

AR: That would be an example of reclassification, yes.

Axiomatic Concepts

"Existence" and "Identity"

Prof. B: I'm interested in the fact that "existence" and "identity" have the same units, yet they are different concepts. In general, would it be true that if two different concepts have the same units, then what makes them two concepts rather than one is that in each case the units are differentiated from something else? For instance, in the case of "concrete" versus "entity," the units are the same, but the concept "entity" distinguishes entities from attributes, while the concept "concrete" distinguishes entities from abstractions.

AR: That's correct.

Prof. B: Then is it the case that what distinguishes the concepts "existence" and "identity" is that the concept "existence" differentiates this object from nothing, while "identity" distinguishes this from that?

AR: You could put it that way. The distinction between these two is really an issue of perspective. "Existence" is the wider concept, because even at an infant's stage of sensory chaos, he can grasp that something exists. When he gets the concept "identity," it is a further step—a clearer, more specific perspective on the concept "existence." He grasps that if it exists, it is *something*. Therefore, the referents of the concept "identity" are specific concretes or specific existents. And, you see, even though it is the same concept, the

240

whole disaster of philosophy is that philosophers try to separate the two.

"Existence" vs. "Existent"

Prof. B: What is the relationship between the concepts "existence" and "existent"? Is it that the concept "existent" is a term which applies a concept to a particular or designates the particular as a unit under the concept?

AR: That's right. Because the concept "existence," at least the way I use it, is in a certain way close to the concept "universe"—all that which exists.

Prof. B: "Existence" is a collective noun almost.

AR: That's right. An existent is, then, a particular which exists.

"Fact"

Prof. B: What is the difference between the concepts "fact" and "existent," and is "fact" an axiomatic concept?

AR: No. "Fact" is merely an epistemological convenience. The term "fact" can apply to a particular existent, to an aspect, to an attribute, or to an event. An existent is a concrete. "Existent" is a very convenient term in that it subsumes entities and attributes and actions and even mental events. They exist.

Prof. B: Relationships too?

AR: Yes—everything that exists on which you can focus, anything which you can isolate, whether it is an entity, a relationship, an action, or an attribute. The concept "existent" refers to something which exists. And it is wider than the concept "entity," because it permits you to subsume under that concept, and focus on, attributes or relationships or actions—on that which depends on an entity but can be studied separately.

Now, "fact" is merely a way of saying, "This is something which exists in reality"—as distinguished from imagination or misconception or error. So you could say, "That the American Revolution took place is a fact," or, "That George

Washington existed is a fact." In the first case you refer to
an enormously complex series of events over a period of
years. In the second case you refer to just one individual.
Both are facts.

Prof. E: You wouldn't say, for instance, that the American Revolution is or was an existent?

AR: No.

Prof. E: Or a war wouldn't be an existent?

AR: You could treat it as that, but in speaking of it you
wouldn't talk that way. Why? Because "existent" primarily
refers to a metaphysical status [such as entity, attribute,
etc.].

Prof. E: And a war or revolution would be an enormous
complex of entities, relations, and actions.

AR: Of all sorts of existents.

Prof. E: So that when you have that complexity, it is
easier to say "fact."

AR: It is easier, and there is a certain subtle distinction.

Prof. E: The term "existent" more implies a particular
entity or attribute or relation, and "fact" a whole conglomeration of them?

AR: "Fact" can subsume both. It can be a particular
narrow detail, or an entity, or an event, or a series of
events.

Prof. E: Would you say that either of those concepts is
wider than the other, or that they don't differ in their
extension but simply in their perspective?

AR: In the perspective.

Prof. B: Is "fact" a concept like "necessity" in the following respect? The referent of "necessity" is the same in a
sense as the referent of "identity"; but "necessity" is a
concept which comes much later in the hierarchy and derives from our particular form of consciousness [i.e., from
its volitional nature—see "The Metaphysical Versus the Man-
Made," in *Philosophy: Who Needs It*]. It is a concept we
need to distinguish things outside our control from things in
our control.

AR: Correct.

Prof. B: Is "fact" like "necessity" then—in that we need the concept "fact" for two reasons, both deriving from the nature of our form of consciousness? Number one is that our form of consciousness, like any, is limited and, therefore, we get information bit by bit, so to speak, and "fact" designates the bit of information or of reality that we have gotten. Or is it that "fact" is a concept which we need because we are capable of error?

AR: It is the second.

Prof. E: Which would not be true of the concept "existence."

AR: No.

Prof. B: So "fact" then designates existents, but it is used in a context in which it is relevant to distinguish knowledge from error.

AR: That's right.

Prof. B: It's not that the fact refers to the knowledge; it refers to the reality known, or possibly known.

AR: That is correct. It is a concept necessitated by our form of consciousness—that is, by the fact that we are not infallible. An error is possible, or a lie is possible, or imagination is possible. And, therefore, when we say something is a fact, we distinguish primarily from error, lie, or any aberration of consciousness.

And it serves another function: it delimits the concept "existence" or "reality." For instance, you may have noticed I often use in writing the expression "facts of reality." What have I added to the term "reality" by saying "facts"? I have narrowed it. I have said: whichever aspects, events, or existents you happen to know, these are the facts of reality—meaning: these are the things which actually exist. So it is like concretizing a very wide abstraction, such as "reality," but it isn't adding any new content.

Prof. B: That's what I was struggling to name by this "bit-by-bit" idea—that we don't grasp reality like God would, all at once.

AR: Ah, that's correct then. In that sense, yes.

*   *   *

Prof. F: Is every fact complex?

AR: Well, as we discussed, "fact" is a very broad term. You can apply it to a single concept, or to a very complex series of events. That depends on what you designate by "fact." The table's existence as a fact is simple. But that the United States has been in existence almost two hundred years—that's a very complex fact.

Prof. E: I think there's a possible equivocation here on "simple" and "complex." In asking whether a fact is complex or simple you can mean it in the sense of difficult to grasp or easy to grasp; or you could mean it in the sense of divisible into components or indivisible, in which case I don't think the distinction applies to facts. Entities are divisible, but how would you divide a fact?

Prof. B: Into the entity and the attribute.

AR: Is that what you meant?

Prof. F: Yes.

Prof. E: But you wouldn't say a fact is metaphysically divisible or indivisible. Neither concept applies.

AR: No, it wouldn't apply.

Prof. E: Bertrand Russell, in one mood, upheld a division between simple and complex facts. But also there were atomic facts and molecular facts, negative facts, general facts, and so on.

AR: Yes. I reject that sort of thing. Because if by "simple" you mean metaphysically primary, then only entities are metaphysical primaries.

The real issue here is always to define your context. Because if you mean how many concepts are necessary to grasp that the table exists vs. that the table is round, you can see that one requires more conceptualized knowledge than the other. But if you mean to ask, "Is 'fact' a primary?" that's different.

This issue bears all the earmarks of Russell, because observe what the mistake is. He is taking a concept out of any hierarchy; he is not concerned with the hierarchical structure of concepts. In fact that is what he would deny vehemently. I don't think he would even be able to grasp what we meant by "hierarchy." He is the man who claims you can take anything as an axiom and work from there—and the result is most of modern philosophy (except I wouldn't ascribe it to his influence). But that is the institutionalization of all the worst anti-existence errors, of starting without axioms, or denying axioms, or—what amounts to the same thing—making axioms arbitrary.

In asking yourself whether any concept is of a metaphysical primary, you have to ask yourself: to what does that concept refer? And once you observe that the word "fact" is a term which can be applied to a very broad category of phenomena, and actually that it is helpful only in order to subdivide a very wide idea, such as existence or reality, you know it is not a primary. It's a complex, derivative concept.

The Physical World

Prof. K: Some philosophers treat our knowledge that existence exists as equivalent to our knowledge that there is a physical world. They hold that to know that existence exists, and is what it is independently of our perceiving it, is to know that it is different in kind from consciousness—to know that things exist which possess characteristics which no consciousness could possess—for example, spatial extension or weight. Then they claim that the propositions "existence exists" and "there is a physical world" are, if not synonymous, two perspectives on the same fact, such that if the first is an axiom, then so is the second. Is any variant of this position consistent with the Objectivist view of axioms and axiomatic concepts?

AR: The answer is: no, emphatically. Not consistent in any way whatever. Now let me elaborate.

When you say "existence exists," you are not saying that the physical world exists, because the literal meaning of the term "physical world" involves a very sophisticated piece of scientific knowledge at which logically and chronologically you would have to arrive much later.

As to the chronological aspect, the construct that you describe here is totally impossible psychologically. You say that to grasp that something exists is to know that things exist which possess characteristics which no consciousness could possibly possess, such as extension and weight. You are talking about an enormously sophisticated level of knowledge. And you are assuming that first a man grasps that he's conscious, à la Descartes, and *then* he decides, "But there are certain things which have properties which consciousness doesn't have." Nothing could be further from the truth.

The simplest way to begin an answer is to point out that animals, who do perceive reality or existence, have absolutely no concept of their own consciousness. The enormous distinction between man and animals here is self-consciousness. An animal does not have the capacity to isolate critically the fact that there is something and he is conscious of it. How does that apply to man? In this crucial sense: neither does an infant. Why is it metaphysically important? Because there is no such thing as a consciousness per se, apart from that of which it is conscious. And therefore no entity could conceivably be conscious first of the fact that he is conscious and then grasp, "Oh, I'm conscious of *something*."

You see, this is a complete inversion of the meaning of the concepts. You can become aware of the fact that you are conscious only after the fact of performing an act of consciousness. Only *after* you have become conscious of something—and in fact long after—can you identify the fact that it is some function in your mind that is performing this process of awareness. Only at a relatively advanced age—after, say, months or perhaps a full year—can an infant grasp the fact that if he closes his eyes he doesn't see, if he opens them he sees. And that if he closes off his ears, then he doesn't hear. That's the beginning of his grasp of the fact that something operates inside of him that permits the process of awareness. But that is an enormously sophisticated step of self-consciousness. You cannot begin by saying, "I'm conscious" and then ask, "Of what?" It's a contradiction—in effect, a process of concept-stealing.

As to such characteristics as extension and weight, how would you grasp those ahead of grasping the existence of an outside world? Because the implication of your question is that you grasp that it is a *physical* world by means of observing that it has certain properties which your consciousness does not possess. But you could not have any concept of those properties ahead of grasping a physical world, nor could you say, "My consciousness doesn't possess weight or extension," ahead of grasping that there is something outside which does possess them.

But now what's the difference between saying "existence exists" and "the physical world exists"? "Existence exists" does not specify *what* exists. It is a formula which would cover the first sensation of an infant or the most complex knowledge of a scientist. It applies equally to both. It is only the fact of recognizing: there is something. This comes before you grasp that you are performing an act of consciousness. It's only the recognition that something exists. By the time you say that it's a world, and it's a physical world, you need to know much more. Because you can't say "physical world" before you have grasped, self-consciously, the process of awareness and have said, "Well, there are such existents as mental events, like thinking or memories or emotions, which are not physical; they are existents, but of a different kind: they are certain states or processes of my consciousness, my faculty of grasping the existence of that outside world." And the next step is: "What is that outside world made of?"

The concept "matter," which we all take for granted, is an enormously complex scientific concept. And I think it was probably one of the greatest achievements of thinkers ever to arrive at the concept "matter," and to recognize that that is what the physical world outside is composed of, and that's what we mean by the term "physical."

Now observe that a savage doesn't have a concept of

"matter." He believes that reality is like his own consciousness, only it is in the power of supernatural creatures or
gods or demons who manipulate it. What permits this kind
of mysticism? Precisely the absence of the concept "physical
world" or "matter." Now those concepts, in historical development and in the development of an individual consciousness, come very late—by which I mean they are concepts
that require a long development before one can grasp them.
And yet a savage grasps that existence exists. He doesn't
grasp all the implications of it. Nor does he grasp the law of
identity. But that something exists, with which he deals,
even he grasps that. To the extent to which he is able to
hunt or to support his life or pray to his gods, he is admit-
ting implicitly the existence of something.

So you see the axiom "existence exists" embraces all
those stages of knowledge, implicit or explicit. Whereas the
concept "the physical world exists" is a very sophisticated
scientific statement.

Prof. E: I just wanted to give a historical corroboration of
that from early Greek philosophy. In the pre-Socratic period many of the philosophers had great difficulty distinguishing between consciousness and the physical world. Things
like wind and breath were equated with soul and consciousness, as something intangible or invisible. They had no clear
idea of the distinction.

AR: Yes, and they ascribed love and hate or attraction
and repulsion to the elements. It was all a kind of groping
chaos, in a state before they clearly differentiated the two.

The original questioner asked whether "existence exists"
and "there is a physical world" are two perspectives on the
same fact, and whether the second is also an axiom. It's not
two perspectives on the same fact. The fact is the same, but
one is a fundamental axiom applying to any level of your
knowledge, and the second is not a different perspective—
it's a statement which is the result of a long and complex
development of knowledge. The facts are the same in the
sense that when you say "existence exists" you have *implicitly*

stated the proposition of omniscience, because whatever exists—even things of which you have no suspicion at present—is included in that proposition. It exists. But you wouldn't say that therefore once you've said "existence exists" you know everything. No, you've merely grasped the principle which applies to everything, but the rest is up to a long, long development of knowledge. And therefore a proposition about the nature of what exists is not the same thing as the axiom.

Prof. A: Does "existence exists" implicitly include consciousness as part of existence?

AR: Here I was very careful in my formulation in *Atlas Shrugged*: "The *act of grasping* that statement" implies consciousness. Existence exists whether there is any consciousness or not. But since you are making that claim, in the act of grasping it you are introducing the axiom of consciousness.

Prof. A: But it doesn't exclude consciousness. That is, when you say "existence exists," you don't mean: "I am only speaking about external reality and I don't mean consciousness."

AR: No.

Prof. A: Which *is* what you are saying when you say "the external world exists."

AR: Yes. The axiom "existence exists" is wider than the concept of the external world. It includes everything, as I indicated, including your mental states, mental processes, and such phenomena as ideas or feelings, which are not in the same category as physical reality, but they exist.

Prof. E: Would it be fair then to say that there are three stages here at least? The primary philosophic one is existence—

AR: Right.

Prof. E:—which covers everything no matter what. Then at a certain point you make the distinction between the "out there" and the "in here," the external and the conscious.

AR: Right.

Prof. E: And then at a later, much more sophisticated stage, you form the concepts pertaining to the nature of what is out there, such as "matter" and "physical."

AR: That's right. And there is the necessary corollary: you also develop the "how"—the "how" you know it. In order to define what constitutes knowledge of what is out there, you have to develop the science of epistemology.

Prof. B: Isn't there a sense in which Locke, Berkeley, and Hume—less so Locke, but all of them—don't really have a concept of existence as a metaphysical fact?

AR: No, they don't.

Prof. B: Their concepts refer to mental states or to other concepts. That's why they all had the problem: "How do we form the concept of 'existence'?" And they went through incredible contortions trying to work that out.

AR: Yes.

Prof. K: Locke is similar to Descartes in that he considers it a special problem to establish the independent existence of the world. In order to establish that existence exists independently of our consciousness we must show that one element of existence is something that our consciousness could not give to existence.

AR: Yes, that is the way they would approach it, but what it literally amounts to is: in order to validate the existence of an outside world, we have to introduce something mystical, something unknowable, something not of this world and not of our knowledge. Locke and Descartes achieve the exact opposite of their intention. Whereas actually what Descartes, and all of them, should have done is ask themselves the origin of the concept "consciousness" —since they meant something by that concept and they referred to something, their inner mental state. They never considered the fact that there can be no such thing as consciousness if it is not conscious of anything.

They put consciousness first—as if that is the absolute, the given—and then we have to prove the existence of something outside of it. Incidentally, in all such theories of the primacy of consciousness, whenever reality doesn't conform to what their consciousness decides is true, it is reality that then is dismissed. Again, it is the absolute negation of "existence exists" as an axiom.

That is the error of starting in midstream. That was my original "Rand's Razor": that in an ideal Atlantis, every philosopher would be asked to name his axioms before being permitted to utter a proposition. And boy would the field shrink.

Prof. B: Teaching would be easier.

AR: Oh, and how! And you would have better pupils.

"Self"

Prof. K: I'd like to ask a question about something which is intuitively obvious to me, but which I couldn't defend in argument: the statement that to be aware of your own consciousness has, as a corollary, that *you* exist possessing consciousness. How does awareness of states of consciousness have, as a corollary, that there is one faculty, namely your self, which unifies or possesses all these states and processes?

Prof. E: In other words, the question is: why does a series of successive states of consciousness imply an entity, as distinct from just a disintegrated series?

AR: You mean Mr. Hume?

Prof. E: Right.

AR: Read the chapter on axiomatic concepts. You don't need "intuition" here, you need to remember very clearly the fallacy of the "stolen concept." What do you mean by a "series of states of consciousness"? Anyone who offers that argument to you is guilty of the crudest form of concept-stealing. There is no such thing as a state of consciousness without the person experiencing it. What does one mean by "state of consciousness"? A state of a faculty possessed by an entity. Consciousness is not a primary object, it is not an independent existent, it's an attribute of a certain kind of existents.

You cannot project what you mean by a state of consciousness—neither by synonyms nor in any way—without refer- ring to the person or the animal who possesses that consciousness: an entity of whom consciousness is a faculty. It is not possible to project it.

Now why isn't it possible? Because such a thing as a state of consciousness is obviously a derivative concept—derivative qua attribute. It's a primary, as far as the conceptual chain is concerned, but in regard to observation, you have no way of experiencing or observing a state of consciousness without the entity which experiences it. It's a concept that could not enter your mind or your language unless in the form of a faculty of a living entity. That's what that concept means. Therefore to ask, "Well, I know I have states, but how does it prove that I am?"—is a question that's not worth discussing.

Incidentally, I know a lady who once gave the proper answer to that kind of question, the kind of question you have been confronted with, so let me quote her with the appropriate answer. Some young college student said to her, "I don't know whether I exist," which is the same issue. She said, "You'd better find out, because I don't want to be caught talking to myself." And that's about the seriousness this question deserves.

The consciousness of self is implicit in [any grasp] of consciousness.

Prof. D: Is the concept of "self" something abstracted from a content of consciousness?

AR: No. The notion of "self" is an axiomatic concept; it's implicit in the concept of "consciousness"; it can't be separated from it.

Prof. D: In other words, what one really has here is something like Descartes' innate idea.

AR: How?

Prof. D: Well, because implicit in the concept of "consciousness" or "I think" in Descartes is "I." That's implicit there, so that you cannot have the one without the other; and it isn't experiential.

AR: Oh, no, but in Descartes you have consciousness without content. He takes consciousness as a primary, not as depending on being conscious of something. In fact he says it is possible to be conscious of nothing, which is a contradiction in terms. We don't say that the "I" is an innate idea.

Prof. D: I know, but I don't see any difference, though.

AR: The "I" cannot be developed without the content of consciousness, and that content is not innate.

Prof. D: But the content is never the "I" itself. And, in fact, Descartes would say all thinking has objects, except—

AR: Wait a moment, let's start at the beginning. Descartes says that consciousness or the "I" is something innate, apart from any content. In other words, apart from perceiving anything, you have that idea of the "I" or of "I think"; you have those ideas before you think of anything or have anything to think about. That's the difference.

Now what I say is: before your conscious apparatus, the faculty of consciousness, is aware of something, it is not conscious, and certainly there is no "I." But when you become aware, implicit in your first sensation are certain axiomatic concepts. And they are what? That you exist, that the outside world exists, and that you are conscious. The baby could not conceptualize this, but it's implicit; without that implication he couldn't be aware of anything. Therefore it's not an "innate idea," it's a corollary of the fact of consciousness.

Prof. D: So when a consciousness becomes conscious of an object, that object will not be the self; but implicit in the consciousness of the object will be the idea of a self having it.

AR: That's right.

Prof. D: That is no different though, essentially, from Descartes.

AR: It has to be different, because if it were the same how would you go from that to the idea that you have to prove the existence of an outside world? If Descartes claimed that implicit in the first sensation from the outside are certain concepts such as "I" and "consciousness," he would be wedded to the primacy of the exterior world. He would say, "Well if the world doesn't exist, I can't be conscious." That isn't what he said.

Prof. D: The idea of an external world wasn't an innate idea, though, in Descartes.

AR: But are you suggesting in any way that we are here dealing with innate ideas?

Prof. D: Well, it looks that way.

AR: Well yes, if you drop the context.

Prof. E: There's an enormous confusion throughout the Rationalist tradition between two things: a concept which has introspective referents as against an innate idea. And these philosophers constantly go from one to the other.

AR: As interchangeable.

Prof. E: As interchangeable. As though if all you have to do is introspect to discover the referents of a concept, it follows that the idea of those referents is innate. Which is a complete non sequitur.

AR: But you see that's what I mean by the dropping of the context.

Prof. E: Descartes can say that we are aware of the self by the sheer act of being conscious and being implicitly aware of our consciousness; he calls that an innate idea, and proceeds to say that in the same way we have an innate idea of God. Because he switches from defining an "innate" idea as a conceptualized recognition of something in advance of experience to calling an "innate" idea any concept which is formed by a process of thought based upon introspective data.

AR: Exactly.

Prof. E: Let's look at the definition of "implicit." On page 6, it is applied to "existence," but the same thing would be applicable to "consciousness." A concept is implicit when one "grasps the constituents of the concept . . . the data which are later to be integrated by that concept."

Prof. D: But if my self is not one of the constituents of the content of consciousness, then "implicit" must have a different sense here from the sense it has in cases where the contents are present but not put together. Or do you want to say that I am put together out of contents of consciousness?

AR: No, you are the precondition of the concept of

"consciousness." In every state of consciousness that you experience, part of it is the fact of the person who experiences. And in that sense you are implicit in every state of your consciousness.

Prof. E: In other words the only fact of reality that you'd have to get in order subsequently to form the concept "self" or "I" would be your being conscious.

AR: That's right.

Prof. B: Is this correct? When you introspect, it's not that what you observe is a state of consciousness, so that when it comes time to form the concept of "self," there's nothing to form it from. When you introspect, what you experience each time is "me being conscious of something."

AR: Yes.

Prof. B: It's not that you experience consciousness and later on you discover a new component: self.

AR: Exactly.

Prof. B: Every awareness *is*: me experiencing something.

AR: Exactly. You know the best example I could give— perhaps this will help. If you brought a dog or a cat into this room, it would be aware of everything that we see here. It would also see the room, the objects, and the people. What it would never be able to grasp is, "I am conscious of this room," although that fact is inherent in its perception. The difference between its consciousness and a human consciousness is that looking at that room we are able to say, "It takes an act of consciousness to be aware of all this, and it's I, my consciousness, that's performing that act." That is, I am aware of this room, and I can project closing my eyes and my awareness stops—at least visually. Or I can project fainting or sleeping and not being aware at all. But an animal cannot do that. If he falls asleep, then that's one state; when he awakens, it's another. But he wouldn't be capable of identifying conceptually material which is present there in his consciousness: that it is he who is aware and at other times he is not aware.

The whole difference between a human type of consciousness and an animal is exactly this. The ability to be self-conscious and to identify the fact of one's own consciousness, one's "I." And then to apply introspection to the processes of one's own consciousness and check them.

Time

Prof. B: On page 56, you say: "The measurements omitted from axiomatic concepts are all the measurements of all the existents they subsume; what is retained, metaphysically, is only a fundamental fact; what is retained, epistemologically, is only one category of measurement, omitting its particulars: *time* . . ." Could you elaborate on the distinction between retaining metaphysically and retaining epistemologically, and does that distinction apply to other concepts, too?

AR: In a sense. What I mean here by "metaphysically" is: in reality, in existence—that is, focusing on the entities subsumed under that concept. By "epistemologically" here I mean psychologically. In the process of cognition, what type of measurement do you retain when you deal with a concept that includes every existent?

Now, there are some very important things I would like to say about the issue of time. In the very next paragraph I say that these concepts "identify explicitly the omission of psychological time measurements, which is implicit in all other concepts." That is an important point to keep in mind. When you form a concept, it is independent of time. That is, if you form the concept "table," implicit in that mental process is the fact that any time you encounter an entity with certain characteristics you will designate it as a table. Or, every time you see the same table you still designate it by the concept "table." In other words, your concept is independent of any particular moment of perception. Whereas a sensation or a percept is strictly dependent on the immediate moment of awareness. One of the reasons why a concept permits us to enlarge our knowledge to such a phenomenal extent lies precisely in the fact that a concept is independent of any given moment. It is a form of classifying and retaining as a mental unit a certain classification of perceptual concretes, which you then hold at all times.

Now, a non-axiomatic concept, such as "table," implicitly holds only this much: that you will always refer to a given type of object as a table. But axiomatic concepts have a wider function. Time is involved in them epistemologically or psychologically in a more important manner: they have to be held in your consciousness at all times. It isn't only that what you call existence today you will also call existence tomorrow, but also that in all future processes of cognition the axiomatic concepts are directing that process. You cannot form another concept or utter a proposition without regard for your axiomatic concepts, once they have been consciously identified. They function implicitly up to the time of identification. Thereafter, they have to be explicit; they have to be automatized psychologically. And all the disasters that you observe in philosophy are due, in part, precisely to not observing the timelessness of axiomatic concepts; they are used while being negated.

*   *   *

Prof. A: Does the omission of psychological time measurements refer to the fact that concepts are open-ended?

AR: The sense in which it refers to open-endedness isn't the primary issue, it's the consequence. When you form a concept, you implicitly state to yourself that you will subsume under this concept any future object of this kind. That's how the omission of time-measurements relates to open-endedness.

But more importantly, the omission of psychological time-measurements, for both normal concepts and axiomatic concepts, refers to the fact that concepts are independent of the time of your awareness. Whereas percepts are dependent on the specific presence of the object of perception before you, concepts are not dependent on time. When you have formed a concept as a mental unit, its existence doesn't depend on any given moment you are using it or considering it. It may be dormant in your memory while you are dealing with other matters. When you need that particular concept, you can deal with it regardless of what you are perceiving out there in reality; it's not dependent on that.

Prof. A: Is the following correct? A percept is of a particular thing at a particular time; and when you later remember a percept, say your view of Mount Rushmore, that would be a memory of the way Mount Rushmore looked at that particular moment in time.

AR: That's right.

Prof. A: Whereas your concept of "man" is not tied to the first three men that you formed that concept from. Is that part of what is meant by saying that concepts are independent of time?

AR: That also. That's a good addition to what I said. You do not have to recall all the particulars in order to use the concept—it's independent of memory in that way. Actually, there are several forms of independence of time: a concept is independent of recalling any particulars or how you formed it, and it's independent of having the particulars before you. You can sit in your room in total darkness and deal with any concept that you know. You don't need a particular event in reality in order to deal with your concepts. Whereas a percept is strictly dependent on a particular event at a particular moment.

*   *   *

Prof. B: What is the hierarchical order of the concepts "motion," "duration," and "time"? First, is "duration" an axiomatic concept?

AR: No, "duration" is definitely a derivative concept—derived from "time." Because "duration" means the time necessary for a certain event or the time-measurement that is involved in a certain process. So duration is clearly a derivative concept, based on the concept of "time."

Prof. B: I would have thought that duration is what time measures, just like extension is what magnitude measures.

AR: No, you have it in reverse. What would you mean by the concept "duration" if you have no such concept as "time"? You couldn't form the concept "duration" first and then derive from it the concept "time." It would have to be the other way around. You form the concept "time," and then in regard to particular processes or events you form the concept "duration"—for example, how long it takes you to cross the room. But, in order to conceptualize the duration of your walk across the room, you have to have a concept of what it is that you want to measure. And that is: time.

Prof. B: I had approached it this way. It is clear that in some sense time is the measure of motion. But motion has several attributes. For example, we measure the rate of motion, and that is the distance covered in a certain time. So I asked myself: what is it about motion that time measures? And I answered: the duration of motion.

AR: Yes, but that is what you grasp after you realize the relationship of time to motion. The two interrelated concepts are "motion" and "time." Because observe, to grasp "motion" you have to grasp a change. A change of what? Of [spatial] relationships among entities. If you see some stationary objects and one object that is moving, you grasp the fact that it is moving by seeing the changed relationship between it and the other objects, and that gives you the concept of "time." At a given moment, let's say it is to the right of the first stationary object, a few minutes later it is to the left, then it passes the next stationary object. It is the progression of the motion that gives you the concept of "time."

But "duration" is already a delimited concept. You would have to ask yourself, "How long will it take this object to pass, let us say, three stationary objects?"

Prof. B: You relate it to some unit of motion.

AR: Yes. And that is already a complex derivative concept because you are consciously measuring a given process of motion.

Prof. B: Then I have trouble distinguishing what is being measured by time on the one hand and speed or velocity on the other hand. Because what is it about the motion that time is measuring?

AR: "Time," as the widest or parent abstraction of all subsequent and narrower measurements of time, is a change of relationship. You observe that certain relationships are changed, and you form the concept "time." Then you can subdivide it into speed or duration or any other measurements. Speed and duration are really two aspects of the same type of measurement. Continue with the example of an object moving past some stationary objects. To measure the duration, you would have to define the beginning and the end of this process—how long will it take this object to pass three stationary points. And you measure the total of the process. To measure its speed, you have to already have established a unit of time-measurement. Suppose your unit is the second. You would say this object is moving at so many inches per second. You have to have a unit, which would consist of the amount of time taken to cover a certain amount of space. And you use that to measure the speed of a given process.

Prof. E: Do you have to form the concept of "duration" before the concept of velocity?

AR: Oh, yes. The concept that there are units of time, that it can be measured.

Prof. E: Duration is just really units of time, stretches of time?

AR: For the completion of a given defined process. You really here have to have the concept of the beginning and the end of the process.

Three Functions of Axiomatic Concepts

Prof. E: After reading the chapter on axiomatic concepts, I tried to list their main functions. I could distinguish three functions, even though I am aware that all of them are enormously interrelated. I wondered if I had omitted anything that you thought was crucial. The first is the continuity function; the second is objectivity, in the sense of focusing on the distinction between existence and consciousness and on the independence of existence. And the third is the underscoring of primary facts. Is it fair to say that those are three main, highly interrelated functions of axiomatic concepts? Have I left out something?

AR: I have never asked myself that question. But offhand, I think you have included the essentials. Name them again.

Prof. E: Enabling human consciousness to preserve continuity, the idea of the continuity of existence and consciousness—the issue of psychological time-measurements.

AR: Yes.

Prof. E: Second: generating the ability to be objective by emphasizing existence, with identity, as independent of consciousness. And third: the issue of underscoring primary facts, which you mention on page 59.

AR: The reason that I asked you to repeat them is that the last one is the one I would regard as most important. The confining of knowledge to reality, to existence, and delimiting it from non-existence, imagination, falsehood, etc. They are all interrelated, but that I would name first.

I would add one more that is also closely related, so it might be a restatement, but it is an important restatement: epistemological guidance.

Prof. A: I don't fully understand the idea of the continuity function. How exactly do those three axioms preserve the continuity of your life?

AR: Not of your life, but of your cognitive operations and your knowledge. The axioms underscore first that these concepts are what they are at any time, independent of any perceptual or existential experience. If you say "existence exists" or "consciousness is conscious," that would be so at any time, that's immutable. That's point one. And point two is that you have to hold them in mind at all times. And that's why I mentioned their function as epistemological guidelines: during any cognitive process, you check your knowledge against those axioms. And if you come out with something that exists and doesn't exist at the same time, you know that you have made a mistake somewhere.

The Explicit Formulation of Axiomatic Concepts

Prof. B: In Chapter 1 you described the stages of development of the implicit concept of "existent." My question is, in the process of forming axiomatic concepts *explicitly*, are there necessary stages of development?

AR: Similar to the variations of the implicit concept "existent"?

Prof. B: Not necessarily. Just in general.

AR: To reach axiomatic concepts consciously, you have to have a certain amount of knowledge about epistemology. You do not need knowledge of a full, philosophical theory of epistemology, but you have to have the self-consciousness to identify explicitly certain elements in your knowledge which have been implicit up to then. It requires a sufficient amount of knowledge and a very significant degree of introspection. The ability to introspect is necessary to begin to identify the implicit explicitly. And for that there has to be the material of introspection. So you have to have a sufficient knowledge both of the outside world and of the process of your own consciousness before you can begin to identify the widest abstractions.

Prof. E: In the development of the human race philosophically, the three axiomatic concepts were explicitly grasped for the first time at definitely different periods of history and in a definite order: "existence" by Parmenides, "identity" by Aristotle, and "consciousness," as far as I know, not until Augustine.

AR: Why would you say not until Augustine?

Prof. E: I don't think there was any actual concept of "consciousness" in Greek philosophy.

AR: But what of Aristotle's psychology, with the concept of "soul" as consciousness?

Prof. E: Yes, but "soul" as he used it is more of a biological concept than a mental one.

Prof. B: Aristotle has "thinking," he has "feeling," he has "imagining," but he doesn't seem to have "consciousness" as an integration of those. The next level of abstraction for him is "soul," which applies to all living things qua living.

AR: You mean Augustine was the first to isolate "consciousness" as a concept in the Cartesian sense?

Prof. E: Yes. "Si fallor, sum."

AR: Oh, that's interesting.

Prof. E: The human race developed the three axioms in the right order.

Prof. B: Good for us!

AR: It's a very interesting observation from another aspect, too. You know it's been said many times that the human race follows in a general way the stages of development of an individual. And this would be an instance of that. But I shudder to think of the time elements involved, if it takes that long. It's an interesting observation, however.

Entities and Their Makeup

What Is an Entity?

Prof. K: I would like to ask you to clarify your use of the term "entity." Specifically, on page 15, in speaking of perceptual entities, you state, "entities are the only primary existents." Now, does this imply that you grant that there is a metaphysical status of entity apart from whether or not something is a perceptual entity?

For example, is it in principle possible for a perceptual entity to be composed of constituents which are metaphysically themselves also entities, such as a brick wall with the individual bricks also retaining their status as entities?

AR: Certainly. What about human beings? Heads, arms, and legs can be cut off and they are entities. But I was speaking here in the context of entity as against attribute or action. Actually, I was speaking here in the Aristotelian sense of the primary "substance"—which is a very misleading term, but what he meant was that the primary existent is an entity. And then aspects of an entity can be identified mentally, but only in relation to the entity. There are no attributes without entities, there are no actions without entities.

An entity is that which you perceive and which can exist by itself. Characteristics, qualities, attributes, actions, relationships do not exist by themselves.

But, now, if you ask me what is the relationship of parts

of an entity to the entity: metaphysically they exist, so that if you, for instance, cut off the legs of this table, the top will exist by itself and the legs will exist by themselves.

Now, epistemologically, you could regard the top and the legs as attributes of the table in the sense that, if you cut them off, what remains is no longer a table. But that would be only an epistemological method of regarding a part of an entity [as if the part were an attribute]. Metaphysically, the separated parts will continue to exist, only they will no longer be in the form of a table.

You know, there is a great validity in looking at it that way, epistemologically, provided you always remember the metaphysical difference [between parts and attributes]. Length cannot exist without something which is long; an action cannot exist without something that acts. But parts of an entity can exist separately; but if they are separated, the entity is no longer the same kind of entity.

For instance, if you remove the picture tube from a television set, you will have a tube on one side and a box on the other. They still exist. But if you regard a television set as an entity, then if you remove that which makes it a television set—the works—what remains is no longer a television set, even though the parts exist separately. Or, if you cut a man's head off, what you have is a corpse; you have parts of a man but it is no longer a man. In that sense, you could regard parts as an attribute of a given entity—as that without which it would no longer be the same kind of entity. But, metaphysically, you must always remember that the parts can exist separately, whereas attributes and actions cannot exist apart from the entity.

Included in the very concept of attributes is the fact that they are parts which you can separate only mentally, but which cannot exist by themselves. That is the difference between "part" and "attribute."

Prof. K: If we separate the organs of the body from the body, not only will the body change but the separated organ will change, decompose, and so forth. But that will not happen to the brick taken out of a brick wall. Can philosophy specify this difference as a criterion for deciding whether or not something could be validly viewed as a part, in addition to being viewed as an attribute?

AR: But you are mixing terms here. The fact that human organs deteriorate but a brick does not has no relation to the issue at all. That is not a philosophical issue, it is an issue of the fact that living organisms deteriorate—well, so do bricks, but it takes them longer. That does not pertain to the question you are asking. It isn't by means of observing what happens to separated parts that you decide whether something is a part or an attribute. If it can be separated for a split second it is a part, it is not an attribute. An attribute is that which cannot be physically separated. Now, what is an entity? It is a sum of characteristics. There is no such thing as an entity without its characteristics, and, for that very reason, there is no such thing as a characteristic without an entity.

Prof. A: I don't want to seize on a formulation which you may not have meant to be taken literally, but you said that an entity is the sum of its characteristics or attributes.

AR: Don't take "sum" literally, no. Not in the sense that you would say "sum of its parts." Usually when I write I say the entity *is* its attributes. To be exact, you'd have to treat them as inseparable.

Prof. A: That follows from "existence is identity"—in other words, there can't be a "substratum" that has no identity with the attributes just inhering in that.

AR: Exactly. You mean the Lockean idea?

Prof. A: Yes, where each attribute—

AR:—is hung on an ineffable substratum. No—the attributes *are* the entity, or an entity *is* its attributes. The attributes are really separable only by abstraction.

When you form concepts of attributes, all you have done, if you are precise about it, is to have mentally stated, "By 'length' I mean a certain aspect of an existing entity, by 'color' I mean a certain aspect of an existing entity"— parenthesis: "which cannot, in fact, be separated from the entity." That is implicit in forming the concept. Therefore, once you say that anything, anything whatever on any level, can be separated from an entity and can exist, it doesn't matter whether it deteriorates in two days or two centuries. If it can exist by itself, it is a part and not an attribute.

Prof. E: I think he is attempting to show that a living thing has a kind of unity that no mechanical juxtaposition of parts could possess, and that therefore there is a metaphysical basis for distinguishing a living whole from any other type of wholes.

AR: Oh, but that is almost self-evident, isn't it? That is implicit in the distinction between inanimate objects and living entities.

Prof. E: Well, he is trying to characterize that distinction by saying that, in the case of inanimate things, you could explain the behavior of the totality exclusively on the basis of the characteristics of the parts, without taking into account the additional fact that they are combined into a whole. Whereas, in the case of living things, you can explain it only by virtue of their combination into a whole; therefore, living things have a kind of unity that the inanimate doesn't.

AR: But you can establish that by other means. In other words, you don't have to go into the issue of relationship of parts to whole, in order to prove something which is apparent by means of other observations. The fact that parts of a living entity will deteriorate without the whole isn't philosophically explicable by a different kind of philosophical category. It is explicable by the nature of what is a living entity as against an inanimate object. And the two concepts have to be established empirically. You have to first observe the difference, then establish what are the essential characteristics of a living entity as against an inanimate object. After you have established the essentials of what is a living organism, as a consequence of that you will be able to explain why the parts of a living entity, if cut off, deteriorate. But if you try to base it all on just that observation about the parts, I'm afraid you would have a Rube Gold-

berg set-up—trying to prove something [philosophically] which
can be demonstrated as a consequence by a different method.

                    *   *   *

AR: A part of an entity is something that can be separated.
Prof. E: And then becomes an entity, when it's separated.
AR: Yes.
Prof. B: Is a pile of dirt an entity? Or a mountain?
AR: A mountain would be an entity.
Prof. B: But it's just a heap or pile of sand.
AR: It's not a pile of sand, no. It's minerals, metals, and
whatever else a mountain is composed of, which are welded
together in a certain form. You know how I would draw the
distinction here? We call an entity that which is welded
together physically and about which we can learn something, to which we can ascribe certain properties, as a whole.

But now as to a pile of dirt, we can only call it a "pile" for
convenience of identification, because there is nothing we
can learn about the pile as a whole, nor does it have any
particular attributes qua pile. It's only separate entities put
together with no consequent change in their status or in
their aggregate potentialities.

Prof. E: Suppose you took that pile of dirt and poured
glue into it so that it became all welded together, and then it
could roll back and forth, you would still not learn anything
about the total that you couldn't tell about the constituents,
but it would be welded together.

AR: It would be an entity then.

Prof. E: Well, what would you learn about the total qua
total?

AR: Only the things which it would do then—that it could
roll but the pile of dirt couldn't (if you tried to make the pile
move, it would spread across the floor).

Prof. E: You're not bothered at all about the fact that the
mountain is not spatially separable from the earth? You
don't regard spatial separability as intrinsic to an entity?

AR: What do you mean by spatial separability?

Prof. E: The mountain is stuck to the earth.

Prof. B: So is a tree.

Prof. E: Yeah, but you could uproot a tree.

Prof. B: You could uproot a mountain, if you were strong enough.

Prof. E: That's true, I never thought of that.

Prof. B: But on the other hand, if you look at the earth's surface, it is continuous—the surface goes across, and up, and down.

AR: And that which goes up is what you define as a mountain.

Prof. B: But the mountain is welded to the crust of the earth—it's just a kind of protuberance of the crust of the earth.

Prof. E: The mountain is an entity and the earth, with the mountain, is an entity—and that's not a contradiction.

AR: Oh, of course not. It's the same issue as inbuilt furniture in a room, like a desk which is built into the room, it doesn't become entity-less by being attached to the wall; it's still a separate entity, only it's attached to the wall.

Prof. F: So is a built-in closet an entity?

AR: Yes, certainly. Because you distinguish it from the room; it's not the room.

But let me give you the arch-example of this type of consideration. What about a square inch of ground? Is that an entity or not? You can, from an epistemological viewpoint, regard any part of an entity as a separate entity in that context. And a square inch of ground would be just that. The entity would be the whole ground; you delimit it and examine one square inch of it. In the context of your examination, it's a specific entity, that particular inch, even though metaphysically, in reality, it's part of many, many other inches like it.

The concept of "entity" is an issue of the context in which you define your terms. So that an entity has to be a material object, but what you regard as an entity in any given statement or inquiry depends on your definitions. You can regard part of an entity as a separate entity. And in that sense all the vital organs are entities, and you have a separate science for the brain or the heart or the stomach. And in the context of that science, you study them as separate entities, never dropping the context that they are vital organs of a total entity which is a human being.

Prof. E: Is it intrinsic to the concept of "entity," in any context, that it be capable of some form of action?

AR: No, not necessarily. Except that everything existing is capable of some form of action.

Prof. F: Would there be any context in which an individual human being would not be an entity?

AR: Almost any of them today.

[Laughter]

Prof. E: That's an equivocation.

AR: I know, that wasn't a serious comment.

Prof. F: You certainly can't subsume an individual into society in the same way that you can subsume the liver into an individual.

AR: Oh, no. That's a very important point.

Prof. F: So there seems to be no context wherein you can say an individual human being is not an entity. Well then, that's an exception to the generalization you made.

Prof. B: No, it wasn't said that everything can be viewed in some context as not an entity. It was the other way around: every part of an entity can in some context be viewed as an entity.

Prof. F: I thought that what Miss Rand said was that whether you view a thing as an entity or not depends on the context in which you are viewing it.

AR: Oh, no. You can view a part of an entity as an entity without dropping the context: you will have to include the context that it is part of an entity, such as the human vital organs. Or: if you cut off an arm, what is it? Well, it's a human arm, but now it will not function as a living part of a living being. Still, it is an entity of a certain kind: a dying part of a human being. In the same way you can look at an inch of ground and consider it an entity, but that doesn't mean that you can then drop the context and say, "This inch is hanging alone in a vacuum, it's not part of a plain." You can narrow or widen your view, but you can never drop the identity—the basic definition—of the entity which you are considering.

Similarly, there is a way in which you can in fact not consider man as an entity—speaking metaphorically: if you discuss a society.

Prof. E: Not an entity!

AR: Now wait. For the purposes of your discussion, if you are drawing certain conclusions about socio-political laws, and you say, "A society organized as a dictatorship will always have such and such consequences." Now, you are not here discussing particular men; you are discussing a collective whole. You are considering it as an entity, but you must always remember the definition of your entity—which is: a number of individual human entities living in the same geographical locality under the same laws, etc.

Prof. E: But how does it differ from the heap of dirt, in that it is not welded together?

AR: But it is welded together when you are talking about a society. It is welded together by certain laws and by geographical location. You can consider it that way, but that doesn't mean you then consider human beings as dispensable cells of it, which is precisely the mistake all the collectivists make. You can discuss society as an entity, never forgetting that what you mean by "society" is a large number of human entities.

Human beings in a society are tied together by, let's say, political laws and by common geographical location. In discussing society, you are discussing a collection of entities tied together by certain kinds of laws. And then you can determine what kind of organization is proper in regard to this entity and what kind is improper.

Prof. E: Just to nail this down: I would always have said against Plato or Hegel, for instance, that society is not an entity, it's a collection of entities. What would you say?

AR: You distinguish the epistemological aspect from the metaphysical in this sense: you are saying, "I am considering this inch of ground or I am studying this human organ, but I know that metaphysically it's part of a wider space of ground or of a living human being." In the same way, you are permitted to regard as an entity, for purposes of study, a collection of human beings such as a society, but you are not permitted then to say that metaphysically it is an organism, tied together by some ineffable means. You cannot say it is anything other than a group of a certain kind of entities, living beings, and you regard them as one entity only from a certain aspect—that they live in the same geographical locality under the same type of government and laws.

So you can discuss the society, but it doesn't mean that while you are discussing it you are dropping its definition and regarding man as a non-entity.

Prof. E: But then I don't see why you couldn't take any disparate collection of entities and in some context regard it as an entity.

AR: They would have to have something in common or be tied together in some way.

Prof. E: What if the tie is only physical location?

AR: That wouldn't produce anything new.

Prof. F: So it would not be correct to pick out as your entity "all the people now walking on Thirty-fourth Street."

AR: No.

Prof. B: Unless they made a mob.

AR: Right.

Prof. E: Or, "all the things in my pocket"—that wouldn't be an entity.

AR: No, but if you glued them together, they would be.

Prof. B: Does that mean that some entities are prior to other entities, or have priority in being called entities? In other words, you can't identify a society as an entity until you have identified the individuals as entities, and the same with parts of the body.

AR: That's right. But the priority here, metaphysically, would be determined according to which is essential. In other words, you would apply the law of fundamentality. Now, epistemologically, the priority is: which do you have to know before you go to the next one? It's the hierarchical structure of concepts. You can't talk about "society" before grasping what man is. And you can't separate an inch of ground without grasping that there's a wider stretch from which you isolate a certain area. Therefore here the priority is both cognitive and metaphysical.

Prof. B: On the metaphysical priority, isn't there a basic classification of things as entities which comes before all these special cases, rather than seeing them all as equal?

AR: Right, they're not all equal metaphysically. A valley, for instance, or society—those epistemologically can be regarded as entities. But a mountain is a primary entity; the valley is not, it's a dependent—it's actually an indentation between two mountains if you regard them together. But then what is the primary entity? Recall what we said about the pile of dirt vs. the mountain: it has to be a unit of some kind, tied or welded or integrated together, which has certain properties, and with actions being possible to it as a whole. Such as, you can climb a mountain, but you can't do anything with the pile of dirt, unless you glue it together.

Prof. B: I would be completely satisfied on this if you could clarify one more thing for me, which is: why call the universe an entity, rather than simply a collection, since it doesn't act as a whole?

AR: Well, you can't really call it an entity in that sense. I don't think the term applies. The universe is really the sum of everything that exists. It isn't an entity in the sense in which you call a table, a chair, or a man an entity.

Actually, do you know what we can ascribe to the universe as such, apart from scientific discovery? Only those fundamentals that we can grasp about existence. Not in the sense of switching contexts and ascribing particular characteristics to the universe, but we can say: since everything possesses identity, the universe possesses identity. Since everything is finite, the universe is finite. But we can't ascribe space or time or a lot of other things to the universe as a whole.

Prof. E: The whole trick in talking about wholes is to remember that they are wholes.

AR: The whole trick in talking about anything is to remember what it is you are talking about, and where your definitions came from, and are they correct. You always look back at reality—what do we mean by a given concept, or how did we get it?

"Entity" vs. "Attribute," "Action," Etc.

Prof. E: In any process of concept-formation, you have to differentiate certain concretes from the field around you. You and I discussed this once in regard to forming the concept of "existence," but how does differentiation apply to forming the concept of these metaphysical categories: entity, attribute, action, and relation? What would you differentiate entity from? Would it be that you differentiate entity from attribute, or attribute from action, in order, as an adult, to form such concepts? Do you differentiate one such category from another?

AR: Yes, except in one respect. To be exact, you would have to say you learn to differentiate those concepts by differentiating them from the concept "entity." Because "entity" has to be the basic concept. And then, as you observe that entities move or change or they have certain characteristics, you isolate those attributes or actions from the concept "entity." So that the concept "entity" serves as the context. But it is basic.

Prof. B: In connection with this, would there be any CCD behind attribute, action, relation?

AR: Well yes, in regard to everything based on or derived from the concept "entity," the CCD is that they all pertain to entities.

Prof. B: But there would be no CCD for the whole group of them, including entity. This is Aristotle's point about the different categories: there would be no CCD of "being" which is behind entity, attribute, action, etc.

AR: No.

Prof. E: There is nothing in common between existence and nonexistence on the basis of which you would differentiate existence from nonexistence.

AR: No.

Prof. G: May I ask, what was that earlier discussion about existence that you referred to?

Prof. E: I had asked the question, "What do you distinguish existence from, since there is nothing else?" And Miss Rand said, "Look at something. Now close your eyes. That is what you are distinguishing it from." And that made it perfectly clear. It doesn't imply, of course, that there is a metaphysical zero which comes into existence when you close your eyes.

Prof. L: Previously you said that the CCD in forming basic categories, such as "attribute" or "action," would be: entity. But a CCD is always a characteristic. So I have a problem in seeing how "entity" could be a CCD in conceptualizing the basic categories, like "attribute."

AR: No, remember that the question asked was how do we form concepts of actions or attributes at all. And I said that we arrive at them from the concept "entity." But to say that "entity" is the CCD in forming "action" or "attribute" does not mean that you differentiate between actions and attributes on the basis of the fact that they pertain to an entity. Because those two as such are incommensurable. But the common element which permits you to interrelate them [once each has been conceptualized] is the fact that they pertain to an entity.

The concept of "attribute" is a concept which you can arrive at after you have identified individual attributes. Such as, for instance, by observing different objects you will arrive at the concept "length." Then by weighing them you arrive at the concept "weight." Then the concept "attribute" will be formed out of these various individual concepts, such as the weight of an object, the length of an object, the color, etc.

Prof. E: Suppose you have conceptualized a whole bunch of individual attributes, and you now want to rise to the level of conceptualizing "attribute" as such, "action" as such, etc. In conceptualizing "attribute," don't you have to differentiate attribute from something, for instance from "action" or from "entity"? And to differentiate the one group from another, there has to be some commensurable characteristic uniting them. The question then is: what is the commensurable characteristic uniting attributes as such with actions as such? Must there be something commensurable in common between attributes and actions in order to follow the rule of the CCD?

AR: No, because you do not form the concepts "attribute" and "action" by considering them one against the other and differentiating attributes from actions. You don't form those concepts that way.

If the question is: "What is the CCD for the concept 'attribute'?" the answer is: "entity." An attribute is something which is not the entity itself. No one attribute constitutes the whole entity, but all of them together are the entity—not "possessed by" but "are" the entity.

Prof. E: Then is this correct? If you separate blue from green, those are two distinguishable things existentially, metaphysically. And therefore the issue of there being a common characteristic which is reducible to a unit of measurement is involved. But when you "separate" or "distinguish" attribute from entity, those do not have the relationship of green and blue because the entity *is* its attributes.

AR: That's correct.

Prof. E: So the concept "attribute" still names, existentially, the same fact—namely, entity, but just from a different perspective. And therefore it's a mistake to think there are two different things—the attribute and the entity—and then ask, "What's the common denominator uniting them?" That's the significance of your remark: an entity is its attributes.

AR: That's right.

Prof. B: So you are forming the concept "attribute" by distinguishing it from entity, not by distinguishing it from action, relationship, etc.?

AR: That's right. By distinguishing it as one aspect or characteristic of an entity, an indivisible aspect or characteristic which cannot be factually, metaphysically, separated and cannot exist by itself.

"Material"

Prof. B: In the theory of concept-formation, you want to identify how the various types of concepts are formed, and it becomes valuable to distinguish the different aspects of reality—entities, attributes, etc. I think that is one of the functions of any table of categories, such as the one Aristotle gave. Now, would you include materials in, as it were, a table of categories the way you include attributes, actions, and relationships?

AR: No, I only included materials as an example here [page 16] because the process by which you form concepts of materials is somewhat different from the process of forming other concepts—it's the same in principle but the actual details are somewhat different. And since I was in fact once asked how you form concepts of materials, I thought it would be valuable to include it here. But "materials" is not a separate metaphysical category, because materials cannot exist except in the form of entities of some kind, nor can entities exist without materials. That is, physical entities.

Prof. B: But in what way is that different from the relation of attributes and entities? Or relations and entities?

AR: "Materials" is an abstraction we use to denote what all physical entities have in common. The things which we call physical entities are all made of some kind of material. But you can't consider one without the other.

Prof. E: Would it be correct to say that "material" is a classification of attributes of entities?

Prof. B: Entities qua possessing certain attributes.

AR: In a way, yes.

Prof. E: And from that point of view, it's a cross-classification to have both "attribute" and "material" as categories.

AR: That's right. You could say that, yes.

Attributes as Metaphysical

Prof. A: In regard to the concept of an attribute—for example, "length"—since the attribute is something which does not exist separate in reality, is the referent of the concept of an attribute in the category of the epistemological rather than the metaphysical?

AR: Oh no, why?

Prof. A: Because length doesn't exist per se in reality. Length is a human form of breaking up the identities of things.

AR: Wait a moment, that's a very, very dangerous statement. Length does exist in reality, only it doesn't exist by itself. It is not separable from an entity, but it certainly exists in reality. If it didn't, what would we be doing with our concepts of attributes? They would be pure fantasy then. The only thing that is epistemological and not metaphysical in the concept of "length" is the act of mental separation, of considering this attribute separately as if it were a separate thing.

How would you project a physical object which had no length? You couldn't. And therefore if to say it is epistemological rather than metaphysical is to say it exists only in relation to your grasp of it, or it requires your grasp of it in order to acquire existence—it doesn't. Surely, if anything is metaphysical, attributes are.

Prof. A: If I ask you, then, what is the referent of "length," would you say "long objects"?

AR: Not the objects, the attribute of length in all the objects which possess that attribute.

Prof. A: Isn't the referent something separated?

AR: It's mentally separated, but it is there in those objects. It doesn't have to be an entity to be a referent.

Prof. A: I don't understand then why the referent of the concept "red," say, isn't all the red concretes.

AR: How about the other attributes of all those red concretes? Is the referent of "red" the length and weight of all the red concretes?

Prof. A: No.

AR: Well then, obviously the concrete itself isn't the referent of the concept, but a particular aspect of that concrete, an inseparable aspect.

Prof. B: You said that the referent must be separated, or something like that. There's no reason why the referent of the concept should be separable from the object.

Prof. A: But in the case of attributes, the referent is not the entity but only an aspect of the entity. And an aspect cannot exist except as an aspect of the whole entity.

Prof. B: Can you follow that one step further? You say that the referent of "length" must be an aspect, and an aspect cannot exist separately—what is the next step?

Prof. A: The referent is the aspect separated. Is that the wrong premise?

Prof. B: The referent is the aspect, not the aspect separated.

AR: Exactly.

Prof. B: Otherwise you switch metaphysics and epistemology.

AR: That's right. The aspect, not the separation. That's very well put.

The Primary-Secondary Quality Dichotomy as Fallacious

Prof. C: I have a question about the primary-secondary quality distinction. A quality like bitterness is not an attribute of an object, but it is caused by an attribute. At least I would be tempted to say that.

AR: I would not accept the distinction of primary and secondary qualities, because it leads you into enormous pitfalls. It is not a valid distinction.

We perceive light vibrations as color. Therefore you would say the color is not in the object. The object absorbs certain parts of the spectrum and reflects the others, and we perceive that fact of reality by means of the structure of the eye. But then ask yourself: don't we perceive all attributes by our means of perception—including length? Everything we perceive is the result of our processing, which is not arbitrary or subjective.

The primary-secondary quality distinction is a long philosophical tradition which I deny totally. Because there isn't a single aspect, including length or spatial extension, which is perceived by us without means of perception. Everything we perceive is perceived by some means.

Prof. C: Would you put taste and smell in the identical category with length?

AR: All of them. Because they would be different forms of the way your particular sensory apparatus works in order to grasp something. Consider taste. It relates to the way your particular nerve ends react to certain chemicals or certain components of the things which you eat. Tastes as such do not exist apart from your sensory apparatus. But that which arouses a certain sensation of taste in you, does it exist or not?

Prof. C: Yes, of course. But I would not claim that the object has the particular taste. I would say that the taste is an effect of the object.

AR: Certain elements in the object, when they strike your taste apparatus, your nerve endings, produce a certain sensation. Now take length. How do you become aware of length, which is usually taken as a primary quality? Are your eyes involved?

Prof. C: Yes.

AR: What else? You perceive the attribute by means of your eyes, but you can also perceive it by means of touch. And both these enter your mind as certain sensations conveyed by certain kinds of nerves and nerve endings in response to certain stimuli. Therefore, if you say that taste is a "secondary quality" but length is a "primary" one, you are open to the same criticism. The primary-secondary distinction in fact starts from the idea that that which we perceive by some specific means is somehow not objective.

Now you can properly distinguish that which is in the object from the form in which you perceive that quality. But that isn't the same thing as saying color is a secondary quality but extension is a primary quality. That isn't the same issue at all. Color is a form of perception—something caused by one existing phenomenon, namely wavelength, acting on another phenomenon, namely, the retina of our eye. That does not make color a "secondary quality," as if one could say color isn't in the object but extension is.

You see, it's the classification of the attributes of reality according to how and by what means we perceive them that is wrong in that whole classification. The same argument can be made against any sensation, anything that you perceive by means of your senses.

Prof. E: Berkeley did exactly that and came to the conclusion that everything is subjective.

Prof. G: Is your position then that all qualities of objects are on an equal footing in this respect?

AR: Not necessarily exactly the same, because for instance, as far as is known (and remember now this is a scientific question, not a philosophical one)—as far as is known, the process by which you establish texture or hardness is simpler than the process by which you perceive visually. So you would have to have some dreadful disaster occur over your whole skin to lose the sensation of touch altogether (in fact I don't know whether that's even possible), whereas you can lose the capacity of sight simply by having your eyes damaged. A more complex and a more delicate mechanism is involved in vision or hearing than in touch. But that's all we can say scientifically.

Philosophically, the issue is reduced to the question: do we make a distinction *metaphysically*, in regard to the object, on the basis of our form of perception? So that in the perception of sight we can identify a particular sensation, color, whereas in the sensation of touch, we identify roughness or smoothness, let us say, which is closer to the actual quality in the object: a given surface is smooth, and an uneven surface will give you a sensation of roughness. So that it seems—and I stress: it seems as far as we know—that the process there is simpler. But you could claim that the object as such is neither rough nor smooth, because those terms refer to your sensation, just as "color" refers to your sensation and not to the actual object. A rough object is merely of an uneven surface. But the difference [between sensory qualities] is only one of the comparative simplicity and directness by which you perceive one kind of sensory data vs. another.

Properties, Actions, and Causality

Prof. F: This question has to do with the concept of "property" and its significance for causality. In Galt's speech, you say every action is caused by the nature of the acting entity. Now, by "the nature of an entity" do you mean the physical properties of an entity—properties like combustible, fragile, corrosive, and so on?

AR: Yes. And also the psychological properties of a consciousness, including free will.

Prof. E: And also the constitutive properties, because the question here specifies exclusively examples of potentialities to act in a certain way. There are also the properties that constitute the entity—size, weight, material, etc.

Prof. F: Yes, I agree with you, but I am trying to phrase it in terms of dispositional properties so I can get clearly the distinction between these kinds of properties. So I am going to go on now as if I don't presuppose that particular distinction. My reason for going on is to get it completely clear in my mind.

AR: What are you calling "dispositional properties"?

Prof. F: When you say, "That glass is fragile," you mean only that if you drop it, say on concrete, it will break; you don't mean it is breaking now at this moment. To say that an entity is combustible at two hundred degrees Fahrenheit does not mean that it is now actually burning. To say that it is corrosive does not mean that it is now actually corroding anything. And so on.

Indeed, most physical-property concepts are concepts of actions which are not actually occurring. They need "counterfactual" conditions for their definitions. I have to say, "If I drop the glass, it will break," but actually I haven't dropped it, so we call that "counterfactual" because as a matter of fact the condition is not fulfilled.

If the physical nature of glass is defined primarily in terms of such properties as fragility, and if the identity of glass is its physical nature, it follows that the identity of glass is determined primarily in terms of its non-actualized relations to other entities. There are two problems here. First of all the relations are not actualized and secondly there is a reference to other entities in every definition of the identity of a thing.

Prof. E: So it leads to the doctrine of "internal relations."

Prof. F: It impinges on internal relations.

AR: You are making an artificial dichotomy. Why divide properties into two categories, first of all?

To straighten out the question, you would have to begin by asking yourself, "How do I determine what is the nature of an entity?" Before you can divide properties of an entity into subcategories, you have to first determine what is a property. Then you can subdivide them. But you cannot say, "I will deliberately take one group of properties and see what it will lead to logically if we consider exclusively those properties." I question the start. Why do we take exclusively those properties? If we do, we have already admitted that we are not looking at the whole picture. Then we have, in effect, edited reality, so that we are trying to define what an entity is on a partial, selective basis.

Where would you properly start here? Not with fragility, because you would have to ask yourself what literally and in reality you mean by this glass being fragile. We say it has the property of fragility. What does that actually mean? You said it means that if you drop it on concrete, it will break. But that isn't what the property consists of. If you drop a metal object on concrete, it won't break. Why? What is it that you know or determine about the glass as it is now, before you break it?

Prof. F: It has a certain structure.

AR: Yes, it has a certain molecular, chemical, or other structure which makes it a certain type of material object. That type will produce certain effects if it acts or is acted upon. So that if you drop it, it will fall to the floor and break. It will not float away. If you drop a feather, because of its constituent chemical, material structure, it will float; where it will land will depend on the nature of the air currents, etc. But when you ascribe particular action-potentials to an entity, you do so on the premise that these actions will result because the entity, materially, physically, chemically, is of a certain kind.

Prof. E: Isn't that another way of saying the following? The so-called "dispositional property" is already a mistaken concept because all there is in actual reality is constituent properties and their effects when the entity acts. The so-called "dispositional property" is simply a package-deal term to cover a certain structure and its consequent potentialities for action.

AR: Exactly.

Prof. E: It simply presupposes and summarizes a causal relationship. Therefore it would be entirely mistaken to say that an entity comprises its constituent properties *and* its dispositional properties.

AR: Exactly.

Prof. E: Because to make that distinction will leave the constituent properties of a thing divorced from its potentialities for action and its potentialities for action divorced from its characteristics.

All there is is the constituent properties and the capacities for action. Some combination of those is occasionally given a name in the language, but there's not a separate property.

Prof. F: Could you give me an example of a constituent property?

Prof. E: Physical structure.

AR: The arrangement of molecules.

Prof. B: The glass is silicon dioxide, etc.

Prof. F: But where you have certain physical laws about the way those molecules will interact, those physical laws themselves are stated in terms of dispositional properties. Namely, if an atom of such and such atomic structure approaches an atom of such and such other atomic structure, the following will happen.

AR: Observe: you have already said, "An atom *of a*

certain structure, another atom *of a different structure.*" Now those are not "dispositional."

Prof. B: I think the point he is after is the following. We explain actions on the molecular level by reference to different kinds of atoms. And when we classify different kinds of atoms, it turns out that they have different electric charges. But that charge is simply a potential for action. Eventually you reach the ultimate stuff, which you can identify only as the kind of thing which acts in this kind of way.

AR: But the mistake is right here. If you go to the subatomic level, you'd have to state, "which we at present can identify only in terms of its action because that's the only way we can observe it." But if we said, "Therefore it's pure action without entities," that would be the worst mistake possible.

Prof. E: So in other words, the whole idea of dispositional versus non-dispositional properties is simply wrong.

AR: It's totally wrong. Professor F is entirely right to bring it up in connection with my statement on causality from Galt's speech. Because actions are caused by entities, and therefore if you divide properties into dispositional properties vs. other properties, you've already denied the law of causality.

Prof. F: But if you talk about the glass merely in terms of the macroscopic level, then don't you need some concept of "dispositions"?

AR: In what way? How?

Prof. F: Because the glass is not acting now, it's not breaking into pieces.

Prof. E: Well, what's wrong with the Aristotelian concept of "potentiality"? An entity has the capacity to act because of its nature.

Prof. F: Well, the reason I was bringing this up was because I thought that you rejected the concept of "potentiality."

AR: No. What made you think that? I have referred to actual and potential in any number of ways in any number of articles. Even if I didn't write on this subject directly, what would make you think that we reject the Aristotelian view on this?

Prof. F: All I can say is that I have memory or a misremembrance of someone saying that Objectivism does not accept the Aristotelian concept of "potentiality."

AR: Specifically, that wasn't me. Unless it was in some context of what Aristotle makes of it, as in regard to his form-matter dichotomy.

Prof. E: Or if "potentiality" becomes the bare possibility of being something—as in his views on ultimate "prime matter." Most of Aristotle's usage of the concept of "potentiality," so far as I understand, is quite rational.

Prof. F: He defines "motion" entirely in terms of potentiality, as the passage from potentiality to actuality. Would you agree with him there?

AR: No. But that's not disagreeing with the concept of potentiality, but only with its application to this particular instance.

Prof. B: Would you say that what they call a "dispositional property"—fragility, combustibility, etc.—is simply naming what an entity with certain properties can do?

AR: Under certain conditions, under the action of another entity.

Prof. F: But most physicists deal in what they call "dispositional properties."

Prof. B: That's just bad epistemology.

AR: That's modern epistemology.

Prof. B: They don't want to get involved with the "why," only the "how."

Prof. E: Not even with the "what."

Prof. B: Yes, exactly.

Prof. F: But now, properties are all constitutive properties, right?

AR: Yes.

Prof. F: In Galt's speech you say, "A thing cannot act in contradiction to its nature." But that does not mean, of course, that every action which is possible to the entity is now being realized.

AR: Oh, no. I only mean that it cannot take an action which is not possible to it by its constituent nature. For instance, if you dropped that glass, it couldn't suddenly float. If it did—what would you do as a scientist? Suppose you took that glass and dropped it, and suddenly you saw it going up instead of down. You would look for other forces operating here. You would immediately say: something is acting on that glass in a manner which is contrary to the force of gravity. Then you have to find out what that something is. You would look for new causes—namely, new phenomena, entities previously unknown to you which caused the different behavior of that glass.

In other words, whenever you observe a phenomenon which seems to contradict what you knew before, you do not discard your knowledge, you look for new information— which is the process by which all science has grown.

Therefore, when you say that a "dispositional property" of this glass is that it will break, what you are really saying, if one keeps full context, is: this glass is of a certain structure which, in the context now known to me, will break if it is thrown with a certain force against another entity with a different, harder structure. If it does something other than break, that means some other entity has interfered, or the action of another entity, according to its nature, has changed the result of this glass's action but not the glass's nature. The action has changed, but the action remains within the potential for action inherent in this glass by its nature.

But if you dropped the glass, and no other force was involved, and it started floating, *that* would be an action contrary to its nature. Or if you dropped a match into a highly inflammable substance like gasoline and it failed to explode—

Prof. E:—without some compensating factor entering—

AR:—without any other factor, but suddenly nothing happened, neither to the match nor to the gasoline, that would be the two entities acting contrary to their nature.

Prof. B: Could you put it this way? It would contradict the fact that entities with these properties necessarily act in certain ways under certain conditions.

AR: Right. Because of the nature of a flame and the nature of gasoline, if you bring the two together there will be an explosion or the gasoline will catch fire. If you drop the same match on a piece of iron, nothing will happen except that the match will burn out and the metal will be slightly heated. That's what I meant by that statement in Galt's speech. ["The nature of an action is caused and determined by the nature of the entities that act; a thing cannot act in contradiction to its nature."]

Prof. F: I noticed that Galt does not say, "A thing must act in accordance with its nature"; he says it "cannot act in contradiction to its nature." I wonder if you had some particular reason for stating it in the negative.

AR: Oh, no, only to make it stronger actually. You could have said "must act in accordance with its nature." But I wanted to stress that one cannot claim causeless actions, or actions contrary to the nature of the interacting entities. I wanted to stress that actions cannot be inexplicable and causeless. If the cause lies in the nature of an entity, then it cannot do something other than what its nature makes possible.

Philosophy of Science

Philosophic vs. Scientific Issues

Prof. B: Is the concept of "matter" a philosophical concept or a scientific one?

AR: In the way we are using it here, as a very broad abstraction, it is a philosophical concept. If by "matter" we mean "that of which all the things we perceive are made," that is a philosophical concept. But questions like: what are different things made of? what are the properties of matter? how can you break it down? etc.—those are scientific problems.

Philosophy by its nature has to be based only on that which is available to the knowledge of any man with a normal mental equipment. Philosophy is not dependent on the discoveries of science; the reverse is true.

So whenever you are in doubt about what is or is not a philosophical subject, ask yourself whether you need a specialized knowledge, beyond the knowledge available to you as a normal adult, unaided by any special knowledge or special instruments. And if the answer is possible to you on that basis alone, you are dealing with a philosophical question. If to answer it you would need training in physics, or psychology, or special equipment, etc., then you are dealing with a derivative or scientific field of knowledge, not philosophy.

Prof. B: I'd like to apply this to the "mind-brain" issue—

289

that is, what is the relation of conscious activity to brain activity? That would be a scientific question.

AR: Yes.

Prof. B: With certain provisos from philosophy, such as that consciousness is causally efficacious and that free will is possible.

AR: Philosophy would have to define the terms of that question. In asking what's the relationship between "mind" and "brain," scientists have to know what they mean by the two concepts. It's philosophy that would have to tell them the [general] definitions of those concepts. But then actually to find the specific relationship, that's a scientific question.

Properties of the Ultimate Constituents

Prof. E: Could you argue, on metaphysical grounds, that all observed properties of an entity are ultimately explicable in terms of, or reducible back to, properties of their primary constituents?

AR: We'd have to be omniscient to know. The question in my mind would be: how can we [as philosophers] make conclusions about the ultimate constituents of the universe? For instance, we couldn't say: everything is material, if by "material" we mean that of which the physical objects on the perceptual level are made—"material" in the normal, perceptual meaning of the word. If this is what we mean by "material," then we do not have the knowledge to say that ultimately everything is sub-subatomic particles which in certain aggregates are matter. Because suppose scientists discovered that there are two different kinds of primary ingredients—or three, or more? We would be in the same position as the pre-Socratics who were trying to claim that everything was air, water, earth, and fire because that's all they knew.

Prof. E: You see the question is whether the concept of "potentiality" might not be irreducible. That is, whether the ultimate constituents of the universe, if and when we ever reach them, would have to be definable solely in terms of their mode of action.

AR: No, in fact the opposite will be true. The only thing of which we can be sure, philosophically, is that the ultimate stuff, if it's ever found—one element or ten of them—will have identity. It will be what it is. You could not say that it is pure action: the concept wouldn't apply. If you come down to the ultimate particles of the universe and say they are pure action, they don't have any identity, they don't have anything except the capacity for action—the term "action" would not apply. By "action" we mean the action of an entity.

Prof. E: But suppose one were to raise the question epistemologically, rather than metaphysically. Granted that the ultimate constituents are something, are entities and have an identity, still is it possible for us in theory ever to know any more about them than the kind of action they take?

Prof. B: They'd have to have size, for one thing, and shape.

AR: *If* they are particles. What if they are solid flows of energy, but each is indivisible, and it moves, but it's one entity, moving from left to right and vice versa?

Prof. B: That depends on what "energy" means, because whatever the nature of energy is, that's the nature it would have.

AR: Exactly.

Prof. E: No, I was switching this to epistemology.

AR: But the confusion there would arise in applying concepts based on the macroscopic level of observation to the submicroscopic, subatomic level. If you use macroscopic terms which do not apply on that level, the misapplication will destroy all your perceptual level and your whole conceptual structure.

Prof. B: So you are saying that the ultimate constituents need not be particles, like sold balls, but whatever they are, one is not to refer to them as being actions without entities.

AR: Exactly. And I was also objecting to your saying

they will have to have extension, for instance, or shape. We can't claim that.

Prof. F: But suppose we agree that whatever they are, they will have identity—they will be what they are and so on. But mustn't we also say something else: that we cannot define this identity solely in terms of their relationship to other objects?

For instance, suppose that one of the ultimate properties of an entity is charge. Suppose you couldn't find any way of defining "charge" except in relationship to other entities. Now wouldn't that be grounds, metaphysically, for saying therefore charge is not an ultimate property of matter?

AR: I am not sure I even understand the logic. Why?

Prof. E: Presumably he would argue that a property which is defined in terms of a relationship between two entities presupposes and is a consequence of the attributes of that entity which give rise to that relationship. And therefore, if charge is definable only in terms of an entity's relation to others—its effects on them—then charge couldn't be a primary, it would have to be a derivative from something else in the entity that gives rise to that kind of effect.

Prof. F: Thank you. That's exactly what I meant.

Prof. E: But then we are in bad shape here, because to grasp what the ultimate entities are, you have to strip off their actions, their potentialities for action, and their relations to other entities—then by what means would you ever get to know what they are?

AR: Not only that, you are obviously making advance conditions for what that primary has to be. You are being Hegelian or Rationalistic in that sense. You cannot say philosophically what conditions you will ascribe to that which is not known. We cannot know by what means we will grasp something not known today. A hundred years ago you couldn't have conceived of the cloud chamber, the first instrument by which scientists could observe atoms simply by observing their effects on something. You couldn't have made the rule that unless you can touch, see, smell, and measure a given entity with a ruler, it cannot exist. That would have been crude materialism of some kind. You couldn't, a hundred years ago, have prescribed the means by which you would discover twentieth-century knowledge. And yet in making any kind of conclusions about the ultimate stuff of the universe, you are necessarily committing that error. You are prescribing conditions of what something not known to you now has to be.

The important thing here is this. You cannot say that you would define an atom by means of its charge, or that you would look further, or what you would do, because you have no way of knowing in what form you will become aware of that primary stuff. It might be through ten different instruments, and the interaction of one upon another, which would only tell you *how* you became aware of it. You wouldn't yet have defined it, metaphysically. All you could say is, "It is a something, which I discovered by the following method."

The only thing that concerns philosophy is that we can say: whatever it is, it will have to be what it is, and no contradictions claimed about it will be valid—as for instance, the current theories about a particle that goes from one place to another without crossing the places in between. Now you see *that* is metaphysically impossible, and you don't have to be a scientist to know that. A philosopher can tell you without ever entering a laboratory that that is not possible. But for a philosopher to attempt to define what kind of particle it has to be, or how we will determine its properties, that is unwarranted and Rationalistic. That is the province of science, not philosophy.

You see it isn't the job of philosophy to tell us *what* exists, it's only to tell us what has to be true of everything that exists [identity] and what are the rules by which you can claim knowledge. And in regard to the constituent elements of the universe, all we can say is that they would have to have identity. *That* we can prove. Any other conclusions we cannot draw philosophically.

Prof. F: So then philosophy should leave open the possibility that the ultimate properties of things are relational properties?

AR: No, because you are using a term from our present level of knowledge. "Relational properties" are what? Properties arising out of the relation of two entities. In calling something a relational property, you are implying the existence of entities. But now if you say the ultimate particles or elements will be defined as relational, what does that mean? You are applying a concept from our present level of knowledge to a level on which you deny it suddenly. What is a "relational property"—relation of what?

Prof. F: Two ultimate elements to one another.

AR: But then it isn't a relational property.

Prof. E: You've already made reference to the elements.

AR: You made reference to the elements. The only meaning it could possibly have is that you will observe it only through a relationship. Let's say that ultimately, through ten super-microscopes, you establish that you can only observe this ultimate particle by means of its relationship to another particle. That's possible. But then you will still have implied the entity.

Prof. E: Suppose it were the case that worse comes to worst epistemologically, that at the outside limit of human cognition in the indefinite future, scientists will never get beyond a knowledge of the actions of the ultimate entities— because in effect human beings' means of cognition doesn't encompass any means of reaching the nature of the entities, except that it is a something which has identity and acts in a certain way. Would you regard that as having philosophic significance, were that to be the ultimate answer?

AR: No.

Prof. E: Would that prove that reality in itself is unknowable to us?

AR: No.

Prof. E: Or that all we can know ultimately is just action?

AR: No. Keep your terms defined. What are you talking about? You are talking about the constituents of what we, to begin with, perceive as entities. And to say we really can perceive only action, because on the sub-subatomic level we cannot grasp the nature of those entities, we can only grasp their actions, doesn't hold. All you are saying is: I can't go beyond a certain level of knowledge. That doesn't mean that all you grasp is action.

And you know what else is crucially important? When you talk about discovering the ultimate constituents of the universe, remember that in order to discover them, no matter by what calculations or by what machinery, you had to bring them to your perceptual level. You would have to say "this particle" is that which acts in such and such a way on subatomic particles, which act in such and such a way on atoms, which act in such and such a way on molecules, and all of that results in a material object such as this glass as distinguished from other material objects such as this ashtray. Unless you bring it back to the perceptual level, it's not knowledge. That is what has to be kept in mind always in speculating about ultimate causes, which have to be discovered by some, at present, unknown means. You still always have to bring it back to your sensory-perceptual level, otherwise it's not knowledge.

Induction

Prof. H: This is a common question relating to induction. Someone is boiling water, and he notices that every time the water gets to a certain temperature, it boils. Now he wants to know: does all water boil at that temperature, or is it only due to some accidental feature about this particular water? How does he determine whether it's accidental or essential?

AR: By whether you can or cannot establish a causal connection between what you have determined to be the essential characteristic of water and the fact that it boils at a certain temperature.

Prof. H: I suppose what I'm asking is: how do you establish the causal connection?

AR: That's a scientific question. But, in essence, what you do is this. Let's say you have to establish the molecular structure of water. How do those molecules act at a certain temperature? And if you see that something happens to the molecules which causes boiling at a certain temperature, you conclude: that's essential to the nature of water, adding the parenthesis: "within the present context of my knowledge." You will later discover that water behaves differently at a different altitude. So you never claim water necessarily, as an absolute, will always and everywhere boil at the same temperature. No, you say, "Within my present context, omitting elements of which I have no knowledge at present, water will always boil at a certain temperature, because boiling is a state depending on certain kind of molecular motions, and water's molecules will always reach that stage at a certain temperature."

Now, with later development, you might discover that maybe there are differences in certain molecules of water when in an impure state. Or with atomic additions, say, something else happens. But then your context has changed. You don't say that water has changed. It's only that your definition of how the essential characteristic of water will function will have to include more: what water will do at sea level, what it will do at higher altitudes, and what it will do under new molecular or atomic influences, or in relation to some scientific phenomenon not yet known to any of us. But the principle there is the same. Does that answer it?

Prof. H: I have to think about it.

AR: Okay, but ask again later, because I don't want to leave you with semi-answers. And that is the rational procedure: think it over, and if a further question occurs to you, then ask me later. This applies to everybody else as well. If any answer is only partial, the right thing to do is to think it over, because one can't discuss it and integrate it at the same time. If you see that there is still an area not covered, then ask me later.

Prof. A: How would you answer this common objection to your answer? In relating the boiling of water to the energy required to break certain molecular bonds, you haven't actually made any progress in regard to the induction, because you've only got the same kind of generalization on the molecular level that you had before on the gross, macroscopic level. You now know, "In a given number of cases, it has always taken a certain amount of energy to break this molecular bond." But that fact has the same sort of status as the fact you started with: "In a given number of cases, I heated the water to 212 degrees, and it always boiled." I know the objection is crazy, because in some way you do have more knowledge when you've gone down to the molecular level. But I can't see what the error is.

AR: But you see, you answered it. When you simply boil water, you do not know that it has molecules, nor what happens to those molecules. When you arrive at that later stage of knowledge, you've discovered something about water and the conditions of its boiling which you didn't know before. And, therefore, within your present context, this is a sufficient explanation, even though it's not the exclusive and final explanation. To reach that you would have to have omniscience. But, if you can say, "It's in the nature of water that it's composed of molecules, and something happens to those molecules at a certain temperature, this explains to me why water boils," that is a causal explanation. It isn't the same thing as saying, "I don't know why it boils, but if I heat it, it bubbles up." That's all that you knew before. And, therefore, your knowledge is now further advanced.

Prof. A: But it seems that the certainty that you were first trying to attach to the idea that water boils under certain conditions is derivative from the degree of certainty you have concerning the idea that a certain amount of energy disrupts the molecules.

AR: If this is supposed to be on the same level, what would the person raising this objection consider to be a different level?

Prof. A: Yes, that's exactly the problem.

AR: That's not the problem. No. That's the method of ruling his objection out. Because you discover that he has no ground for his conclusion that you're on the same level. Look at the facts. You observe that water boils. You discover something in the constituent elements of water that causes it. You know more than you did before. But he tells you, "No, you're at the same place." Then you ask him, "What place do you want to go to? What do you regard as knowledge?"

Prof. E: And then his answer would be that he wants a mystic apprehension of "necessity," which he hasn't yet received. All he has is "contingent" facts.

AR: Yes. And you ask him what does he regard the facts of reality as: a necessity or a contingency? He'll say, "Of course it's a contingency, because God made it this way, and he could have made it another." And you say, "Good-bye."

Prof. F: But I am not clear why it is a significant step when one goes from the macroscopic phenomenon, boiling, to the molecular level. Why does one then say, "Aha! Now, within our present context of knowledge, we've made a satisfactory advance."

AR: Let's ask something wider: what is knowledge? And what is study, what is observation? It's the discovery of properties in the nature of certain objects, existents, entities. All knowledge consists of learning more and more about the nature—the properties and characteristics—of given objects. So first you see only water—just that. Then you observe that it boils at a certain point. Your knowledge is advanced. You know more about water than you did when you only observed it in a lake. Then you discover such a thing as molecules, then you discover the molecular structure of water. Your knowledge about what water is is still greater. Now you observe what happens to those molecules when you apply a certain amount of energy. Your knowledge is still greater. If it isn't, what do you mean by knowledge?

Prof. F: Both you and your positivist opponents would agree that the knowledge is greater. But they would then raise the question of whether one has to go a further step or not—or why one should have made this step in the first place. Why does the breaking of the macroscopic down into the molecular constitute a significant step, whereas the addition of some other type of knowledge—

AR: Such as?

Prof. F: Such as the knowledge of, say, the shape of the water at present, or the electrical charges involved.

AR: All that is knowledge. The knowledge of anything that can happen to water—what temperature it will freeze at, how it reflects light—any characteristic of a given object of study is knowledge. If you can establish that this characteristic pertains to water, you have learned something new about water.

But if the problem here involves the issue of necessity vs. contingency, then it's a prescientific problem, a strictly philosophical problem. What do you mean by "necessity"? By "necessity," we mean that things are a certain way and had to be. I would maintain that the statement "Things are," when referring to non-man-made occurrences, is the synonym of "They had to be." Because unless we start with the premise of an arbitrary God who creates nature, what is had to be. We have to drop any mystical premise and keep the full context in mind. Then, aside from human action, what things are is what they had to be.

The alternative of what "had to be" versus what "didn't have to be" doesn't apply metaphysically. It applies only to the realm of human action and human choice. For instance, will you wear a gray suit or a blue suit? That's up to you. You didn't have to wear either one. Let's assume you have only one suit. Even then you can't say you had to wear it. You chose to wear it rather than be naked. Anything pertaining to actions open to human choice raises the question: "Is it necessary or is it volitional?" But in regard to facts which are metaphysical—that is, not created by a human action—there is no such thing as necessity—or, the fact of existence is the necessity.

Prof. A: I think that was exactly my problem. I was assuming that the fact that a certain entity had always done a certain thing had no significance in itself—that it could be otherwise tomorrow. But actually, something would act differently tomorrow only if a new factor entered in.

AR: Yes.

Prof. A: And by going to the molecular level, you tend to exclude any new factor; you have more awareness of the mechanism operating, so you have more knowledge of what is going to affect it and what isn't; you understand what the process is that's happening. I was assuming exactly what you were saying, that the fact that the energy required was so-and-so today, might change tomorrow, because of God knows what. So the answer lies in the point that necessity is just identity.

AR: Exactly.

Prof. C: On this issue of boiling water and finding out that it must boil because of understanding its molecular structure: isn't it related in some way to the issue of unit-economy in concepts? Because in theory-formation one attempts to condense a vast amount of knowledge into a smaller and smaller number of principles. And when one is able to explain the boiling of water in terms of the electrons and protons, not only does one explain boiling as necessary from these few facts, but also one explains a vast number of other characteristics, properties, and set of behaviors for water and a whole scad of other substances.

AR: Oh yes.

Prof. C: So when you go to that level, you have widened your knowledge to a much larger scope by integrating the data to a few simple laws, such as, in this case, the properties of the electrons.

AR: You mean, it is also applicable to more than water, and if you discover how the molecules of water react to heat, you then open the way to discoveries concerning how other elements react to heat, and you learn a great deal about other elements that way.

Prof. C: Right.

AR: Oh, of course.

Prof. C: So the objection of the logical positivist would be valid only if one learned nothing else relating water at the molecular level to other substances. Then one would say one has additional knowledge, but one doesn't have a more fundamental knowledge.

AR: No, the objection wouldn't be valid even then. To begin with, the supposition is impossible. Everything that you discover about one kind of subject or element opens the way for the same type of inquiry and discovery about other elements.

But let's assume for a moment that it had no other applications. Even then, you learn something about water and how to handle it and what you can obtain from it. If you discover that its molecules move in a certain way and that causes boiling, this can lead you to discover other things you can do with water, such as what happens under a deep freeze or what happens with liquid oxygen—which is all derived from the same type of knowledge, from the same category of science.

And don't forget—it is important here—what the purpose of knowledge is. The purpose is for you to deal with that which you are studying. And if you discover why water boils, you will know something more and will be able to do more things with water than the primitive man who knows only that if he holds it over fire a certain length of time it will boil. By discovering such issues as temperature and molecular structure, you have made yourself infinitely more capable of dealing with water and using it for your purposes than the primitive man who only made the first observation.

Scientific Methodology

Prof. M: Would you consider the following method of confirming a scientific principle to be valid? One formulates the principle being guided by one's knowledge of fact. Using the principle, one next deduces how entities under certain conditions should act. Then, if one observes such action and, within the context of one's knowledge can account for it only by the principle which predicted it, it follows that the principle has been confirmed. In summary, one induces the

principle, deduces its consequences, and if only that principle is known to give rise to those consequences, which in
turn exist, then the principle is confirmed as a contextual
absolute.

AR: This is outside the province of my book; this is the
theory of induction. But within this context, I would say,
no, this would not be the right procedure, and there is a
danger of a very, very grave error here. Because if you
follow the procedure you outline here, and you make certain predictions on the basis of a hypothesis, and the entities
do act accordingly, you conclude that you can hold as a
contextual absolute that it was your hypothesis that was
operating and that it is therefore true. You are assuming an
omniscience that contextual knowledge cannot permit. Because since you are not omniscient, within the context of
your knowledge you cannot say that your particular hypothesis was the *only* possible cause of the entities acting the
way you predicted. You would have to say this offers great
confirmation of your hypothesis, but it still remains a hypothesis and cannot be taken as knowledge. Why? Because
so many other possibilities are involved. And I don't mean
unknown or unknowable factors—I mean that it would be
impossible, for any complex principle of science that you are
trying to establish, to eliminate, even within your own context of knowledge, all the other possibilities.

What I would question is this part of the procedure: "if
only that principle is known to give rise to those consequences"—that's the mistake of arrested knowledge, right
there.

Prof. M: Even though it is relative to what you know at
that time?

AR: Even though it's at that time and it's your full
context of knowledge. Because you cannot conclude that
something which is not fully known to you can be produced
only by one hypothesized factor. On the basis of that same
context of knowledge, any number of hypotheses could be
constructed. Which is why we need hypotheses. If it were

otherwise, then your hypothesis to begin with would almost have to be a certainty.

Historically, some dreadful errors have resulted from that method. One of them is the denial of the existence of ether. I don't mean that ether necessarily exists; I mean the process by which they denied it, was of this type. They predicted something with an artificial absolute or ultimatum delivered to nature—if light bends in a certain way (or something on that order), then it proves that space is a vacuum. It certainly does not, and I am no physicist, I am just an epistemologist. You cannot arbitrarily restrict the facts of nature to your current level of knowledge. In other words, you cannot take the context of your knowledge, as if reality were confined only to that which you know, and deliver ultimatums, saying, "If my hypothesis predicts correctly, then it is only my hypothesis that can be true."

Prof. M: Take the example of Newton's theory of universal gravitation. He said that if the theory is true, then the planets will exhibit elliptical orbits with the sun at one of the foci. Now it is found in astronomy that the planets do follow that path. So what can one say then about Newton's theory? Is it a possible explanation? Is it correct, or what?

AR: After it has been verified by a great many other observations, not merely the verification of one prediction, then at a certain time one can accept it as a fact. But taking your example as an illustration of what you are asking, if the sole validation for Newton's principle was that it predicted that orbits will be elliptical, and then we observed that they are elliptical—that wouldn't be sufficient proof. Epistemologically, it wouldn't be enough. You would have to have other observations, from different aspects of the same issue, which all support this hypothesis. [Historically, Newton validated his theory by means of a great many observations of widely differing phenomena.]

Prof. M: The question is: when does one stop? When does one decide that enough confirming evidence exists? Is that in the province of the issue of induction?

AR: Yes. That's *the* big question of induction. Which I couldn't begin to discuss—because (a) I haven't worked on that subject enough to even begin to formulate it, and (b) it would take an accomplished scientist in a given field to illustrate the whole process in that field.

* * *

Prof. C: Some mathematicians claim that there is such a thing as an "imaginary number." How do you determine whether it is correct or not to include imaginary numbers within the same category as real numbers?

AR: By defining the essential characteristics of the units. After you define what a real number is and what an imaginary number is, if you see from what you mean by those terms that there are essential differences, then you can't include them in the same concept.

But this is really a question concerning theory-formation, not concept-formation. You are in the realm of epistemology of science. I will just say on this topic that you have to treat scientific concepts in exactly the same way, in principle, as you treat "table" and "chair." If somebody decided to put tables and chairs into one concept—on the grounds that you always see them together—but beds and automobiles in another because he can lie down in either, you would object to that. Why? Because you would say that he has organized his data by non-essentials. He has ignored essential similarities and essential differences and arbitrarily coupled certain existents into certain groups. That error comes under the general category of definition by non-essentials. It is disastrous conceptually to try to integrate objects by non-essential characteristics.

Exactly the same thing, in principle, would apply to a scientific theory. Suppose somebody tries to couple neutrons and pancakes. The same objection applies. If you ask him to define what he means by "neutron" and what he means by "pancake," you will find volumes of differences that do not permit them to be grouped into one concept.

Prof. C: An imaginary number is supposed to be that number which when multiplied by itself is equal to minus one. There is, in fact, no real number which when multiplied by itself gives you minus one.

AR: What is its purpose?

Prof. C: It turns out that it has a great usefulness as a device mathematically for solving problems of a real kind—for instance, problems involving electrical circuits. But I personally do not see the validity of this concept. There is nothing in reality to which it corresponds. Nothing is measured except by real numbers.

AR: But here there is a certain contradiction in your theoretical presentation. If you say that these imaginary numbers do serve a certain function in measurement, then—

Prof. C: Excuse me, not in measurements of anything, but in computation—in solving an equation.

AR: The main question is: do they really serve that purpose?

Prof. C: In practice, yes.

AR: If they serve that purpose, then they have a valid meaning—only then they are not concepts of entities, they are concepts of method. If they have a use which you can apply to actual reality, but they do not correspond to any actual numbers, it is clearly a concept pertaining to method. It is an epistemological device to establish certain relationships. But then it has validity. All concepts of this kind are concepts of method and have to be clearly differentiated as such.

Whenever in doubt, incidentally, about the standing of any concept, you can do what I have done in this discussion right now. I asked you, "What, in reality, does that concept refer to?" If you tell me that the concept, let's say, of an imaginary number doesn't do anything in reality, but somebody builds a theory on it, then I would say it is an invalid concept. But if you tell me, yes, this particular concept, although it doesn't correspond to anything real, does achieve certain ends in computations, then clearly you can classify it: it is a concept of method, and it acquires meaning only in the context of a certain process of computation.

Therefore, when in doubt about the classification or nature of a concept, always refer ultimately to reality. What in reality gives rise to that concept? Does it correspond to anything real? Does it achieve anything real? Or is it just somebody's arbitrary theory?

You see, the danger here is the method of saying, "What if?" That is a very widely held and disastrous error today— not only in mathematics but in every science. And, of course, philosophy is the author of that error. I mean the idea that it is legitimate to form arbitrary hypotheses. Never try to justify or to tie to reality—or to negate for that matter— some hypothesis, or some "What if?" proposition for which there is no basis at all. That is the dead end of human epistemology, and worse than that. That is a mind-destroyer.

Prof. C: On the preceding point, how would I answer the charge that I am now accepting the validity of imaginary numbers on merely pragmatic grounds—that is, just because "it works."

AR: Yes, but if it works, it is your job as a scientist to find out why it works. If something works you want to know the reason why. For instance, there are cases where people used certain things, such as potions in medicine, which worked—only they didn't know why. That's not science yet; that is a stage of pre-science or of pragmatic observations. But you don't dismiss them. If they work, you inquire why. But only after you have established why they work does this kind of inquiry enter the realm of science or of philosophy.

Concluding Historical
Postscript

Prof. B: You said you might discuss how you arrived at your theory of measurement-omission. That might be a fitting way to close.

AR: All right. Historically, it happened this way. Somewhere in the 1940s, so it's over twenty years ago, I was discussing the issue of concepts with a Jesuit, who philosophically was a Thomist. He was holding to the Aristotelian position that concepts refer to an essence in concretes. And he specifically referred to "manness" in man and "roseness" in roses. I was arguing with him that there is no such thing, and that these names refer merely to an organization of concretes, that this is our way of organizing concretes.

We never really finished the argument. But after this conversation, I was dissatisfied with my own answer. Because I felt, "Yes, I have indicated where concepts come from, but I haven't indicated what is the process by which we organize concretes into different groups—because I certainly don't agree with the modern nominalists who claim that it's an arbitrary convention or an arbitrary grouping."

And then I asked myself, "What is it that my mind does when I use concepts? To what do I refer, and how do I learn new concepts?" And within half an hour, I had the answer.

Now it took me longer than that to check it, to apply it to various categories of concepts, and see if there are exceptions. But once I had the answer, by the logic of it, I knew that that's it. And that's it.

INDEX

Prepared by Linda Reardan, Department of Philosophy
California State University, San Bernardino

308

Perception (*cont.*)
  objects of, 22, 205–209
  role in knowledge of, 5–6,
    14–16, 49–50, 112, 179–181,
    198–199
  validity of, 3, 136
  See also Animals, awareness
    of; Sensations
Philosophy, 74, 120–121, 189,
  235, 289–295
  See also Modern philosophy
Physical world. *See* Matter,
  concept of
Plato, 2, 53–54, 90, 95–97,
  101–106, 155–156, 173,
  271–272
Potentialities, 282–288
Pragmatism, 306
Prepositions, 17
Pre-Socratic philosophy, 248,
  290
Primacy of consciousness, error
  of, 53–54, 245–252
Primary-secondary quality dichot-
  omy, 279–282
Pronouns, 17
Proper names, 10–11, 175
Properties, 282–288
  See also Attributes
Propositions, 75, 100–101,
  110–111, 177–181, 183
  See also Analytic-synthetic
    dichotomy
Protagoras (c. 490–c. 421 B.C.),
  8
Pythagoras (c. 582–c. 507 B.C.),
  90

R

Rationalism, 112, 252, 292–293
"Razor" of concepts, 72
"Razor," Rand's, 250–251
Realism, extreme. *See* Plato
Realism, moderate. *See* Aris-
  totle, epistemology of
Russell, Bertrand (1872–1970),
  50–51, 201, 244–245

S

Sartre, Jean-Paul (1905–1980),
  60–61
  See also Existentialism
Science, 286–295, 304
  and measurement, 38–39
  vs. philosophy, 189
  See also Induction; Knowledge
Scope (of a psychological
  process), 31–32
Self, concept of, 251–256
Sensations, 5–6, 57, 136
  concepts of, 40–41
  See also Perception
Sense-perception. *See* Perception
Similarity, 13–15, 139–141,
  217–222
Skepticism, 79–82, 96
Some-but-any principle. *See*
  Measurement-omission
Space, 273
Stolen concept, fallacy of the,
  3, 59–61, 214, 246–247,
  251–252
  See also Hierarchy, of concepts
Subdivision of concepts, 23–28,
  217
  See also Abstraction, from
    abstractions
Subjectivism. *See* Intrinsic-
  subjective dichotomy
Subsumption (of new concretes),
  27–28
Supernaturalism, 109–110,
  114–115, 247–248
  See also Mysticism

T

Theory-practice diochotomy,
  190–191
Thought, concept of, 32,
  223–225
Time, 56–57, 256–260, 273
Truth, 48, 100–101, 110–111
  See also Knowledge;
    Propositions